P9-AER-830

Law and Social Process in United States History

Da Capo Press Reprints in

AMERICAN CONSTITUTIONAL AND LEGAL HISTORY

GENERAL EDITOR: LEONARD W. LEVY

Claremont Graduate School

Law and Social Process in United States History

Five lectures delivered at The University of Michigan

November 9, 10, 11, 12, and 13, 1959

by

JAMES WILLARD HURST

Foreword by

ALLAN F. SMITH

DA CAPO PRESS • NEW YORK • 1972

Library of Congress Cataloging in Publication Data

Hurst, James Willard, 1910-
Law and social process in United States history.
(Da Capo Press reprints in American constitutional and legal history)
Originally published as the 9th series of the Thomas M. Cooley lectures.
1. Law – U.S. – Addresses, essays, lectures.
I. Title. II. Series: Michigan. University.
Law School. The Thomas M. Cooley lectures, 9th ser.
KF358.H8 1972 340'.0973 74-173669
ISBN 0-306-70409-9

This Da Capo Press edition of *Law and Social Process in United States History* is an unabridged republication of the first edition published in Ann Arbor, Michigan, in 1960. It is reprinted by special arrangement with the University of Michigan Law School.

Published by Da Capo Press, Inc.
A Subsidiary of Plenum Publishing Corporation
227 West 17th Street, New York, New York 10011

Manufactured in the United States of America

Law and Social Process in United States History

The Thomas M. Cooley Lectures

Ninth Series

Law and Social Process
in United States History

by

JAMES WILLARD HURST

The Thomas M. Cooley Lectureship was established for the purpose of stimulating legal research and presenting its results in the form of public lectures. Thomas M. Cooley, for whom the lectureship was named, was a member of the first faculty of The University of Michigan Law School, when it was organized in 1859, and subsequently became its Dean. At the time of his death in 1898 he was one of the most distinguished legal scholars of this country. These lectures are made possible through the endowment for legal research at The University of Michigan, established by the will of the late William W. Cook, a member of the New York bar and an alumnus of The University of Michigan.

Law and Social Process in United States History

Five lectures delivered at The University of Michigan
November 9, 10, 11, 12, and 13, 1959

by

JAMES WILLARD HURST

Foreword by

ALLAN F. SMITH

The University of Michigan Law School
Ann Arbor 1960

Foreword

Everyone who enters the legal profession is exposed to some aspects of legal history, and to many the study of legal history becomes a fascinating end in itself. It is fairly common to find individuals who seek for particular purposes to enlarge their perspective by resort to historical materials which throw light upon the evolution of existing institutions or help to provide an understanding of the source of some of society's problems. It is rather less common to find an individual whose breadth of knowledge and whose understanding of social institutions permit him to perceive relationships between the past and the present which can serve to guide the development of institutions needed to make society function. Even more rare is the person whose perceptive insights permit him to observe the interaction between human behavior patterns and the institutions which both mould and respond to such behavior and to evaluate the role which those institutions play in society. One such rare individual is Professor James Willard Hurst, and his skill is once again demonstrated in this volume of lectures.

At least since 1940, when, with Lloyd K. Garrison, he published a book "Law and Society," Professor Hurst has been recognized as an outstanding legal historian. In addition to numerous articles, his contributions to literature include "Growth of American Law: The Law Makers" (1950) and "Law and Conditions of Freedom in the 19th Century" (1956). The last-named book, which received the James Barr Ames prize of the Harvard Law School, established him as one destined to provide leadership in filling the awesome gap in literature relating to the social history of the law in the United States. His personal work at the University of Wisconsin and the influence he has had upon those who have worked with him have commanded the attention and admiration of all those who seek to clarify the relationships between human behavior and the legal order.

One of the delightful results of the kind of study exemplified in these lectures is that the product is enlightening both to laymen and to the professionally trained lawyer. The former will find that Professor Hurst has chosen the ordinary cases for his observation and not the celebrated or complicated landmarks which so often make up the grist for the historian's mill. By so doing, he is able to focus his reader's attention upon the social import of the law's action rather than having it diverted by the drama of the fact situation or the glamour of the noted participants. Thus the layman finds himself drawn to an awareness that the legal order is not something apart from himself but rather a framework which at once bounds his behavior and is also susceptible of remodelling to meet his social needs. The lawyer, already aware of the general role which legal order plays in society, will find a perspective which only an historian can supply and will find ample challenge for the exercise of his professional talents in making the law perform its tasks for the society in which it operates. He will be sharply reminded that although the law can so operate to encourage changes in social and economic behavior, and although the law can, within limits, coerce patterns of behavior, yet wide areas remain where directed policy is lacking; and our society moves in erratic steps toward unstated and ill-defined goals. Simultaneously, however, he will be reminded that cultural change, as well as changes in economic order, will inevitably occur from forces other than law, and that the capacity of law to induce changes is limited. Throughout, both layman and lawyer will be reminded of the human values which must be preserved in the manipulation of man's activities.

These lectures, in short, constitute another fine contribution from a distinguished scholar, which will be welcomed by all who are interested in the factors which affect our societal operations.

ALLAN F. SMITH, Dean
The University of Michigan Law School

Ann Arbor, Michigan, 1960.

Acknowledgment

I am indebted to Dean Edwin Blythe Stason and to the law faculty of The University of Michigan for the privilege and opportunity they afforded me by their invitation to give the lectures on which these essays are based. I am under particular obligation to Professor Allan F. Smith, for hospitable arrangements in connection with the lectures, and to Miss Alice J. Russell, assistant editor of Michigan Legal Publications, for shepherding the lectures to publication.

These essays are a product of a program in United States legal history research made possible initially by a grant from the Social Science Research Council and brought onto a long-term basis by the continuing support of the Rockefeller Foundation and the president and regents of the University of Wisconsin. For encouragement in the work my debts run also to Dr. Joseph H. Willits, and to Deans Lloyd K. Garrison, Oliver S. Rundell, John Ritchie III, and George H. Young, and to my colleagues of the University of Wisconsin law faculty. Of course the essays do not purport to speak for any of these men or agencies, and I take sole responsibility for what I write.

JAMES WILLARD HURST

Table of Contents

Analytical Table of Contents

I

The Subjects of Legal History

These essays examine some operations of law among processes of social change and stability in United States history. If legal history were a more developed field than it is, this might be a sufficient definition of the enterprise. But little has been done relative to what waits doing. Most work by lawmen has concentrated on one kind of legal agency, the courts—upon one kind of legal process, the development of public policy by judicial choice and exposition of values—upon one type of raw material, doctrinal argument and analysis in lawyers' briefs before courts and in courts' opinions—and upon that range of social cause and effect that finds reflection within the frame of reference provided by this agency, this process, and this material. Others than lawmen have ventured a little into other subjects. General historians and political scientists have examined constitutional history—with main emphasis upon form and upon parties. Leonard White's magnificent history of 19th century developments in federal administrative structure and operations stands so conspicuously alone as to emphasize the narrow limits of venture generally. Sociologists have begun to interest themselves in fitting law into theories of social structure and function, but there is no significant body of product about the social history of law in the United States.[1]

This state of affairs enforces on legal historians a greater concern than they have shown to define their subject. There would be naiveté painful to contemplate, either in the position that existing concentrations of work reflect the range of relations that have, in fact, existed among law and other social institutions, or in the position that the potential subject matter of legal history is so obvious to common sense that no one need ask its dimensions.

Whether its immediate focus be wide or narrow, any serious essay in the legal history of the United States ought to have as its background subject the further definition of legal history. It is a compulsive busyness rather than the study of history that brings men to collect records when they do not know what to seek. Legal history needs philosophy of history. It will never need philosophy more than when the catalog of work done is so relatively small as now. The philosophic dimension of historical writing is not only critical for the meaning of work done. It is even more important to raise challenges which will recruit more than the small company so far gathered in the field.

What is "the law," or what are the aspects of men's experience to which we refer when we talk of the "legal" part of their history? It inheres in the historian's purpose that these questions have meaning for him only in contexts of time and space. For these essays the question is not what

[1] See White, THE FEDERALISTS (1948), THE JEFFERSONIANS (1951), THE JACKSONIANS (1954), THE REPUBLICAN ERA (1958). See, generally, Boorstin, "Tradition and Method in Legal History," 54 HARV. L. REV. 424 (1941). Compare Hurst, "Research Responsibilities of University Law Schools," 10 J. LEGAL ED. 147 (1957).

"law" and the "legal" have meant as a distillation of all human experience or what they are capable of meaning out of the energy of men's wills and the speculative capacities of their minds anywhere, anytime, but what they have meant in the experience of people in the United States.[2]

Four features shape the distinctive roles and character of law in United States history: (1) *Force.* Law has meant possession in identified hands of a legitimated monopoly of violence. Generally it is only the policeman who lawfully goes armed. By close corollary, law has meant possession of a legitimated monopoly of secular authority to call to account all other forms of secular compulsion which some men undertake to wield over the wills of others. (2) *Constitutionalism.* Law has been constitutional law. This means that legal order has been valued not as an end in itself but as a means to serve human life. Community consensus accordingly has held officials accountable for their use of power, however high their position or however important their declared objectives. Whether the life served by legal order is viewed as gaining value primarily in its aspects of individual or of social experience has been another matter. There has been enough fluctuation in men's behavior so that one cannot, with assurance, fix either the individualist or the social emphasis into the definition of this legal order as a constitutional one. Indeed, this ambiguity itself provides a major theme of United States legal history. However, the idea that official power is accountable has continued so much a working reality in the country's life that the constitutional character of law is still a useful point of definition, notwithstanding tensions between indi-

[2] See Linton, THE STUDY OF MAN 268 (1936).

vidual and group ends. (3) *Procedure.* Law has meant defining values and allocating means by procedures which (a) have enforced legitimated forms of fact finding and legitimated forms of choosing among scarce satisfactions, and (b) have maintained creative tension between general propositions and particular instances. Our law has emphasized forms as a basis for the legitimacy of substance; it has been a legal order which puts a high value on procedure. This concern with the relation of form and substance has had close operating connection with an equal concern for the relation of generals and particulars. The shirt-sleeves philosophy of our working lawmen and of our people has mingled rough-hewn kinds of nominalism and idealism. Much in our law —not least its constitutionalism—has expressed conviction that the unruly or appealing uniqueness of human situations cannot supply the values or the continuity needed to give meaning and lasting satisfaction in life; we look for general principles—for justice, but for justice within a "concept of ordered liberty."[3] Yet it is no less true that our way of life taught us to distrust large generalities as guides of conduct and to put faith in wisdom and technique learned by doing. The practicing beliefs out of which we defined our law were more or less adequate brands of pragmatism. We insisted on formal procedure as a way of effectively relating generals and particulars. (4) *Resource Allocation.* Consistently we treated law as a major means for allocating human and other than human resources among competing life satisfactions. This role has provided central tensions in the social history of our law, especially because of the great

[3] Cardozo, J., for the Court, in Palko v. Connecticut, 302 U.S. 319, 325, 58 Sup. Ct. 149, 152 (1937).

emphasis we put, in contrast, on market allocation of resources. The interplay of law and market has expressed a good deal of our way of life, reaching into values and attitudes that concern much more than merely doing business. The larger the questions, the more alike are the modes of analysis of economists and lawmen; the older designation, "political economy," carried insight that we should not lose amid the specialization of our day. This means that a simple regulatory, prohibitory, narrowly policeman-role concept has not adequately described our legal order, certainly not since our society began to grow to any complexity after the opening of the 18th century. If to be "conservative" is to limit law to uttering restrictions and laying penalties, our approach has always been "liberal." Despite much contrary rhetoric our main operating philosophy has always been to use law to allocate resources positively to affect the conditions of life wherever we saw something useful to be accomplished by doing so.

This, then, has been the distinctive character of the law which has made the legal element in our history. Law has meant organization for making and implementing choices among scarce sources of human satisfaction—organization marked (1) by successful assertion of a legitimate monopoly of violence, (2) by constitutionally ordered power, (3) by procedures which emphasize adherence to legitimated form and to continual cross-check of generals and particulars, and (4) by its regular use to allocate resources to affect conditions of life in society. Let me repeat that I single out these elements of definition for my purposes as historian. I do not claim that these are universal elements of legal order, either in the sense that they are essential to any meaningful idea of law or that they are universal in human experience. These are simply factors which form a significant institutional cluster which provides "legal" elements in United States history. The subject matter of United States legal history cannot properly be limited to telling of the form and working of legal institutions as if they were self-sufficient and self-contained entities.

There is valid ground for criticism if legal history develops no hyphenate interests, as in legal-economic, or legal-religious, or legal-social relations. Again I should caution that these comments refer specially to the North American experience. There may be some ideas of law which meaningfully abstract it from relation to other than legal ideas. There are societies—usually very simple ones—in which law has little relation to general living, or scarcely exists as a distinct focus of interest. But these things have not been significantly true of our experience; at least since our more developed colonial years and certainly since we became a nation, we have woven law into a wide range of living. Indeed, this has been itself one of the striking features of our experience. Ready use of law expressed a deep-seated instrumental attitude toward institutions that came naturally to our peculiar situation on the North American continent; we found legal organization not only a handy but a specially necessary tool in our circumstances. Few in numbers, scarce of working capital on an immense, rich and unsettled continent, we needed every workable device we could contrive to muster men, money, and tangible movable resources for realizing our opportunities.

Partly our attitude toward law expressed the values which added up to constitutionalism. We believed that legal order should justify its costs by serving life. We believed that the state and society existed to fulfill and enlarge individual life, and not individual life to nourish the strength of particular rulers or of some mystic social whole abstracted from people. It would be a mistake to think of the constitutional tradition as consisting wholly of limits on official power, though certainly this has always been its more obvious element. Less dramatic but no less real was the insistence that law serve the commonwealth, the general or public interest. These were vague terms, subject to twisting to gloss over pleas of special interest. Yet, even in their most reduced meaning, these terms recognized that individual life depends on some health of social context for its quality and sustainment. Law's legitimacy required that it maintain constructive, living relation to the course of life in society outside the law. So, for example, the framers wrote into the United States Constitution that Congress should have power "to regulate commerce . . . among the several states . . . ," and Hamilton truly characterized the attitude back of this grant when he said that its proper use was "to give encouragement to the enterprise of our own merchants, and to advance our navigation and manufactures."[4] Again, consider some revealing decisions written into the Wisconsin Constitution of 1848. Wisconsin's leaders knew the financial embarrassments into which neighbors had been led by an excess of promotional enthusiasm. So they wrote into their new constitution sharp limits on contracting state debt and firmly forbade the state to be a party in carrying on works

[4] "Opinion as to the Constitutionality of the Bank of the United States," rendered to the President, Feb. 23, 1791, 4 REPTS. SEC. TREAS. 105 (1837), 3 WORKS OF ALEXANDER HAMILTON 180, 214 (Lodge ed. 1885).

of internal improvement. But they also provided that, should the state receive any federal bounty in lands or other property for particular works of internal improvement, it might accept these and use them accordingly. And they put on the state the affirmative duty—no mean charge upon its undeveloped resources—to establish a system of public schools to offer free, nonsectarian instruction to all between the ages of four and twenty years of age. Moreover, they made this duty an obligation upon the state's largest present asset, its public lands derived by general grant from the United States.[5]

Both the instrumental and the constitutional character of law in this society mean that an adequate history of law's roles must relate legal order to social order generally. Of course this does not mean that legal history overlaps all social history. Plainly law played a large role in some aspects of United States history and a much more limited role in others. Uses of law and disputes over uses of law so wove into economic growth in the United States that legal and economic history cannot be separated. In contrast, more difficult and subtle problems are posed in assessing the law's relation to religious life or to the content of the family. Compared with economic affairs, direct legal intervention in these realms was marginal. Yet, law may be potent by indirection. In legislation about incorporated associations, compulsory schooling, the property rights of married women, and the control of child labor the legal order gave authoritative form to points of view important to the role of church and family. We can gain some of our most revealing insights into the effective uses and limitations of law out of the variations in direct and indirect influence of legal order

[5] WIS. CONST. art. VIII, §§ 3, 4, 6, 7, 10; art. X, §§ 2, 3, 8.

in different areas of living. Such comparative area studies should be an important category of legal history.

An activist bias may enter the study of any human institution if it is examined only from within. What I have said about studying law in relation to the life outside of and around and about the law might be taken to imply that the question was always simply of law's effect upon other interests—upon the economy, the church, education, the family, social status. But this would run counter to obvious reality as well as to what in principle should have prevailed if our system worked at all according to its declared values. First, on this matter of principle: because we valued law as a means to ends of life, and not as itself representing end values, we should expect to find insistent pressure of lay demands upon law, and so it was. Moreover, principle gained drive from the varying strains of pragmatism that made up our working philosophy. Preoccupied with settling and developing the continent and achieving status in a busy, mobile society, people found it natural to demand that law be useful. Thus, for example, legislative development of the forms of the 19th century business corporation responded to the practical demands of businessmen more than it expressed the originating genius of lawmen. Further in the background was another kind of influence, probably more potent than all the force law exerted directly on lay affairs or all the influence that men's purposed strivings laid on the law. This was the compulsion of the situations in which men found themselves at given times and places—a pressure the more compelling in the hard-paced, many-sided growth of the 19th century United States. Other institutions besides law entered into the constitution of social order in the United States. Such institutions as the market, church, or family consisted in large measure of patterns of conduct grounded in ideas, attitudes, habits that originated apart from law's influence. These institutions had their own internal logic, or at least inherited accretions of function, and therefore generated demands upon legal order. Full-dimensioned legal history must tell of the shaping force exercised upon the law from outside it, by what people wanted, by the functional needs of other institutions, and by the mindless weight of circumstances.

Is legal history in the United States properly confined to aspects of men's lives which are "public" rather than "private" and related only to what they do overtly and not, as well, to what they think and feel? It would not be surprising if all attention went to what is public and overt. The law's formal apparatus most obviously symbolizes interests capable of generalization; indeed, if the legislature passes a statute for advantages that seem too specialized or unique, a court may hold that the statute violates due process of law for want of a sustaining public concern. The everyday operations of law almost always deal with conduct that can be seen, smelled, touched, or measured, at least in result if not in origin; indeed, the law generally insists on proof of an overt act in finding a crime, a civil wrong, a contract, or a transfer of goods or land, and the shadow of unconstitutionality hangs over legislation which purports to penalize states of mind apart from behavior or visible consequences. Thus doctrine may seem to conspire with appearance to leave out of the subject matter of United States legal history what is not so obviously public and overt—law's relation to the ideas and emotions which constitute people's feeling of life, its fire or its tedium, its hope or its despair, its energy or its weariness, its quality as experience uniquely met and individually shaped or as circumstance faceless and impersonal, compelling surrender of all original and particular response.

Man's human-ness lies in his capacity to think and to feel, with awareness of himself as a thinking and feeling being, and in his capacity to criticize and order what he thinks and feels and to develop his thought and emotion by exchange with others. These attributes of man make the growth of idea and attitude essential parts of his history. This is no less true even if one believes that his ideas and feelings are illusion or that they are always responses to the stimuli of more basic causes produced by chance or out of some mindless pressure of events. If what man perceives is illusion or is merely derivative and of slight effect, nonetheless it holds all that life means to him or can mean, and thus it is inherent to his history. This is not so because it ought to be so, or because we wish it so, but because the idea that man has a history loses meaning otherwise; a god could write a history of men on other terms, but men cannot.

The law should supply rich and, in large measure, unique portions of the history of ideas and attitudes that have given character to life in the United States. This follows from what law has been like in this society.

Because we confided to law the measure of the legitimacy of secular power of all sorts and were ready to use law to muster and dispose of large resources for fashioning the frame of economic and social behavior, the law held out great prizes for men's striving. Because it could bestow sanction or grant means, law became a prime focus of men's wants and plans, a great target of opportunity. This legal order possessed the legitimate monopoly of violence and demonstrated a considerable capacity to police types of power created by other than political means. Thus the stakes were large in contests to control the legal apparatus, and the consequences of legal intervention were of a weight that induced sober and deliberate, if not always principled, thought about using law to affect what went on outside the political arena. Hence, when men strove for the prizes law offered, they were likely to do so with an uncommon amount of thought and calculation and with uncommon manipulation, if not discipline, of feeling. Moreover, this legal order emphasized framing issues and choices and ordering evidence within formal procedures—in the legislative and judicial branches and in the processes of constitution making, if not so much in the executive branch, until well into the 20th century.

For all its frailties and fictions, law operated with force not matched by any other major institution of social order to press men to define ends and means. Hence its product of constitutions, statutes, judicial opinions—and, later, administrative rules and orders—yielded the largest single body of articulated values and value-oriented contrivances in society. At once more diffuse and particularized and partisan, and yet likewise presenting exceptional definitions of values and attitudes, was the vast body of more fugitive documents produced in administering legal order: lawyers' briefs, contracts, deeds of trust, articles of private association, documents evidencing personal status, such as adoption papers or naturalization certificates, and official forms reflecting the manifold aspects of life involved in tax returns, licenses, and license applications, or the census. Nowhere else did men undertake so much to explain themselves. Certainly this was true in contrast to the informality and preferred fuzziness of principle which characterized business. At least through the 19th century neither school nor church matched the law for detailed output of value definitions and judgments of ways and means. Where education was not narrowly technical, it did little more than spell out the private morality of middle-class, production-oriented individualism. In some ways the church influenced main currents of life in the 19th century United States, sometimes with strong, if indirect, impact on law—as in the emotional underpinnings which evangelical Protestantism supplied to Jacksonian Democracy. But on the whole, like the school, the church focused on highly individualized aspects of life and added much less than law to defining choices and directions implicit in developing large patterns of social relations.

This, it may be said, is all true enough. It shows that legal history of full dimension should deal with the growth of ideas and attitudes that pertain to men's social relations. But it may still be true that by nature history of law deals only with what was public (general) and overt, though this domain is somewhat larger than we may have first understood. It is relevant and important for understanding man to inquire with what philosophy and what feeling he has experienced life as an individual. But this might be thought stuff of life too subtle to be affected by the large and formal processes of law, save perhaps at those extreme points where law killed or imprisoned or enslaved.

There is a valid line of distinction here. It was the nature of law in this society to deal with the general context of living. This was no less true, though it was inherently the business of law also to bring general policy into particular application. In our constitutional legal order law was not supposed to enter into shaping the unique particularity of a life. Indeed, no value was more basic in our constitutional tradition than that of privacy, the legally defined and protected right of an individual to be let alone in as wide a range of experience as he chose, consistent with maintenance of a like right in others and consistent with the maintenance of a social context essential to a human existence. But this last qualification inevitably introduced the law's generality into the unique feel and pattern of the individual life. Man is man only in society, and the quality of man he is is materially determined by the kind of society in which he lives. True, in our constitutional frame of reference, law could legitimately enter the individual experience of life only as it dealt with the general conditions of social living. But this did not mean that law did not, in fact, affect the nature of the individual's life experience, for the ideas and feeling that the individual built into his life were created in part out of the legal order in which he lived; even his privacy was itself inescapably in important part the product of his social context, including the law.

Certainly it is difficult to relate law to the character of individual experience, all the more so when we try to recreate the felt quality of life long past. We may have to be satisfied with little in this telling, simply because we cannot find enough reliable evidence. But we cannot leave out this part of the matter on the ground that in principle or in fact it is not within the range of human relations that legal order encompassed. To hold so would be to ignore plain implications of our constitutional tradition and of our pragmatic insistence on using law wherever we found it a handy tool for fashioning ways of life that made sense to us as individuals. The hold that constitutionalism had on substantial opinion in this society—the practicing belief that all power should be accountable to serve life outside the formal power structure itself—meant that observance of law and belief in law were themselves ingredients of a way of life. Aspects of the country's growth which seem to contradict this mostly express the improvising, rule-of-thumb instrumental attitude we also took toward law as a tool. However, so far as contradictions exist from this cause, they do not divorce law from close connection to the feel and drive of the individual life. This impatient, often narrowly focused instrumentalism expressed a great deal of what made sense in living to individuals in the United States. Both when we examine the full implications of our constitutional tradition —in its broad meaning, not limited to the high politics of the separation of powers or the alignment of a federal system—and when we study the bluntly instrumental ideas and attitudes taken toward law and expressed through legal manipulation in the growth of the United States, we are following legal history into the intimate experience of men and women.

The intangibles of men's experience which fell within the scope of legal history included feeling as well as idea, emotion as well as calculation. Perhaps the point needs still more emphasis. Constitutional tradition created sustained pressure to justify the uses of power. Emphasis on formal procedures of fact finding and choice making assigned prestige to rational ordering of affairs; this was no less so though the prestige might accrue to rationalization as well.

Our cultural inheritance included popular respect for science, or at least for a popular image of science, which exalted reason.

In this culture it pleased man's vanity to see himself as a reasoning creature. Both the legal and the general social environment might bias us to exaggerate the rational element in legal history; scholarship itself might contribute to this bias, because it wanted to make sense of what happened. Yet the record is plain that large currents of feeling affected the course of law in the United States. This showed itself in very broad movements, as in the abolitionist crusade, in the Jacksonian insistence upon a wider suffrage for men, and in the later campaigns for votes for women. It showed itself with like sweep in the emotional reactions to loss of old-style middle-class individualist independence which moved farmers to revolt against the railroads and small business and professional men to revolt against "the trusts." It showed itself in more specific expression in such highly charged episodes as the impeachments of Mr. Justice Chase or of President Johnson, the contest over the Second Bank of the United States, the trial and aftermath of the trial of the Haymarket bomb defendants, the Pullman strike injunction, the Ballinger-Pinchot controversy, and the battle to confirm the nomination of Louis D. Brandeis to the United States Supreme Court. Feeling might move men toward results indicated also by reason, as in the demand for a broader suffrage. It might move them to results that did not make sense, measured by relation of means to ends, as fear of subversive influences drove "respectable" people to applaud the subversion of fair trial processes in the Haymarket case.

Of course there might be no subtler bias in favor of reason than to believe that we could achieve rational understanding of emotion. But emotion was so patent a reality in the course of United States legal history that the historian must try to take it into his reckoning.

Law offers special insights into the growth of this North American society because so many forces for stability and change came into focus at points of legal action. The character of law in this society—its monopoly of legitimate violence and scrutiny of other forms of compulsion, its constitutionalism, its procedural emphasis, its functions in allocating resources—gave it a large role in supporting and invigorating other institutions of social order. This was so, though typically law worked only to exert limited but critical leverage upon situations; its effectiveness in this culture not only depended upon but consisted in its playing a limited part. The distinctive content of United States legal history derives in large measure from the course of doctrine and practice in which we defined the proper and effective marginal incidence of law in social affairs.

Granted its marginal incidence, law nonetheless dealt at many levels and in many spheres with the processes of change that determined the growth of the country. This discussion has pursued a good many generalities. It may add dimension and bring some general propositions into sharper view to end with a specific instance.

I choose a rather ordinary matter, rather than an issue of high politics. There is a degree of bias in my choice. I confess to some irritation that the writing of legal history tends to take the cream off the top of the bottle and let the nutritious skimmed stuff flow down the drain because it is bulky to handle and not so immediately pleasing to taste. With intelligent diligence and some literary flair anyone can make a good story out of the spotlighted star acts, like the Federal Convention or the Legal Tender Cases or the Court-packing bill. But the spotlighted acts could not go on without stage crew and audience, and without a complicated environing pattern of activity which produced a theatre, a city, and an economic surplus sufficient to allow the luxury of star performances. The reminder that such environments surround the moments of high drama should relieve me of the criticism that I choose an example from the ordinary only out of bias.

Of course, one may look at what is ordinary and see only what is obvious. This is the fair criticism that may be made of a great deal of legal history writing that has dealt only with the internal structure and the formal doctrine and techniques of legal agencies, usually only of the courts. There is nothing more deceptive about the ordinary than that it is likely to appear obvious. Herein lie the uncommonly attractive challenges in studying ordinary events.

Let us, then, define some features of United States legal history which appear more or less clearly in the opinion of the Massachusetts Supreme Judicial Court in 1908 in the case of *Doherty* v. *Inhabitants of Ayer*.[6] The example will not illustrate all the themes this essay touches—the crude flow of events rarely contrives any single matter so neatly—but it will identify a fair range of factors.

[6] 197 Mass. 241, 83 N.E. 677 (1908).

Mr. Doherty sued the town of Ayer to collect money damages after his automobile suffered a broken axle in bumping over a stretch of public road under repair. He rested his claim on a statute of the state first enacted in 1786 and carried forward into successive revisions of the Massachusetts statutes in 1836, 1860, and 1882. The statute required that towns keep their highways "reasonably safe and convenient for travelers, with their horses, teams and carriages at all seasons of the year." The Massachusetts Supreme Judicial Court held that the statute did not give Mr. Doherty a right to recover.

Speaking for the court, Mr. Chief Justice Knowlton made two principal points. "[O]f course," he conceded (quoting an opinion in an earlier case which refused to extend the statute to bicycles)—"[the statute] . . . is not to be confined to the same kind of vehicles . . . in use" when it was enacted in 1786.[7] But it should be confined to vehicles of the same kind as then known. True, "an automobile" . . . is a carriage in a broad sense of the word. But its features as a piece of machinery are far more striking than those which it possesses as a carriage. It is commonly spoken of as a machine.[8] The court thought that, "It hardly can be contended that locomotive cars of many tons' weight, propelled by a gasoline engine or a steam or electrical engine with complicated machinery, capable of developing fifty or seventy-five horse power, and sometimes even more, are vehicles *ejusdem generis* as the carriages known to the legislators of Massachusetts in 1786." [9] The court looked at the words in their total context: "Horses, teams and carriages

[7] *Id.* at 245, 83 N.E. at 678.
[8] *Ibid.*
[9] *Ibid.*

are grouped together in the statute, and the carriages referred to are those drawn by animal power."[10]

Persuasive in themselves, these aspects of the case pointed to a second consideration. When the statute was enacted, "there was no thought of putting upon [the towns] . . . such a burden as would be imposed if they were compelled to keep all of these ways in such a condition that automobiles could pass over them safely and conveniently at all seasons . . . . In some parts of the State that are very sparsely settled there are vast stretches of sandy surface, traversed by roads that are but little used, where the small wheels of a heavy automobile might sometimes encounter as great an obstacle to progress as the plaintiff's vehicle encountered on the smooth, level sand at the place of this accident. To be obliged to harden all such roads would be a burden upon towns heavier than could be borne . . . . No reasonable expenditure by towns would be enough to make all such roads [in the more mountainous areas] convenient for the use of heavy automobiles, with their small wheels, at all seasons . . . . Such roads could not be made safe and convenient for use by automobiles [when frozen into deep ruts after muddy spells] . . . without entire reconstruction." [11] Hence, the court concluded, "if their ways are reasonably safe and convenient for travel generally, [towns] . . . are not liable for a failure to make special provisions, required only for the safety and convenience of persons using automobiles or bicycles." [12]

Given its character and complexity, at least from the 18th century on, law in the United States responded to

[10] *Ibid.*
[11] *Id.* at 245-46, 83 N.E. at 679.
[12] *Id.* at 246, 83 N.E. at 679.

social change on at least three levels. So we may appraise *Doherty* from three points of view. Adjustment between law and changing circumstance might be viewed in its own time—and may subsequently be appraised by the historian—first, as a technician's problem in using professional doctrine and procedure to reach and justify a particular result; second, as a statesman's problem in apportioning responsibility and achieving an effective relationship among available official agencies, for deciding what ought to be done by law and how to do it; third, as a practical philosopher's problem in perceiving reality in and outside of the law and relating this perception to some pattern of life values and to some working notions of cause and effect and economy in realizing values. This is to say that law's response to social change may be viewed as it resolves issues (1) of professional technique, (2) of the separation of powers, or (3) of the integration of all relevant aspects of the human experience of change. This range of issues was in fact present wherever law and social change were in play in United States history.

First, then, the situation in *Doherty* poses questions of the state and development of legal techniques. Here was a statute. One may inquire what it reflects as to the level of draftsmen's skill and sophistication, whether the legislation adequately defined a general standard, whether its statement was cumbered by too specific reference to the horse and carriage incidents of the draftsman's day, whether the limits of the statutory policy should have been indicated more firmly in some money limit on the town's liability. Here, too, was an appellate court's reading of the statute. One may inquire what conception of interpretation and what stage of technique in interpretation are represented in the opinion. There have been times when judges commonly insisted on the literal scope or limits of a statute's words. But, with a flexibility increasingly marked in 20th century interpretation, the Massachusetts court here is not content with literal context. The decision looks for the substantial purpose back of the words. Nineteenth century judges tended to shy from construing a statute primarily out of its own language and with reference to the particular situation out of which it grew or the particular problem with which it dealt. Instead, 19th century opinions tended to cloak the court's responsibility of choice in abstract canons of construction, so that not the judges but some impersonal principle seemed to determine decision. If the canon bore a Latin ornament, so much the better; the sonority of the old language helped suggest that the result flowed not from the reading of this particular statute by these particular men but from compulsion inherent in venerable doctrine. The Massachusetts opinion pays deference to the maxim *ejusdem generis.* About the court's marked disfavor toward an extensive construction of an act that imposes liability upon the sovereign's agent there may hang some implication of the rule that commanded strict construction of a statute in derogation of common law. But the analysis is dominated by a hardheaded factualism; automobiles are heavy, fast, and contain complicated machinery, and roads must be expensively surfaced to bear them under all conditions. The emphasis is pragmatic, particularistic, focusing on the distinctive facts of the particular setting. This is an approach of interpretation that spells a shift in judicial technique. In proportion as analysis becomes thus more overtly factual and particular, the approach gives new importance to another technical issue, that of judicial notice of matters of fact not put in evidence; realistic appraisal of what the judges are doing now calls for observing more closely how they weave into their determinations their assumptions as to facts of social life and technology, and invites closer scrutiny whether in doing so they stay within bounds of proper judicial notice.

The statute and the lawsuit raise other questions within the law's own institutional context but dealing with more basic problems of power. The statute traces to 1786. The date is a useful caution against the typical bias of men trained in a common law system, toward exaggerating the role of judge-made law. Legislation in fact entered early into fixing the content of important areas of public policy. There is historic significance, too, in the nature of the legislature's intervention here. The statute creates claims upon a public purse. True, the claims are of a rather humdrum order, not about great issues of ship money or supply of the troops. But the fact that it is statute and not case law that creates these claims points up the already firm, pervasive monopoly of the legislative branch on public finance. Moreover, the 1786 statute points up the legislature's key role in the use of law to allocate resources within the community. Given its power of the purse, and its important related authority to inquire into social facts, the legislature was naturally the agency about whose work this development centered.

The United States was a country of large distances. Even within the older and smaller states, relative to the conditions of their founding, distance presented substantial problems for legal order. These problems gained point and urgency because the country was constantly in growth, reaching out to extend settlement and experiencing under the prod of technological change a recurrent increase in the scale of its capital commitments. These facts meant that the relation of political authority at the center to political authority in constituent units provided one of the organizing themes of the country's legal development. *Doherty* comes to this issue in the end. There was a third party in interest which did not appear formally in the lawsuit but whose relation to the issue determined the judgment. This was, of course, the Commonwealth of Massachusetts, whose statute was in effect an allocation of economic burden between the state and its towns as well as between towns and aggrieved travelers. Measured by what turned the balance, *Doherty* was more a decision upon the relative public responsibilities of the Commonwealth and its subdivisions than upon the rights and duties between Mr. Doherty and the inhabitants of Ayer.

By its 1786 statute the Massachusetts legislature provided a frame of reference for fixing rights and duties. But general propositions of law gain content in use. *Doherty* v. *Inhabitants of Ayer* involved the interplay of legislative and judicial responsibility for making law—here brought to a point of tension because there was need to adjust an earlier value choice to a drastic change of circumstance. This was a situation typical and important to the separation of powers in a country undergoing the turbulent growth of the United States, especially under the impact of great scientific and technological change. The first pinch of change was likely to be felt in the executive branch or in the courts, as in *Doherty*, because these branches dealt with law at the point of application. These situations posed separation of powers choices to tax the wisdom of lawmen. Conceivably executive and judicial officers could turn back to the legislature for fresh directives every time they encountered circumstances materially different from those that confronted the makers of earlier statute law. Conceivably they could regard themselves, in contrast, as charged to promote economy and flexibility in legal order by determining for themselves what old policy meant in new situations. In a society characterized by the range and depth of change that marked the United States, choice between these attitudes decided a good deal of the practical content of separation of powers doctrine. The *Doherty* opinion represents what emerged as the typical judicial reaction. With the confidence of men backed by generations of bold common law growth, the Massachusetts judges assume their authority to adapt old statutory rules to considerable change of fact so long as change relates to the means rather than the ends of policy. But where change calls in question the relevance of the basic objectives set by the old statute, they return choice to the legislature. Obviously we deal here with a standard and not a rule for working out the separation of powers. Issues of this subtlety and variety can be handled only in broad terms.

By its nature the separation of powers issue brings us to other aspects of *Doherty* that concern not the internal dispositions of the law, but rather the reflection in law of attitudes, values, and problems rooted in the general experience of the community. "Of course," say the judges, the statute should not be restricted to the types of situations that existed in 1786. That "of course" is revealing of a set of mind. These men take for granted that this is law for a society which expects substantial change as the norm, which is not shocked or afraid of this reality, and which expects its legal order to take the reality in stride. Law might be expected to play a very different, and particularly a more active, part among people of such attitude than in a culture which found the meaning and values of life in observing and enforcing tradition. The matter of fact way in which the opinion comes to terms with relevant technology—the mechanical nature of the automobile, the need and cost of hard-surfaced roads —expresses an approach to public policy making which takes for granted that it should proceed, where it can, by rational cost accounting; among people taught by cumulating technological revolution, political decision becomes in truth political economy. Finally, and related to a cost accounting approach, in its treatment of the relation of state and local government fiscal responsibility, *Doherty* v. *Inhabitants of Ayer* reflects issues of economic and social function which were peculiarly characteristic in the growth of the United States and left marked impression upon its law. These are problems of special economic costs that attend major, rapid social change, and problems of cost and organization that attend large-scale organization of activity and commitment of large resources to long-term investment in social overhead capital. Science and technology, and the ways of life which people bred in a striving middle-class tradition derived from the teaching and promise of applied scientific and technological advance, conspired steadily to enlarge the time span and the physical and dollar quantities of our arrangements. Problems of scale increasingly generated problems of legal order in United States history. In *Doherty* the judges present us this generalization in the tangible form of their concern that the towns cannot finance the network of hard-surface roads by which the law must subsidize the new economy and the new society developing out of the automobile. So they turn the problem of resources allocation back to a more central source of decision.

Let us come back to where this discussion began: These essays examine some operations of law among processes of social change and stability in United States history. The enterprise rests on ideas about the meaningful scope of legal history which needed statement as preface to more particular themes. I propose now to define some hypotheses about the roles law has played in the growth of the country, (1) in affecting the shifting balance between deliberation and default as determinants of affairs, (2) in shaping general situations within which particular courses were channeled, (3) in contributing to the education in mind and will of leaders and their supporting publics, and (4) in exercising or standing ready to exercise ultimate force.

II

Drift and Direction

The three essays which follow this one are about ways in which law exercised or might have exercised direct influence on conditions of social stability and change in United States history. To keep close to the realities of the record, and to avoid even the appearance of exaggerating the law's effect, the present essay will talk mainly about circumstances, ideas, and attitudes originating outside the law, which created demands or situational pressures upon law which materially affected its use and character.

1

I focus on two points: (1) There were features about the growth of the United States which made change so much more the norm than stability as to create heavy demands and pressures on legal order. (2) (a) A great deal—perhaps the most influential part—of what happened in the growth of this society, including the growth of its law, came about out of the cumulative drift of circumstance or in response only to the most immediately perceived functional demands of social institutions, rather than out of effort directed at basic decisions. (b) Nonetheless this society and its law participated in a great and accelerating increase in man's capacity to control affairs; this increase in directive capacity stirred the law and provided new criteria by which to measure the worth and adequacy of law's role among other factors of social order.

The first point deals with successive Presents in time, the second with the causal relation of Past with Present with Future. Of course this is not a distinction that holds up if one presses it beyond the point of a helpful device for organizing complicated data. The Present may be whittled down to so instantaneous a point in the flow that it loses meaning. But men did contrive purposes, motives, and means on an assumption which produced overt results—the assumption that there was so high a degree of continuity among a part of the recent Past, the succession of instant moments, and a part of the immediately impending Future as to give them the working room which they called the Present. This working Present incorporated larger or smaller amounts of the Past and Future which environed it, depending upon the area of men's concerns that was in question in a given operation. Thus in a very active market of many striving buyers and sellers—of grain futures, say—the Present might be a very short Present. However, if one's interest were not in the particular course of dealing but in the institution through which the dealing was done—the market itself—there might be such stability of behavior and arrangements and it might take such a sustained accumulation of incident to make up the working reality of the complicated institution that "the present market" would be seen as a reality which existed only in a considerable span of calendar time.

The first point (the change in successive composite pictures of the social structure as it existed in particular Presents at different intervals) and the second point (the dynamics of passage from the condition shown in one of these composite pictures to the condition reflected in a later one) merge when one looks at certain massive facts. There are facts which come into existence, or events which happen, only in the span of generations or centuries. If one's interest is primarily in the processes by which they come into being, he may find it analytically useful to distinguish between (temporarily) achieved equilibria and the dynamics of passage from one (temporary) equilibrium to another. If he is interested primarily in the total result, he may have to take a composite photograph in a focus broad enough to treat the whole process as a single present reality. Thus if one looks at 1850 Wisconsin public policy he finds reflected a dominant pattern of wants, ambitions, and working notions of how to get things done which add up to what may fairly be called the 19th century middle-class mind. This pattern of ideas and attitudes had its own history of origins stretching back at least three hundred years. But in the realities of Wisconsin law making this pattern was a given fact which had influence because men treated it as "given" and took it for granted as the sensible way to look at the world. The influence of this "present" fact was felt, for example, in the confidence with which Wisconsin courts embraced the doctrine that every contract should be presumed valid and enforcible, so that a heavy burden rested on one who claimed some reason why a particular contract should be deemed illegal as against public policy.

There is practical reason for noting that our history included these massive facts which existed only in terms of long periods of calendar time—long periods, at least, as measured against the short lifetime of Western culture or the still shorter lifetime of the United States. Such a fact was the development of a pattern of sectional and nationwide marketing which came into being over the span of three generations after 1800. Such a fact was the moral prestige of rural life and values grounded in three hundred years' experience in settling new country. Such a fact was our preoccupation with operating technique (the "practical") and our relative impatience with understanding (the "theoretical") developed out of constant pressure to improvise, contrive, and manage as we opened up a rich continent. Insofar as such facts entered into the condition of social structure, regarded in cross section at different intervals, so far there was involved an element which profoundly affected passage from one condition of structure to another. From the presence of such facts in men's minds and habits derived much of the force of drift and institutional pressure upon law. To assess the net significance of such facts is not easy. Their more obvious impact was to limit men's capacity to direct affairs. Less obvious but no less real was the point that without the stability given by such massive facts of social existence men's limited energies of mind and will would not suffice to create any directed order at all.

This essay, then, and those which follow look at the growth of the United States and the role of law in that growth partly in cross-sectional views at different intervals —with affairs caught and frozen as in a photograph or X-ray —and partly in motion, or if one prefers, in processes of succession. This is not to deal with different realities, but with different ways of examining the same reality, as an historian can see it.

The last qualification is important to estimating the pretensions of an enterprise like this. An historian needs philosophy, but of course his need does not make him a competent philosopher. These essays use ideas of time and cause which have their own classic and difficult history in the world of thought. There is no way to organize data to treat the questions posed here except to use such concepts. But I claim no more than that I use them in ways that help make sense out of raw materials of United States legal history. History may be useful at least because it furnishes new sources from which philosophers can expose the naiveté of ordinary perception.

2

Let me tell three law stories which will cast into more visible form the general themes I have stated for this essay.

Consider, first, *Libby* v. *New York, New Haven* and *Hartford Railroad Co.,* decided by the Massachusetts Supreme Judicial Court in 1930.[1] Since 1871 the Massachusetts statutes had required that "Every railroad corporation shall cause a bell of at least thirty-five pounds in weight, and a steam whistle, to be placed on each locomotive engine passing upon its railroad." The statutes also provided that the railroad should be liable for all damages caused by a grade crossing accident caused by the railroad's "neglect" "to give the signals required" by the act. In *Libby* the court held that the railroad was not liable because of these statutory provisions for a collision involving its self-propelled gasoline passenger coach, which was equipped with an air whistle rather than a steam whistle. Obviously the "locomotive

[1] 273 Mass. 522, 174 N.E. 171 (1930).

engine" here had given no warning by blasts of a steam whistle; it had none. But, said the court, the gasoline coach could not be included within the statute "without rendering the words 'steam whistle' superfluous."[2] Moreover, "If the statute is to be literally enforced against such motor cars it would follow that a steam boiler must be kept in operation on them for no other purpose than to sound the whistle."[3] That new types of railroad equipment had come into use since the statute was written did not warrant the court in applying the statute; the legislature might have amended the act, but it had not. "The fact that a statute affects public safety does not warrant an interpretation which will make it comply with changed conditions and different modes of travel when the plain language of the statute makes it inapplicable to new conditions and different modes of travel."[4]

My second story begins with Article III, Section 2 of the Federal Constitution, which provides that the judicial power of the United States "shall extend . . . to all cases of admiralty and maritime jurisdiction." Like many important provisions of the Constitution, this one comes to us from the hand of the Convention's Committee on Detail and bears no helpful gloss. How far this admiralty jurisdiction runs has important consequences, if we turn for guidance to the English precedent, as the Supreme Court has always done where the framers used language familiar in our English legal inheritance. Admiralty law involved substantive doctrines not found in common law, notably comparative negligence; admiralty law conferred maritime liens; admiralty procedure was flexible, dispensed with the jury, and allowed

[2] *Id.* at 526, 174 N.E. at 173.
[3] *Ibid.*
[4] *Ibid.*

proceedings *in rem* against a vessel. But English precedent set limits to admiralty jurisdiction. In particular, as the United States Supreme Court read the record in 1825 in the case of *The Steamboat Thomas Jefferson,*[5] the admiralty jurisdiction did not extend to inland waters like the Missouri River, beyond the ebb and flow of the tide. But doctrine stood so for less than a generation. In 1852 in *The Propeller Genesee Chief* v. *Fitzhugh*[6] the majority of the United States Supreme Court (Daniel, J., dissenting) held that the admiralty jurisdiction must be deemed to embrace the libel of a vessel for a collision on Lake Ontario. For the majority, Mr. Chief Justice Taney pointed to the facts of inland marine commerce. The Great Lakes were "in truth inland seas". "A great and growing commerce is carried on upon them between different States and a foreign nation, which is subject to all the incidents and hazards that attend commerce on the ocean."[7] To limit the benefits of admiralty jurisdiction to the commerce of the Atlantic coast would not only produce great public inconvenience, but run counter to the policy of this federal system to afford equal rights in the laws and their administration to the people of all the states. The tidewater limitation announced by English doctrine was sensible enough in a country which had no great inland waters of commerce beyond the movement of the tide. But it was a limitation arbitrary and unreasonable with reference to the situation of the United States. As to the ruling in *The Thomas Jefferson,* with due deference the majority thought it had no option but to overrule that decision as an error. It was an error "into which the court fell, when the great

[5] 23 U.S. (10 Wheat.) 428 (1825) (Story, J., for the Court).
[6] 53 U.S. (12 How.) 443 (1851).
[7] *Id.* at 453.

importance of the question as it now presents itself could not be foreseen; and the subject did not therefore receive that deliberate consideration which at this time would have been given to it by the eminent men who presided here when that case was decided. For the decision was made in 1825, when the commerce on the rivers of the west and on the lakes was in its infancy, and of little importance, and but little regarded compared with that of the present day."[8] It was not "until the valley of the Mississippi was settled and cultivated, and steamboats invented," that a great inland marine commerce developed. Had this development occurred earlier, the earlier decisions on admiralty jurisdiction would have been rendered in the light of such facts, "before the English definition had become the settled mode of describing the jurisdiction, and before the courts had been accustomed to adhere strictly to the English mode of pleading, in which the place is always averred to be within the ebb and flow of the tide. . . ."[9] In light of these considerations, and since *The Thomas Jefferson* did not decide any question of property or define property rights, the majority felt entitled to overrule it and to bring the definition of the admiralty jurisdiction into meaningful relation to the economic and social growth of the country.[10]

My third story is not one which I can bring quickly into focus with a quotation. Its point is implicit in a chronology and formal record. The story is of the sequence of growth in

[8] *Id.* at 456.

[9] *Id.* at 458.

[10] See the recitation of this history by Clifford, J., dissenting in *The Lottawanna,* 88 U.S. (21 Wall.) 558, 583-89 (1875), and in Conover, "The Abandonment of the 'Tidewater' Concept of Admiralty Jurisdiction in the United States," 38 ORE. L. REV. 34 (1958).

Wisconsin public policy toward industrial accident between 1860-1861 and 1911.

In 1860 and 1861 the Wisconsin Supreme Court first confronted cases which required it to define the law regarding an employer's legal responsibility for accidental injury to his employee on the job. The legislature had shown no interest, or indeed awareness, in the matter. Law was made here according to familiar common law pattern—out of the initiative of litigants, the argumentative energy and ingenuity of opposing counsel, and the exercise of the ultimate responsibility of decision by appellate judges. The judges worked partly with what the facts of the cases and the effort of counsel provided them, partly with their own knowledge and assumptions about relevant general facts of life in the community—machine hazards, and the costs and risks of labor and of financing industry—and partly with the guidance given by previous decisions of other courts in this country and in England. The result was to adopt as Wisconsin law a body of doctrine which made it very hard for an injured worker to obtain a judgment against his employer. The injured man must prove some sort of negligence on the employer's part. In his turn, the employer might retreat behind one or more of three strong defenses—that the injured man had assumed the risks of the job, or had been guilty of negligence which contributed to his injury, or had been hurt by the negligence of a fellow servant.

The first departure from this pattern of policy making came in 1875. Railroads had emerged as Wisconsin's Number One heavy industry, and railroad work was specially hazardous. Railroading was also the area of heavy industry where trade union organization first gained a foothold. An 1875 statute abrogating the fellow servant defense in railroad job accidents reflected this added pressure on public policy. Significantly, this group "litigant," the union, sought relief in a new forum—the legislature. However, the balance of power shifted among interest groups; the 1875 act was repealed in 1881. Not until 1889 did railroad labor again succeed in putting on the statute books the first of a new series of laws imposing safety duties on railroad employers and limiting their common law defenses. Meanwhile other unions developed in other fields and pressed for legislation on a wider front. General factory safety legislation began with a fire escape requirement in 1878, and with an 1887 act for minimum sanitary protection and the guarding of dangerous machinery.

So from 1860-1900, policy developed in the legislature and in the courts by maneuver of those most immediately concerned; given the activity of lobby groups, there was somewhat broader representation of the immediately involved interests before the legislature than before the courts. Through these decades supplementary law making went on by judicial interpretation of the statutes. In earlier years the Wisconsin Supreme Court gave the legislation rough handling, construing it strictly as in derogation of common law. Later, judges chafed at the harsh results which application of the fault principle produced within the limits of the narrow legislation. In pointed dicta the state's high court contributed its weight to suggestions that the legislature release the law from its bonds and put the subject into a new frame of reference. But until the turn of the century the legislature operated in a fashion almost as passive as the courts, in effect acting only upon the issues framed before it by parties most closely involved.

Then, in the first decade of the 20th century there occurred an explosion of new creative energy in the policy making process. Several fresh sources of initiative came into play. One development had been foreshadowed since the legislature in 1883 created in the executive branch a Bureau of Labor and Industrial Statistics. For its first twenty years the Bureau showed little force, hampered as it was by the legislature's penury and the want of energetic and imaginative Bureau leadership. But the agency was there, and it did grow. Now, aided by a 1905 law which required report and collection of industrial accident data, in 1907 and 1909 the Bureau laid before the legislature such a background of information on the problems of industrial accident as had hitherto not been seen for any Wisconsin legislation. The executive branch contributed more positive direction to events. In these years Governor Robert M. LaFollette was using his influence as party leader as well as the forum provided by his office to create for the state's chief executive a policy leadership of unprecedented vigor. In repeated messages to the legislature and in background dealings with legislators the governor pressed for more and more liberal industrial accident legislation. Moreover, the governor drew into the policy process another state agency of great potential. The 1907 report of the Bureau of Labor and Industrial Statistics acknowledged the "invaluable assistance" of Professor John R. Commons. Commons joined the University of Wisconsin economics faculty in 1904. Soon after, responding to the governor's requests for university help in legislative research and drafting, Commons was at work and was putting his seminars to work on workmen's compensation, factory safety regulation, and the proposal of a new kind of executive agency to administer statute policy in these fields.

Amid these activities, the legislature itself added new sources of policy initiative and deliberation. In 1901 it provided for a Legislative Reference (research and bill drafting) Department within the Free Library Commission. The state was fortunate that the director of this new staff agency was a man of great creative energy and courage; one of the key bills out of which were shaped the eventual workmen's compensation act was that drawn in 1905 by Charles McCarthy of the Legislative Reference Department at the request of Milwaukee's trade union and Socialist Assemblyman Brockhausen. Throughout, McCarthy and Commons worked in close team play, fusing the contributions both of executive and legislative staff to the making of a statute. Nor did the legislature's procedural contribution end in the creation of the Legislative Reference Department. Confronted with several proposals of major policy importance, the 1909 legislature created five joint interim committees to investigate designated problems, hold hearings, and draft and report bills to the 1911 session. Never before had the legislature set up such an ambitious effort at preparatory work. One of these joint interim committees was charged to deal with "industrial insurance." From its work came Laws, 1911, Chapter 50, Wisconsin's basic workmen's compensation act, and Chapter 485, creating an Industrial Commission charged not only to administer the compensation system but also to develop industrial safety codes that would emphasize prevention over reparation.

For my present purpose this story may properly end with the enactment of these laws, save in one particular so closely tied to the growth of policy making procedure that it needs to be included. John R. Commons made no more distinctive contribution to the construction of the new system than when he suggested that the statutes authorize the Industrial Commission to appoint advisory committees representing employers, unions, casualty insurance companies, and the public, to help the Commission draw safety rules for various fields of industry. This brought interest groups into a new, legitimated working relation to legislative process, involving them directly with specialists who had no particular interest ties as well as with the responsible public officers. It was a very different, more flexible and matter-of-fact, more sustainedly communicative process for policy decision than the common law or the 19th century legislative traditions of making policy through *ad hoc* clash of partisans. Without romanticizing the results, one may note that the advisory committee system worked well enough that it became the normal channel for exploring changes in the underlying statutory pattern as well as for exercise of the Commission's rule making powers.

Of course, while these new sources of influence were coming into play from 1900-1910, policy making still was done in large part by the pull and haul of the adversary process in the legislature. The political parties, the governors, individual legislators and candidates for office continued to play roles of middlemen or brokers among divergent interests. Manufacturers' and trade union lobbies were still prime movers. Yet there was change also in this realm, for these years saw a gathering tendency for more formal organization and planned effort by such interest groups, not only at the state capitol but back in the home districts. It was part of the movement of events that the judicial branch, formerly so prominent in the growth of public policy, now fell into the background, to come forward again in the more restricted, though essential role of helping give living content by interpretation and application to the general pattern set by legislature and commission. However, if the established agencies continued to work in familiar ways or at least in ways analogous to earlier operations, it was plain that in the course of this growth of the law of industrial accident new sources of initiative, influence, and direction had entered the policy making process.[11]

These, then, are my three stories—of the gasoline coach and its air whistle, the admiralty jurisdiction and the collision on Lake Ontario, the shifting procedures for making a law of industrial accident. All three reflect important legal elements in the patterns of social living in the United States at different times. All three, for example, reflect the extent to which the machine generated problems for law over the span of 125 years. The three stories reflect, also, three major types of dynamic processes of change in law and its relation to the society. In one aspect the railroad air whistle case reminds us of the influence of drift and inertia in men's thinking. A lawsuit had to go to the highest Massachusetts

[11] The outlines of this story of changing procedures in Wisconsin policy making, as reflected in the growth of policy concerning industrial accident, may be seen in Garrison and Hurst, THE LEGAL PROCESS *passim* (Auerbach and Mermin rev. ed., 1956). See also Commons, MYSELF 95, 96, 110, 133, 154-58 (1934); Fitzpatrick, MCCARTHY OF WISCONSIN 41, 43 (1944); Haferbecker, WISCONSIN LABOR LAWS 19-24, 32, 38-42, 185 (1958); McCarthy, THE WISCONSIN IDEA 214 (1912); Schmidt, "History of Labor Legislation in Wisconsin," pp. 50-51, 55, 65, 69, 73 (unpublished thesis in University of Wisconsin Library, 1933).

court because a draftsman who wanted each railroad engine to carry an adequate warning signal did not say so, but said it must have a steam whistle; in his day that was the known long-distance warning device, and his imagination did not exert itself to envisage that changing technology might bring new devices. *The Genesee Chief* shows us drift or inertia in a context closer home, the easy acceptance of familiar professional phrases and doctrine—the pleader's habit, borrowed from English precedent, of alleging that the cause arose on tidewater, whether or not the point was necessary to his issue. But *The Genesee Chief* points up a different source of impetus for change or stability in social relations—the logic of function. The definition of the admiralty jurisdiction had to be expanded to include the navigable inland waters because the admiralty jurisdiction existed to serve the functional needs of ship-borne commerce and a trading population; and where the commerce and the people went, the admiralty court needed to follow if it was to fulfill its reason for being. Finally, the course of Wisconsin policy making procedure as it dealt with the industrial accident problem shows us a third type of dynamic for social change or stability—the impact of inquiry, debate, and decision proceeding out of awareness and calculated effort to define ends and means. This is direction, as contrasted with the impetus of drift or of function, and it is the type of response to life which most truly belongs in the law and to which the law belongs.

3

The uses of law in the growth of the United States were determined largely by the pattern of other factors in the country's life. Social context was peculiarly influential upon this legal order. This followed from the values which gave this legal system its character: its scrutiny of the distribution of power, its concern with constitutionalism or the legitimacy of power, its procedural emphasis, its role in resources allocation.

When governing opinion charged law with these tasks and accepted its legitimacy in these terms, the effect was to import into law potential concern for all major power relations in the community or at least to incline all such relationships to acquire some legal aspect or produce some expression of themselves in law. True, within any given area of life outside legal institutions, the law's role was typically to make only a marginal (limited) increment to the sum of factors operating. That it should be so was integral to our concept of constitutional (limited) government. But to say that the law's actual or potential contribution in any given sector was typically marginal does not mean its contribution was unimportant. Because its role was to deal with the relations of power, law provided marginal increments of influence which significantly affected the quality and content of life—or if it did not do so, or did not do so effectively, this fact was no less important for the quality or content of social experience. We need draw another distinction, however, which brings us back to where we started. That the law had important relation to social context did not mean that law shaped the social context. It did mean that popular expectation and demand upon this legal order made it specially sensitive to pressures generated out of the total situation.

The distinctive character of this legal order was itself the product of social context. This was new land; the Englishmen who came into it found no substantial indigenous culture. The situation called again and again for the conscious contrivance of order. This making of order proceeded from the trading company charters and royal grants of colonial years to the new state constitutions and the first effort at federation in the Revolution, to the classic model of the Federal Convention and the ratifying conventions in the states, on into the organization of successive new states through the 19th century. Not until the release of nationalist feeling after the disruptions of World War II did the world again see such a quantity of state making. The blunders of the old order and the energies the new middle class derived from England's commercial and industrial revolution brought rending civil war to the home country in the 17th century. Our English inheritance thus included hard learned lessons in the importance of legitimacy of official power and the monopoly of violence by a legitimate government. On the other hand the victors were a class whose power depended upon private property and large scope for maneuver in market. Thus our English legacy included strong notions about rights of privacy and limits upon the extent and manner of use of official power. The vitality of these factors showed itself in our own classic period of constitution making. The shock which Shays' Rebellion gave leading opinion up and down the new states in 1786 was a large factor in producing the Federal Convention and attested the weight that sober men assigned to issues of legitimacy and the legitimate monopoly of force. The insistence which brought the Bill of Rights by amendment into the new Federal Constitution expressed the pervasive middle-class belief in limited government. Much social unsettlement inevitably attended the American Revolution—in the clash of Tory and patriot, the jailings and the seizures of property through Committees of Public Safety, the leveling enthusiasms of the more radical wing of the patriots in some states. Such experience helped translate into local terms general attitudes born of the Parliamentary Revolution. Constitutionalism, the legitimate monopoly of force and the scrutiny of all other power arrangements were characters stamped upon this legal order by the general experience of the people who gave first form to the new society.

Cross-sectional views at later intervals, say in the 1830's or the '70's, or in the "Progressive" years from 1900-1915, or again in 1933-1937, show that the conditions of the country's growth continued to press upon law these concerns with constitutional ordering of power. Tone and emphasis varied with period. Through much of the 19th century—the great sectional controversy apart—one senses that men attended to these questions of the organization and control of decision outside the market with impatient desire to get on to more interesting challenges of private economic development. If one takes his cross-sectional view around 1900 or 1912, for the first time since 1789 he senses the presence of a prime preoccupation with the general organization of power, as again in the middle 1930's; these differences pose basic questions of the dynamics of social change and stability affecting law's role.

Social context likewise pressed law in the United States into its emphasis on procedure and into its considerable concern with resource allocation. One need not take a position of economic determinism to see that the condition of the economy was of prime importance in shaping these features of the legal system. The point is clear enough in explaining why we turned to law as much as we did to muster and direct the use of manpower, money, and the real wealth that lay in soil, minerals, forests, and waterways. Until the '90's the country was rich in fixed natural wealth, but hard-pressed to find mobile capital sufficient to realize on its opportunities. This situation spelled the great importance of the power of the purse—the power to tax and spend—and the power to dispose of the public lands. Given our political inheritance from the rise of the House of Commons and the leadership of our own popular assemblies in the years of tension that built up to the split with England, it was axiomatic that these primary powers lay in the legislature. At any period in which one takes a cross-sectional view, he will find an extent of Congressional and state legislative activity which at first seems surprising in view of the obvious crudity of the legislative process. However, given the gross imbalance that long existed among the factors of production, this was an understandable legal response to the pattern of the economy. Under the imperious demands of the total situation, legislators were pressed into a role which the immaturity of our legislative institutions left them ill-fitted to play. This situational pressure for legislation in itself channeled effort into formal decision making processes. This was so, though emphasis on form did not fit easily the prevailing temper of this mobile, striving people, whose image of practical accomplishment was that of the entrepreneur. At any period our legal process bears the stamp of a people whose prevailing preference was to improvise and to make opportunistic use of the means closest at hand. Nonetheless, a statute was inherently a formal act. This was so not only as a matter of definition but out of need. A considerable minimum of formal procedure and formal validation was practically necessary to get decisions out of a representative body in a society whose fluidity exposed its representatives to so wide and shifting a range of informal pressures. Outside the realm of taxing, spending, and public lands disposal, however, the crudity of 19th century legislative processes was such as to leave to state appellate courts a big job of law making. From about 1810 to 1890 the courts defined a large part of the law needed to provide a framework of expectations and administration for operating the market, adjusting the play of private associations, validating personal status in marriage and the family, policing or redressing personal injury, and protecting social order. The growth of population, of economic activity, and of closer-knit living created the need for doctrine at the same time as men turned their prime energies and interest away from public policy to focus upon their private concerns. The litigious process was fueled by the private interests of suitors, however, and the judges were available as a body of law makers relatively more trained and disciplined, more continuously in session, than legislators. The natural result was the relative prominence of common law in 19th century policy making. In turn, this reinforced the attention given procedure, since the traditional business of courts in our system was to determine adversary issues brought to as sharp definition as the wit of pleaders could manage. This traditional emphasis on form rose to a still higher point as 19th century appellate judges grew increasingly conscious of their function as law makers; in the attention to points of pleading, the elaborate mustering and distinguishing of precedent, the frequency of the calculated dictum in 19th century opinions, the disposition of the actual lawsuit often seems lost to view and a reader sometimes gathers that the judges saw the real significance of the case in the opportunity it gave them to add to the body of law for the community at large.

Consider how some of these large currents move within the space of a particular, quite ordinary lawsuit, *Smith* v. *Wood*,[12] which the Wisconsin Supreme Court decided in 1860. The case is relevant because in it the judges weigh form and informality with reference to the values of a reliable market in land titles and against the background of some typical resources-allocating statutes. The lawsuit arose in the southwestern lead-bearing section of Wisconsin. The land in question originally belonged to the United States. At the time pertinent to the controversy Congress' policy was that the United States should realize on the mineral wealth of the public lands by leasing rather than selling. Hence the federal statutes directed the local federal land officer to reserve lead-bearing land from sale and forbade its entry for the transfer of a fee simple title. The lead miners did not want to be lessees of the United States, however, and in a fashion familiar in the informal, self-willed ways of the new country, for years they went ahead staking out mining claims and treating the claims among themselves as property which they bought and sold. Smith, a lead miner, paid the handsome sum of $2500 for such a claim which another miner, Jamison, had thus illegally staked out. Wood subsequently entered the land at the federal land office and obtained a land office receipt of

[12] 12 Wis. 425 (1860).

entry for it, though if it were in fact lead-bearing land, the land office should not have made the entry. Smith went to Wood, protesting that he was already working the "Jamison lot" which Wood had entered, and persuaded Wood to execute what purported to be an agreement that Wood would convey the tract to Smith when Wood obtained a final patent for it from the United States. The United States Land Office issued Wood the patent, and when he failed to convey to Smith, Smith sought a decree for specific performance of the promise to convey.

The case required the judges for the first time to define certain terms on which Wisconsin law would grant specific performance of contracts to convey land. Drawing on New York cases and on Mr. Justice Story's treatise on Equity Jurisprudence, the Wisconsin court declared that a decree for specific performance was not a matter of right, but lay in the discretion of the court, and that one determining factor in the exercise of that discretion was whether the promise to convey had been given for an adequate consideration. Denying specific performance, the court decided that there was no adequate consideration for this promise:

> The United States lead mines, on the upper Mississippi, were early reserved from sale, and, in pursuance of an act of congress, were leased for limited terms, by agents acting under the direction of the President. There was great opposition to the system among the miners, and many never applied for or received any leases from the general government, but went on to the public lands, made claims, worked upon them and sold the mineral discovered and taken from their diggings. These claims were generally respected by the miners, even in cases where there was no lease, and were a

> subject of bargain and sale among them. We infer that [Smith] . . . purchased one of these claims, paying therefor a large sum of money. But it seems this claim, or mineral lot, was embraced within a forty acre tract, which had not been reserved as mineral land [by the local Land Office], and therefore was subject to entry. Every one at all acquainted with the early history of the lead district of the territory of Wisconsin, well knows that many lands containing rich veins of mineral, were entered. These entries were valid, unless the general government saw fit to vacate them, and the purchaser acquired an absolute title. So there can be no doubt that Wood . . . obtained a good title to the tract entered by [him] . . . What obligation . . . [was he] under to recognize any claim upon the land thus entered? What legal or equitable right had [Smith] . . . to call upon [Wood] . . . for a conveyance of this land? We cannot perceive that . . . [he] had any whatever. And although Wood . . . gave a bond for a conveyance, yet as this was without consideration, why should a court of equity now enforce a specific performance of it? It is a voluntary agreement, and, although under seal, ought not to be enforced.[13]

[13] *Id.* at 427-28. Compare, generally, Lake, "Legal Profile of the Mining Industry—Part 1," 1955 WIS. L. REV. 399, 401-03. The liveliness of both legislative and judicial lawmaking and some of the interplay between them amid the bustling growth of 19th century Wisconsin are reflected in characteristic settings in Hunt, LAW AND LOCOMOTIVES ch. VI (1958); Kimball, "The Role of the Court in the Development of Insurance Law," 1957 WIS. L. REV. 520; Kuehnl, THE WISCONSIN BUSINESS CORPORATION part III (1959); Laurent, THE BUSINESS OF A TRIAL COURT xx, 34-38, 46, 49, 50 (1959); Mills, "Government Fiscal Aid to Private Enterprise in Wisconsin: A Quantitative Approach," 1956 WIS. L. REV. 110; Page, "Application of the Derogation Rule to the Code of Civil Procedure," 1955 *id.* at 91; ———, "Statutes in Derogation of Common Law: The Canon as an Analytical Tool," 1956 *id.* at 78.

There are interesting balances of judgment here, reflecting the procedural and the resources-allocation emphasis which the situation pressed on the law. In the mineral land leasing statute Congress had shown a rather unusual attention to the choice of means for realizing on the special wealth of the public lands. It had cast its choice in sufficiently formal terms that the court could not ignore; hence the judges refused legal effect to the miners' unlawful trading custom. On the other hand, Congress had left the specific reservation of mineral bearing lands to the local land office and had not provided a procedure for collateral attack upon entries allowed by the land office, though a given entry might be vulnerable to direct challenge by the United States. This was a community in which land titles were a prime subject of market dealing. The court would recognize Wood's entry and the subsequent patent as conferring a valid, saleable title. But ordinary market regularity should prevail. The court would not decree away Wood's title merely because Wood had made a promise to the holder of an illegal mining claim. Since the mining claim itself lacked validity, Wood had done no wrong to Smith in making his entry and hence there was nothing of substance given for his promise to turn over his entry to Smith. The ruling was the more striking because by it the court overrode an old and respected form in the law, a promise under seal.

In its various aspects *Smith* v. *Wood* reflects characteristic interplay of legislative and judicial roles and of political and market values. Congress had created a general framework for public lands disposal, including general terms for the extent and manner of passage from public to private title. Alongside this machinery for determining the use of a massive public resource there existed the market—an institution for private decision making on the allocation of resources, deriving its institutional character primarily from social practice, but given sustaining form by the law of contract, tort and property. The market gave scope for an infinite variety of individual and group activity, more complex than any legislation could anticipate. Moved by the zeal of individual suitors, the litigious process was the natural means for making the supplementary law needed to give reliable form and sanction to this infinite variety of private interest. It was the style of lawmaking which naturally tended to focus most sharply and most continuously on market values and the functional needs of market operations. Thus in *Smith* v. *Wood* the court treats its prime task as that of supplementing statute policy on the shift from public to private title by more detailed judge-made rules to support what the judges deem the desirable substance of market dealing.

If social context fashioned the distinctive tasks and methods of this legal order, it also largely determined the kinds and relative urgency of problems brought to law. Later essays note particular examples of this situational influence. Here it is relevant to observe a more general effect. Through 175 years of national existence the structure of the country's situation produced a tendency for change to prevail over stability in large social relationships. The balance of factors that brought this result shifted in different periods. But the prevailing tendency remained, itself a remarkable constant which profoundly affected the uses of law in the life of the society.

Among the structural elements which favored change in

United States society, five had special bearing in generating opportunities and demands for law. Circumstance, idea and attitude weave together in constituting these elements of the situation. The five elements relate to the land, the people, the state of knowledge, the opportunity for constructive change, and the scale of operations.

(1) *The land.* The land was vast and richly endowed with physical wealth—but, most important, it was new; for all practical purposes it was culturally unoccupied territory. In the state of communications technology for nearly three hundred years after the first English settlement the land was sufficiently separated from English and European influence to foster and require a great deal of independent invention by its settlers. Its interior diversity and distances promoted diversity of social contrivance among its own regions. Of course the people of the United States drew heavily upon inheritances from England and Europe; such cultural continuity is the essential framework for any society. *The Genesee Chief* dramatized this interplay of inheritance and fresh creation, as the novel conditions of growth in a new land pressed the judges to reconsider and reject the English definition of admiralty jurisdiction. However, clear-cut as it was, this was change only within a quite limited area of values. The newness and novelty of the land made themselves felt in much more drastic changes of direction. Great discontinuities do appear in history; quantity, timing, and reach of change sometimes combine to produce qualitative differences between the life of one period and that only shortly preceding it. At least over its first 175 years as a nation, the United States experienced qualitative changes in its patterns of living which represented important discon-

tinuity in the record of so young a country. Three such times of qualitative change stand out: the constitution-making generation, 1765-1800; the generation of growth of private financial and industrial power after the Civil War; the years of impact of the depression of the 1930's and World War II. The land's newness and relative isolation provided a favorable setting for drastic and original change. Other factors in the situation helped realize the potential of the setting.

(2) *The people.* The firstcomers who enjoyed the opportunity to fix the mold of western values that shaped the new society were people whose working philosophy was that of middle-class Englishmen. They believed that life's meaning would be found through the creative will of individuals, that individuals were responsible to God for what they made of themselves, that they should work hard and try to improve their lot, consistently with the like efforts of others, that men could get most effective leverage on their world through the economy, that contract and property dealings in market offered the most productive procedures for private economic activity, that law like other social institutions was legitimated by serving individual life and that all official power was accountable to serve this end, but also that men might properly employ law for common purposes wherever good sense showed that it must be useful. This was a pattern of ideas and attitudes that promoted striving, invention, and mobility in individual and group power and status. Ambitions and attitudes that fit this pattern provided the background for the contriving that produced our 1860 Wisconsin mineral land lawsuit of *Smith* v. *Wood.* The same temper made it natural that Wisconsin law making on the industrial accident problem

proceeded through the 19th century by the most narrow adversary processes in court and legislature—that is, proceeded by the law's nearest analogue to market competition. The conditions of settlement gave sustained impetus to the middle-class bias in favor of change. For nearly three hundred years the hardships of building communities in a raw country continually taught men a sharp awareness of how much they were on their own in a novel situation that demanded originality, ingenuity, and effort. Though in the long run the population grew mostly by native births, prevailing attitudes were set in generations deeply affected by the presence of millions of immigrants who came here in the expectation and hope of change. And for three hundred years people in North America experienced at firsthand the excitement and the promise of manipulating their environment, or at least of seeing a society grow before their eyes. A bias for change was a legacy from the founding middle-class English. The bequest was the more readily accepted by succeeding immigrants under the teaching of a massive common experience.

(3) *The state of knowledge.* What men know changes their world. At whatever point of its national history we take a cross-sectional view of social structure in the United States, the state of knowledge appears a prime factor for change. This country spent its whole national life amid the turbulence of a vast, cumulative, accelerating expansion in western man's knowledge of his material environment and how to use it. Successive explosions of knowledge proceeded out of the interaction of basic and applied science. Though the process gained imperious pace and momentum in the 19th century, it affected the occupation of the North American

continent from the beginning, as developing knowledge of navigation and ship building fixed the time and extent of permanent settlement. The single most potent instrument of the changeful drive of science and technology was the machine. True, social invention and institutions formed by social practice were part of the pattern, especially the market and the almost infinite variety of private associations. But machine-spurred production and machine-geared timing and organization were factors powerful enough alone to insure that the society would move continually from one stage of disequilibrium to another. This was so if for no other reason than the dynamic presence of a constantly rising material productivity. The force of expanding basic and applied science made itself felt, likewise, in an unprecedented development of the division of labor. This spelled an increasingly wide and sensitive interlock of processes, not only in the economic but likewise in the social and political aspects of the society, as well as greater productivity of human resources—again with the result of strengthening the bias of the total situation toward change. The state of knowledge directly affected law's capacities, as we shall note later. The state of knowledge and the dynamic thrust it gave to events also had profound indirect effect upon legal order by determining the problems brought to law. Consider, again, the machine. Machinery radically changed the tempo and relative balance or imbalance of social growth; the coming of the steamboat to the inland rivers and lakes precipitated the changed definition of admiralty jurisdiction in *The Genesee Chief*. Machinery brought new hazards to life and property, and spurred the elaboration of social cost accounting definitions in law—as for the automobile's broken axle in *Doherty* v. *Inhabitants of Ayer,* the grade crossing collision in *Libby* v. *New York, New Haven and Hartford Railroad Co.,* and the general problem of industrial accident with which Wisconsin policy makers grappled after 1860. Machinery affected the relative balance within the constitutional separation of powers; the law which responded to machine-created problems tended to be statute-based law, as fitted matters that were novel, involved a wide range of interests and, more likely than not, required for their solution the spending of public money upon new executive or administrative processes to supplement legislation.[14]

(4) *Opportunity.* My fourth and fifth points derive from the first three. But of their own force they inclined our situation toward change. By gift of circumstance this society lived far above the margin of subsistence. There was so much room in which to grow that it was unusual for any one interest to feel that its existence depended on destroying another; men contended out of hope and not out of despair, taught by rising productivity and expanding markets to be confident that there was more to come; bargain, compromise, adjustment, and co-operation developed as natural working approaches for people who could see the future in terms of getting ahead rather than merely of surviving or holding a position. All this was largely an unearned increment. The land was naturally rich. For a long time it was peopled far below its productive capacity, not because of legal restrictions but because there was so much more living space than people to fill it. Because of cheap raw materials,

[14] See cases and authorities cited in Chapter 1, note 6, and in the present chapter, notes 1, 6, 10, and 11 *supra.*

because of the steady growth of human resources and of the demand for goods that booming population brought, because of the primacy that prevailing middle-class opinion gave to effort and contrivance—and because, too, of a legal order which helped these other factors to expression—this society enjoyed great practical freedom to take advantage of the explosion of basic and applied science. These elements reacted on men's attitudes to generate optimism and confidence that change would be for the better and that change was the natural course of affairs. They reacted on men's attitudes, also, by turning energies of mind and will substantially away from plotting hostility to planning competition and from venting hatred to bargaining for position. On the whole there was never substantial reality to the notion of class war in the growth of the United States, unless we count so the tensions of Negro-White relations. Our history was not unmarked by bitterness. But it was typically that of family quarrels within the frame of middle-class values; this was true of agrarian "radicalism," for example. That all this was, likewise, largely unearned increment—the product more of plenty of life space than of self-discipline or direction—made it no less the fact. Despite its basic riches, the country knew scarcity as it grew. But this was scarcity of a degree and kind calculated to spur ambition by the visible disproportion between opportunity and present means, rather than the damning scarcity which breeds despair or resignation.

Wisconsin policy making from 1860 to 1911 on the industrial accident problem showed in miniature how this society used its opportunities for change by constructive adjustment rather than by merely destructive tests of strength.

Two points in this Wisconsin record deserve special note. First, was the willingness of the most immediately affected interests to use political processes to fix the framework within which they contended. This might seem the less notable so far as concerned the attitudes of businessmen; in this entrepreneurial-minded society, armed with independent resources won in market, they might expect generally to control government. More striking, in this light, was the readiness of the trade unions to go to law and seek power by political means. In Milwaukee men representing various strands of German Socialist thinking competed for labor leadership with the native-born Knights of Labor. In the tense May of 1886 which saw the Chicago Haymarket bombing, the drive for the Eight Hour Day combined with general discontent over wages to explode into some forty labor disputes in Milwaukee. Militia fired on strikers. Most of the strikes failed and the Knights of Labor quickly lost position. So it was Socialist leadership that directed the significant trade union policy in Wisconsin at the turn of the century. But it was a leadership which sought to improve labor's bargaining strength in market or its effectiveness in the lobbies of the legislature, to achieve such practical goals as higher wages and a workmen's compensation act, rather than the dictatorship of the proletariat. It is revealing, too, that John R. Commons persuaded politicians and lobbyists to incorporate his management-labor-public advisory committees in the structure of the new Wisconsin Industrial Commission, and that the device worked.

All was not net profit in this approach to social issues. This pragmatism had appealing humanity; men fulfilled themselves better by arguing and lobbying over a workmen's compensation act than by shooting each other to enforce a political philosophy. But this pragmatism could also turn into complacently narrow practicality which wasted opportunity and let small problems grow big by default. Our situation inclined us to constructive rather than destructive change. But because this was an unearned increment of our good fortune, we were the more likely to misuse the way of life it allowed.

(5) *The scale of operations.* Bigness was typically a determining factor of change in North American growth. The bias of events for or against change, the force and pace of tendency, the nature of opportunities and tensions were formed largely by the great size of some elements in the situation. Bigness first made itself felt in the great size of the unoccupied land mass. In the crude beginnings this factor limited rather than promoted social change. The early colonies were isolated, trusted little in co-operating with each other and pursued narrow ambitions as they struggled for bare foothold on the edge of wilderness. Given the continent's potential for growth, however, we witnessed repeatedly that when cumulative development reaches some critical point, quantitative change can pass sometimes rapidly into qualitative difference. Partly from general growth, partly under the prod of difficulties with England, after mid-18th century we grew bolder about our future and, ceasing to regard the land's size as a threat or barrier, began to regard it as an opportunity and challenge. The achievements of joint revolutionary effort, the Articles of Confederation, the Northwest Ordinance, the Federal Constitution, the Louisiana Purchase, the steady succession of new states testify that the challenge of bigness drove for change

through expanding political organization. For one hundred years after 1820 a new kind of bigness became a persistent structural feature of the society, as the country accepted the largest movement of settlers in western history. This element was compounded by a high native birth rate and by massive internal migration. Wisconsin's experience was not at all uncommon in showing increases from 3200 people in 1830 to 305,000 in 1860, to 775,000 in 1870, to nearly 1,700,000 in 1890, to 2,600,000 in 1920 and to 3,400,000 in 1950. The state gained about 300,000 persons for each decade. Rates of increase showed great variation, trending downward; thus Wisconsin's 1850 population was almost 900 per cent greater than that of 1840, 1860 was about 150 per cent greater than 1850, the increase to 1870 was about 35 per cent, and thence the rate fell steadily lower. Consistent with the fact that land mass was the first element of size to affect the country's history, large-scale heavy industry investment began in transport—in turnpikes, canals, and above all in railroads. From the first really large railroad investments of the 1850's the economy moved with accelerating speed into bigger and bigger commitments of capital, first in production and then in distribution. With increase in dollars committed went increase in time committed. Public works investments showed like trends as urban population climbed toward parity with rural and then passed far beyond into the rise of metropolitan areas, as the automobile was subsidized by tax-built hard-surfaced roads, as the need to limit the swings of the business cycle brought new fiscal functions to government, and as two world wars and their aftermath produced unprecedented burdens for national security. The sheer scale of operations generated change upon change, creating new relations of power, new vulnerability to disturbance, a new reach of consequences, more complicated problems in apportioning the gains and costs that attended larger commitments of social and private overhead capital. This spelled greater pressures upon social order—hence growing demands upon legal processes. The two Massachusetts cases reflect problems generated by the large scale of events. In *Doherty* v. *Inhabitants of Ayer*[15] the immediate issue was whether the town should pay for the automobile's broken axle; the more basic issue was whether the scale of costs of a hard-surfaced road system required reappraisal of policy at the center, where drafts might be made on a wider tax base. In the railroad air whistle case (*Libby*)[16] the background problem was whether statutory cost requirements should be so administered as to allow an ailing public utility to experiment with cheaper modes of operation to meet the overhead cost of a great fixed investment imperiled by shifts in the general economy.

4

What we have just examined are some persisting features of the relation of men and environment which made change of large order, rather than stability, the norm of experience in the growth of the United States. There may seem paradox in finding that the society's course was marked by a stable bias for change. But for a legal historian, this is reality which profoundly affected law's roles. However, the structure of the situation indicated only the potential course of events. It remains to inquire about the dynamics of the social change that in fact went on.

[15] See Chapter 1, note 6.
[16] See note 1 *supra.*

From a lawman's viewpoint it is useful to analyze the processes of major social change or stability as proceeding out of (1) drift, (2) function, or (3) direction. Drift and direction are in a measure polarities; but there is a sense in which drift is prerequisite to direction. Function has some of the character of each of the other styles of cause.

We tend to exaggerate the relative importance of conflict or conscious contrivance in United States legal history. Most of what happened in the growth of this country—as probably in all man's history—happened without plan or intent or purpose or desire or even awareness of what was in process of happening. There was massive change. Some exaggerated attention to conflict and contrivance may be justified if it saves us from viewing law's role as that of defining or administering a set of static relations. The search for sense in the unruly flow of events subtly biases us to believe that of their own motion men's affairs seek equilibrium or that equilibrium is the normal state of social forces. On the other hand the preponderance of drift did not mean that all was formless motion. There were relative constants which provided a framework for shared experience in the country's growth. Coming to terms with scarcity, men farmed, traded, manufactured. Men and women married and reared children in families. People pursued their daily lives relying on reasonable expectations of the conduct of others according to accepted roles of sex, age, and skill. They sought conventional satisfactions of acquisition, prestige, and communication. It is tempting but very dubious speculation to see "laws" of human behavior expressed in some of these relatively constant factors. We are on surer ground if we note simply that there were persistent trends of fact and process in social relations. A trend is not a "law" but a cumulative weight of fact or momentum, subject to change upon a change in circumstances—as, for example, a trend toward male control of the job market, of church and school, and of family decision making underwent considerable modification toward broader sharing of power with women in the United States from about the 1830's on, with considerable impact upon law. Most of the content of life and decision was carried in these trends of fact and process. These trends were mainly the unpurposed result of drift and default or the unpurposed general product of specialized function. Where trends took on form and procedural regularity, they became institutions of social order—the market, the family, the schools; but only a small part of such institutions was ever consciously designed for the uses they in fact served.

In a sense that concerned the most important function of law, it may be said that in this North American society men felt that the human meaning of life lay in their search to create meaning. Hence, men here were continually involved in conflict or at least in creative tension—conflict or tension with infinite physical phenomena that cared nothing for man's finite being, and with the incidence of numberless small events which weighed down men's limited energies of mind and will; conflict with their own dark, undisciplined fears and drives and with the constricting habits and commitments of their own past. And, then, too, men searched here for meaning through conflict and cooperation with each other over perceived and willed ends and means.

This last area—of perceived conflict and cooperation—is only a small and probably the smallest part of man's record, but the part which tends to pre-empt the writing of history.

Our culture encouraged men to look upon their history in terms that exaggerated the causal importance of conscious conflict and cooperation. The value we put on individualism inclined us to look upon men as dramatic actors; competition in market and mobility in status as well as our pragmatic genius for association fostered a homespun dialectical view of life—an everyday faith that some positive resolution would issue from the interplay of diverse elements; social mobility promoted a high level of personal discontent in this society, and when hopes met frustration this so deeply involved men's sense of self and dignity that they must personalize the explanation and look for villains—a line the more easily followed because people who lived in a constant, restless bustle to get on had no time or patience to examine large and impersonal causes. The character of law in the United States itself inclined observers to exaggerate the relative importance of conscious conflict and contrivance in legal history. This legal order emphasized direction of force, in asserting its legitimate monopoly to validate power allocations; it emphasized deliberate choice, in its constitutionalism and its formal procedures of decision, especially in the drama of lawsuits; it emphasized design, in using public lands and public revenues to help shape social and economic growth. So far as the use of law added to the amount of directed effort in social affairs, this fact—in a society which tended anyhow to translate its problems into constitutional terms—raised men's estimate of the relative importance of conscious conflict and contrivance in their lives—even as, ironically enough, the broader use of law added new quotas of unpurposed result to the general drift of things.

The sources of drift as a major determinant of affairs ran deep in United States legal history. Philosophers or psychologists may detect eternal essences, but historians can furnish them no corroboration out of the North American record. On the evidence the core reality was constant, open-ended, irreversible change. In a society fast growing in its rich and almost unoccupied theatre of action, life found infinite points of contact with environment; the variety of men and the novelty of events barred recurrence of any given large conjuncture of circumstances; new customs and habits of behavior were learned fast under stimulus of an open situation and, once learned, meant that men could not go back to older patterns; the society was caught up in a great accelerating explosion of basic and applied knowledge that was constantly fresh shaping the total situation and again and again putting the past beyond recall. Physical and biological fact oriented life within certain cyclical regularities; rivers ran to the sea and people were born, matured, aged, and died. These cyclical realities were not irrelevant to law. They provided its setting, as they provided the setting for all other human action. But even in physics and biology, reality included irreversible movement along lines projecting into infinity, in geologic change and in the evolution of species. The cyclical regularities in nature conditioned law's operations. But they were irrelevant to law's nature and functions, and hence did not form themes of legal history. As this society used it, law represented one of man's greatest efforts to realize his distinctive quality as man, to use his mind and to discipline his feelings to create meaning in life by ordering life according to his perceptions and wants. Of course his energies and will were far too limited to allow him to master the turbulent growth of North American society. Nonetheless—whether we regard the ways in which law moved events or was moved by them—because law was the creation of man's special qualities of mind and feeling, law was not part of the cyclical monotony of nature but was borne rather in the onward flow of non-cyclical change.

Continuing, open-ended, irreversible change spelled enormous force for drift rather than direction in this society because of the added effects of cumulation, context, and pace.

Even in the crude beginnings of settlement, we were inheritors of a complex western culture which both freed us and restrained us. We did not have to spend the energy our English and continental ancestors did, to move from feudalism to individualism or from absolute to constitutional government; we had already in hand by mid-18th century an array of tool concepts immensely useful in providing the legal context of our growth—representative assemblies, an independent bench, the jury, the notion of contract and of the fee simple title in land, for example. Man's capacity to develop culture—to cumulate and communicate experience and practice and transmit these down the line of generations—is the special endowment of his brain which has given him his peculiar leverage on life. Otherwise ill equipped to survive, by his culture he is strong because he adds to his intelligence the compound interest earned by his experience.

But because culture is cumulation it also creates severe limits on man's ability to direct his affairs. There is an economics of creative capacity. Men have limited stocks of mental and emotional energy which they husband—but also confine—by developing habit and custom and precedent. The customary content of culture shapes people's perception of the world, providing them with taken-for-granted notions of cause and effect, of relevance and irrelevance, and of what is desirable and what undesirable. These customary attitudes limit men's imagination and will, and do so the more powerfully because they enter the logic of everyday speech and thought without having been subjected to examination. Such cultural drift helped a New York court in 1911 to the naive conclusion that the state's first workmen's compensation act must be unreasonable because it changed a familiar common law rule.[17] The easy familiarity of cultural inheritance helped the United States Supreme Court in 1825 to follow the conventional language of English pleaders to fasten the tidewater limitation on admiralty jurisdiction under the new Constitution.[18]

Another aspect of the economics of creative effort is the fact that conscious direction and invention are bound to be marginal. This has various features, but they all favor drift over direction. For one thing, man's general competence has grown mostly by infinite small steps of accomplishment. Most of his invention has proceeded by cumulating small perfections of technique, most of this done by people of limited creative capacity; speculative reason had a substantial history perhaps no older than 2500 years when North American settlement began, and it was outweighed by habits of practical reason (shrewdness directed to limited objectives) which ran back into pre-history. Bias toward narrowly practical reason, inherited from man's oldest past,

[17] See Ives v. South Buffalo Railway Co., 201 N.Y. 271, 293-94, 94 N.E. 431, 439, 441 (1911). *Cf.* New York Central Railroad Co. v. White, 243 U.S. 188, 37 S. Ct. 247 (1917); Silver v. Silver, 280 U.S. 117, 50 S. Ct. 57 (1929); International Harvester Credit Corp. v. Goodrich, 350 U.S. 537, 547, 76 S. Ct. 621, 627-28 (1956).

[18] See notes 5, 6, and 10 *supra*.

was fostered by all the conditions of crudity and challenge to improvise for immediate operations which this unopened continent offered for three hundred years. One consequence was that men conceived and acted on the possibilities for manipulating material techniques much more readily than they invented or accepted changes in life values or social organization. Practical reason dealt more flexibly with mining and making and farming and selling than it did with the intangibles of relation which were the peculiar business of law. Thus ambitious Wisconsin readily embraced the opportunities offered by the railroad; within less than a generation the people revolutionized their economy by promoting a trunk line system that grew from about 1000 miles of railway in 1867 to about 5600 miles of principal track by 1890. In about twenty years the federal and state governments joined in disposing of nearly a twelfth of the state's land surface to aid this railroad boom, while Wisconsin municipalities taxed and spent liberally to help construction. People would put law in action fast and boldly where they saw tangible stakes in improving physical productivity. But it took until the turn of the century to muster the ideas and the will to create minimally effective railroad rate regulation. And the problem of fair and efficient incidence of industrial accident costs, though it took on major importance from the start of railroad building in the 1860's, followed a fumbling course in courts and legislature for fifty years before the first broad-scale direction was applied, to produce the workmen's compensation act of 1911.[19]

At any given period conscious direction could represent only a marginal increment to the total influences on affairs,

[19] Hunt, LAW AND LOCOMOTIVES chs. I, III, and IV (1958); Raney, WISCONSIN chs. X and XIX (1940). Compare note 11 *supra.*

even in a mobile middle-class society which found life's meaning in striving and contrivance.

This was inherent in culture, which is cumulation of learned experience. Culture is as broad in reach and as deep in emotional attachment as the human record. It is the more powerful because so much of it operates below the level of awareness, in the sense of *self* which each person forms from the earliest ideas with which he tries to order the confusion of stimuli which his world presses on him. Oddly, the inertia derived from culture's immensity weighed heavier on direction the more dramatically man advanced his knowledge. From the late 19th century on in the United States this factor worked with accelerating force to insure that even the most spectacular advances in control of environment would represent relatively small marginal increments to the total of causes operating. For as men expanded their knowledge, they enlarged their ignorance, too—specialization drove creative minds farther apart rather than closer together—and they laid heavier demands upon limited stores of will and imagination. Great advantages accrue to the older elements of culture, because in time they weave tough, complex nets of connection to other elements; in contrast, innovation must depend more on its own immediate force, unless by accident or by someone's genius of organization the innovation is pushed by, rather than pushing against, the momentum of the older combinations. In the second half of the 20th century man's creativity opened up the energies of the atom to his use. But emotional as well as intellectual inheritances—nationalism, imperialist ambition, out-dated class-war ideologies and the day-to-day preoccupations of stubborn practical reason—made even this spectacular advance seem a relatively marginal increment to the total influences that would determine whether legal order could compass the new relations of power that the situation unfolded.

Culture weighed against fresh direction in affairs not only by cumulation but also by context. At any given time the interlock of cause in North American growth was manifold and intricate; this baffling complexity of current context was the cultural weight which successive Presents laid upon creativity, as cumulation was the cultural weight of successive Pasts. Again we encounter the economics of marginal increments. Where the network of contemporary cause ran wide, any particular exercise of directed effort could have only limited effect. So Congress' declared policy from 1807-1847 to lease rather than sell the lead-bearing public lands came to little or no practical effect in Missouri and Wisconsin, among other reasons because the contemporary development of the federal budget and the federal executive branch was inadequate to provide the vigorous action in the field which alone could give the leasing program reality. Where many causes were at work with interplay hard to foresee or understand, frustration of some hopes and generation of some unpurposed results were sure consequences of any directed effort. This not only added to the relative total of drift in affairs, but tended to rob original creativity of its élan. Thus, with crusading confidence, in the generation 1905-1935 men added a large administrative apparatus to the legal order both in the states and in the nation. Administration would be a new system which, like Equity in other times, would supersede outmoded values and encrusted technical limitations. Administration would give vitality to new fields of regulation and exercise the positive influence of law to reshape conditions which set much of the framework of living—the regularity and honesty of market operations, the provision of essential transport and communications, the management of the money supply and long- and short-term credit, the security of individuals against insurable hazards of accident, disease, unemployment, and old age. Much was done. But, likewise, by the 1950's there was gathering disenchantment with the administrative process. Out of their focused concerns and their preoccupation with mounting technical problems, specialized regulatory agencies tended to become partners if not captives of the regulated. Familiarity could breed complacence; the self-satisfaction we felt for having contrived workmen's compensation made us inattentive to the adequacy of awards or the efficiency of procedures. Belatedly we began to realize that the administrative process was no substitute for legislative vigor in investigating or taking responsibility for basic policy choices. We had given calculated "independence" to new federal and state administrative agencies; by custom and the specialized complexity of their business older executive officers likewise gained considerable independence *de facto.* Now concern grew that this formal and practical independence of specialists was undesirably narrowing the policy leadership of legislatures or chief executives. Such issues were particular expressions in law of the pressures which social context laid upon directed effort. Reaching far wider in effect were more massive facts of our situation which set the framework of our growth, some of which we have already noted as creating a bias for change over stability: the size of the continental area open to occupation, the scale of population growth, the shift from rural to urban predominance, the baffling interplay of short-run scarcity and long-run abundance which marked the exploitation of our continental opportunities.[20]

A swift pace of change likewise increased the influence which a complex social context exerted for drift and against direction. When events moved very fast, and at the same time moved through a bewilderingly complicated network of relations, the situation favored unpurposed results, if only because of the limits of men's imagination and energy. In a measure this was a condition as old—and as young—as civilization. As contrasted with primitive culture, civilization meant that man steadily enlarged his direction of life by organizing discovery and invention and communication and by keeping written records. Up to mid-20th century civilized culture had occupied only about one per cent of the time that had passed since man began to emerge as a species. In this perspective we see the civilizing enterprise for the relatively new and hurried business that it has been. Men settled North America as heirs of a civilized culture which equipped them to exert uncommon leverage on their situation. But, measured against the whole human span, this culture was of too recent emergence to be understood in all its complexity. Only our vanity conceals from us how uncertain is the net balance between the direction and the drift produced by this relatively new and high-paced development.

Moreover, a special acceleration in the pace of social change profoundly affected the role of law in the growth of the United States. This was particularly true from the

[20] See notes 12 and 13 *supra*.

opening of the 19th century, and most markedly from the 1870's on. Science and technology were the prime movers, especially by developing and applying new sources of physical energy. In large part the machine created the frame of reference for the specific examples of legal-social adjustment that I have used in these first two essays. This is not because I selected my examples to this end, but because this was a pervasive element of our situation. The steamboat pressed the need to redefine admiralty jurisdiction in *The Genesee Chief*, the railroad produced the first major incidence of the industrial accident problem with which Wisconsin policy makers grappled after 1860, the automobile required reconsideration of local and central government responsibilities for the highway system in the Massachusetts case of 1908, and railroad and automobile together produced the issues of public safety and cost allocations among competing transport interests involved in the air whistle case in 1930.[21] Second only in dynamic thrust to the movement of science and technology was the growth of population, which constantly redefined markets and living areas and the play of cause and effect in social relations. A third major factor for rapid social change was a matter of popular attitude. With the advances in basic and applied knowledge and the experience of participating in successive generations of highly visible growth, people expanded their expectations of the quantity and quality of life experience they might find within reach, and they grew in confidence that matter-of-fact engineering of human relationships, whether by private or public means, was the way to realize expanded expectations.

[21] See Chapter 1, note 6, and in the present chapter notes 1, 5, 6, 10, and 11 *supra*.

Such was the trend of attitude reflected in the shift from wholly *ad hoc,* adversary proceedings to more generalized and rationalized policy making that marked the development of Wisconsin industrial accident law from 1860 to 1911. These factors converged to produce not only more and more change, but also change in accelerating tempo. It took only about twenty years for the steamboat to revolutionize internal water transport sufficiently to overturn the tidewater definition of admiralty jurisdiction. It took only about twenty years to produce a five-fold increase in primary railroad trackage in Wisconsin and thus to generate out of industrial accident a prime issue of justice and politics which had had no prior existence. There were 8,000 automobiles registered in the United States in 1900; by 1908—when the Massachusetts court confronted *Doherty* v. *Inhabitants of Ayer*—registrations for the country stood at about 194,000 plus 4,000 truck registrations; by 1920 they had climbed to 8,131,000, plus 1,107,000 truck registrations; in 1930 the United States showed nearly 23,000,000 automobiles registered, and over 3,500,000 trucks; by 1950 automobile registrations stood above 40,000,000 and registration of trucks well over 8,000,000.[22] One among many indices of change related to this dramatic rise of an automobile culture was the rural-urban population balance, which shifted from 54.3 per cent rural and 45.7 per cent urban inhabitants in 1910 to 41 per cent rural and 59 per cent urban dwellers in 1950. When social configurations altered on this scale and at this speed, pace joined to context and cumulation to increase the odds against directed effort and purposed result in men's affairs.

[22] *Ibid.*

5

With characteristics akin both to drift and to direction, the demands of function created another kind of influence upon the growth of the country and the role of law in that growth. Human relations sometimes fell into a process or pattern—of men with men or of men interacting with their physical or biological or social environment. Where such a process or pattern served important uses this utility depended upon some minimum interplay of parts, some internal logic of operations, which made the process or pattern stable enough to be of continuing worth and to constitute a reasonably predictable basis of behavior. Such a large process or pattern was a social institution, like the family, the market, the church, or organized education. It developed out of diverse causes, many of which had little relevance to the uses the institution served in its full growth. There was dubious value in asking what was the purpose or end of such an institution, if by the question one meant something other than what uses it served, for no one nor any body of men had ever constructed one of these complex patterns or processes of behavior by conscious decision out of a master plan. On the other hand, if a process or pattern of relations achieved enough continuity to become an institution of social order, this meant that people valued what it did for them enough to do what they saw as needed to keep the institution in working order. Thus the presence of an institution like the market or the church generated additions to the amount of directed effort which men gave their affairs. Typically, however, this was effort directed to rather immediate operational problems, rather than to fresh examination of larger values or results. This was natural in the economics of creative effort—given the limits of men's energies of mind and will as they confronted the range and diversity of relations that constituted a social institution. Thus social institutions had influence partly by drift—because they represented values and procedures which men most of the time took on faith or habit—and partly by stimulating conscious decisions within the limited frames of reference provided by the perceived needs of operations. An institution was constituted both by inertia and by conscious direction. Law was such an institution in United States history. It was also an institution of peculiar interest because its structure put uncommon emphasis upon direction.

The demands of function influenced affairs by forces analogous to those that powered the wholly unpurposed drift of events—through continuous, open-ended, irreversible development, weighted by cumulation, context and pace. Indeed, in large part the influence of institutions simply added to the amount of unpurposed drift in the country's growth. Infinite variables entered into the composition of an institutional way of life. There was always some imbalance among so many factors, hence always some entrance of novelty, to create continuous cumulation of change. This cumulation was too various and too hard to estimate in final incidence to enable men to control all that went on within an institutional frame. No one planned the unprecedented trans-Atlantic movement of people which in so many ways shaped the growth of society in the United States. From the 17th to the last quarter of the 19th century the law rather reacted to this movement than directed it. The dynamics of movement flowed mainly from unpurposed results of the operation of diverse social institutions: for example, the inadequacy of agricultural techniques and rural social organization to support peasant populations in Ireland and Germany; the loosening of the bonds of established churches, the generation of new concepts of self by market experience, and the rise of religious dissent, with pervasive increase in personal discontent and personal ambition; the invitation to bold decision held out to millions of people through cheap printing, improved transport, and the more common use of money. Thus the restless growth of institutions of economy, religion, communication, and social class produced far-reaching, unpurposed results which time and again unsettled public policy. Carried on this great undertow of events, for example, was the Wisconsin lead lands title suit of *Smith* v. *Wood,* in 1860, which reflects in miniature the bending of federal lands leasing policy before the impatient growth of a people.[23]

Institutional influence which derived primarily from cumulation of experience found commonest expression in habit and in the sense of vested interest. Of the first, consider changed concepts of the relation of land title to social order. Under feudalism title to land was primarily significant in defining the arrangement of political power and the hierarchy of classes. In the first century of North American settlement, land title arrangements were likewise used in considerable measure to order political and social power. This responded to the problems of creating original patterns of order in a wilderness rather than to any substantial inheritance of feudal notions. But the emphasis was still largely political. This tradition lingered until the New York constitutional convention of 1820 marked the turn away

[23] See notes 12 and 13 *supra.*

from property qualifications upon the right to vote. Meanwhile, however, for three centuries habits of trade and of tradesmen's thinking had pre-empted larger and larger areas of Anglo-American life, as the market grew in relative importance as a nonpolitical institution of social order. By early 19th century dominant public opinion took for granted that land should be treated as a tradeable commodity little different from grain or manufactured goods; the normal destination of the public domain should be to come to rest in private hands; title to land should be such as to pass freely in market; title should give the holder substantially unchecked discretion in using the land for his own profit. The point relevant here is not whether this was a good or bad pattern of policy. The point is that this was a pattern developed with a minimum of debate and with minor controversy, because it so completely expressed a market-oriented view of society. The passing effort to reserve from sale the federal mineral lands highlights the broad contrasting policy and its unquestioning acceptance. The mineral lands policy went on the books in 1807 before the greatest push into the West had developed; as soon as western growth became substantial both popular disobedience and public outcry condemned even this narrow deviation from prevailing market attitudes. Not until the early 20th century, when the country's growth pressed harder on its natural resources and metropolitan living raised new issues of public health, order, and economic efficiency, did we begin to assess land title as more than a trader's commodity and to regard its significance for the broader ordering of power.

Those who derive a livelihood or valued privileges from the operation of a social institution provide the obvious examples of vested interest created by cumulated expectations. The railroads represented a new style of concentrated, administered power. But they had a vested interest in preaching the gospel of individualism, for this supplied the moral basis for the common law doctrine which for a generation effectively shielded them from liability for injuries suffered by their employees on the job. Clergy of the early established churches in Virginia and New England resisted separation of church and state. Substantial male opinion opposed sharing political and social prerogatives through the married women's property acts and the extension of the vote. Small retailers and wholesalers fought back both in the market and in the legislature against the rise of new channels of goods distribution. Less obvious but no less potent were broad currents of public expectation bred by institutional development. The cumulative workings of science, technology, and expanding markets taught people to expect a rising standard of living and secure employment; the presidential election of 1936 made plain to practical politicians that this attitudinal by-product of our institutions had made irrelevant older lines dividing "liberal" and "conservative" notions of the proper fiscal role of the federal government. Again, in this society cumulated institutional growth ran to a scale of capital and emotional commitment which after some point of development set rigid limits on the range of policy choice. By 1950 this was an automobile culture; the sense of individual well-being and status was intimately tied to ownership of an automobile, and the automobile industry in all its ramifications was so central to the economy that any substantial decrease in its business threatened a general recession. In this context popular expectations of personal status and economic security promised massive opposition if programs of urban land use planning, for example, should materially limit use of the automobile, or if proposals to spend more tax money on schools and scientific research threatened highway budgets.

We must not view the inertia of institutional cumulation simply as a source of resistance to directed effort. As in the case of general social drift, institutional inertia was a factor of ambiguous import for change or stability. Where directed effort ran counter to the cumulative drift of an institution, the problem of achieving purposed direction was largely one of overcoming resistance. This was the case of the federal lead lands leasing program. In such a situation the odds were likely to be against successful direction. But a determined and aggressive group could move policy far and fast toward its special objectives, if its effort moved along with cumulative institutional drift. Such, for example, was the social context that favored the passing of the Robinson-Patman Act,[24] whose strictures against price discrimination expressed the fears with which old-style retail and wholesale distributors confronted the rise of the chain stores. The strategy of directed effort lay often in aligning a program with the cumulative flow of some institutional process, as the strategy of opposing it lay often in sharpening people's perceptions that it ran counter to comfortable habit or prized expectations created by institutional cumulation.

Cumulation was an important source of the influence which demands of function exercised on social and legal growth in the United States. But it was not the most distinctive expression of functional drive, for its operation was

[24] 49 Stat. 1527 (1936), 15 U.S.C. § 13.(1958).

often closely akin to that of general unpurposed social drift. The most distinctive force of functional demands in our history was felt through the pressure of functional context and through the increasing pace of change derived from the functional role of knowledge.

No fact became more determinative of the quality and content of life in the United States than the high and increasingly complex organization through which life moved. By definition a society consists in some measure of organized relationships. But here the lines of social growth converged to press organization far beyond minimal requisites, to make organization the factor that gave the society its most distinctive character. This was implicit in the early conditions of the country's development. The size of the unopened continent invited and required an unusual expenditure of organizing effort, to establish communications and connecting ties of interest. From an early point our people lived by producing for market, and in large part for distant markets; this trading orientation fostered division of labor and a bent of mind for contrivance. When our ways were still formative and our potential hardly explored, the steam engine, the factory, and attendant functional pressures for increasing commitments of capital entered our experience, to stretch the will and ingenuity of entrepreneurs and put new problems to public policy makers. Even before the Civil War these and other factors had moved us far into more complex orders of economic and social organization. The financing and supply of the North's war effort then produced an acceleration of change which constituted one of the great discontinuities in the growth of the United States. The 1870's saw the emergence of a society qualitatively different from that which had before existed. The qualitative difference lay in the nature, size, and complexity of new arrangements of economic, social, and political power. From the late 19th century on, this was an economy, a community, a polity in which organization had become in itself the principal productive asset, determining the quantity and quality of most of the satisfactions by which most of the people found meaning in their lives. It was a society whose way of life was shaped by a rising material productivity, but its material foundations rested on a steadily heightened dependence upon intangible relationships. Because of this contrast the economy offered the most striking symbols of this direction of social development. For example, organization required increased written communication. The value of the country's output of newsprint, magazine paper, and paper for stationery, records, and miscellaneous supplies rose from about $28 millions in 1870 to $120 millions by 1900, to $479 millions in 1919; paper and paperboard production climbed from 2,167,000 tons in 1899 to 14,483,000 tons in 1940. Growth in organization produced shifts in the status and functions of human effort in production. In the early 19th century probably 80 per cent of the occupied population were self-employed entrepreneurs, by 1870 about one third, and by 1940 about 20 per cent; the converse growth in the proportions of people who earned wages or salaries mirrored the extent to which livelihood was caught up in organization. A related fact was the tendency to transfer labor from primary productive operations to dealings with people and paper procedures. In 1870 over three fourths of workers were engaged in extraction and production of things; in 1940 a little less than one half of the total employed were engaged in producing things, while the proportion of those engaged in service, distribution, and coordination of economic activity had risen from about 23 per cent in 1870 to about 44 per cent in 1940.[25]

The increasing importance of organization was reflected in various aspects of life in the United States which had direct bearing on the role of law. Life processes became more and more interwoven, so that both gains and costs accrued at greater and greater distance from any impact of change, and through networks of cause and effect increasingly complex to trace. The trends of growth that made the society more complicated also made it more powerful; yet its greater complexity made it more vulnerable to basic disturbance. Second, to say that this became a society of increasingly elaborate division of labor (interlock of functions), is to say that its operation involved increasing overhead costs. This was true not only of private activity—in larger commitments of capital to railroads and steel mills—but also in spheres of public spending, for highways, an expanding civil service, public sanitation, schools, and defense. Productivity rose, but production of satisfactions proceeded through more and more indirect processes, hence depended increasingly on good social order. Third, the wider and tighter interlock of social relations increased the number of key points or relational intersections of strategic significance both to the immediate operations and to the deeper values of the society. In the United States of 1800 there were few unofficial individuals or groups whose func-

[25] U.S. Bureau of the Census, STATISTICAL ABSTRACT OF THE UNITED STATES: 1958, at 700 (79th ed., 1958); ———, HISTORICAL STATISTICS OF THE UNITED STATES, 1789-1945, at 183 (1949); Mills, WHITE COLLAR 63, 66 (1951).

tions or relative positions made their decisions or conduct of immediate importance to great numbers of other people; in the span 1870-1900, one need only list the names of Andrew Carnegie, John D. Rockefeller, or J. P. Morgan, or the Pennsylvania Railroad, the Standard Oil Company, or the Equitable Life, to mark changes of great consequence. Fourth, associated action of specialized types and for specialized ends grew steadily in importance to the working of the society. This increased problems of controlling power —groups tended to wield more influence and for larger objectives than did individuals—and of adjusting to each other's programs and ambitions whose specialization bred conflict or confusion. Man's general growth from primitive to civilized culture has moved by increasing functional differentiation of associated activity. In the United States this trend took on an importance which made it a distinctive feature of our growth. Through the 19th century we confronted a rich natural potential with manpower and mobile capital far inadequate to our impatient reach. The facts urged us to combine our means. Machine technology developed in ways that required mobilizing larger and larger amounts of capital and labor. The size of our markets and communications areas invited special group organization—in trade associations, churches, reform efforts—to overcome the challenge of space and numbers.

In a society of intricate organization, marked by these phenomena of interlock, key point, and specialized association, social context generated powerful functional pressures to shape events. It is hard to speak of such matters except in metaphor. But we must be careful that metaphor does not trick us into some mystical or biological conception of what we are talking about. This society was not a spiritual entity whose immanent logic commanded things to happen thus and not otherwise. Nor was this society some kind of organic being, making physiological or emotional demands upon its environment. On the other hand, without falling into mystical or biological fallacies, we can see that there were operative causes derived from men's relations with each other, as distinct from causes derived from the nature of individuals. Like any other, this society was more than an aggregate of individuals; life in society was life in relationships among individuals and groups; because of these relations man perceived and acted differently than he would alone or in other contexts. Least of all in United States legal history, however, should the record be read as realizing an Idea or expressing organic needs or faculties of a social Body. Preoccupied with power allocation, constitutional order, procedure, and the direction of resources, law here found its whole legitimacy and meaning in dealing with values, opportunities, and tensions taken as created wholly by men's overt relations. This was no less true even though in our working philosophy the ultimate relevance and legitimacy of social arrangements lay in what they gave to the content and quality of individual life.

In a society as rationalized as this one became, the logic of social relations exerted causal effect in many and subtle ways. Let me note two aspects of this force, one general, the other particular.

The most general influence of functional logic was on popular attitudes. Taught by the heady impact of the industrial revolution on a rich, unoccupied continent, this people learned faith in the beneficent shaping effect of a rising standard of living; in the context of an increasing division of labor, they learned, as corollary, to believe in specialization of function and in the common sense of doing what was needed for functional efficiency; in consequence they put a high value on organization and upon faithful and efficient performance of function, and gave their consent and respect to demands made in the name of function and organization. These attitudes could favor standpattism or drastic change in political and legal arrangements, according to situation. Where events moved with enough speed and scale to jolt popular opinion out of ordinary ways, recognition that effective organization was the key asset of this society could produce major rearrangements of power. Such an instance was the rapid development of public utility regulation in a new context of administrative law in the early 20th century. Another was the command which public opinion gave in the 1930's, that the federal government use its fiscal powers to limit the downswings of the business cycle. These, however, were results—and each belated by a generation at that—of unusual shocks of change: first, the alarmed reaction to the power which the railroads exercised at key points of the economy from the 1870's on; second, the concern at the deepening disturbances which business depression brought to a society which was making larger and larger commitments of private and social capital and of popular expectations for achieving a prospering future. In more ordinary circumstances the popular esteem for functional efficiency could breed a massive indifference toward large questions, and total acceptance of familiar institutions. Patterned ways and comforting busy-ness were everyday products of preoccupation with function. So far as the value put on functional efficiency looked toward improvement, this was most easily thought of simply as change concentrated upon immediate means to ends which could be left unexamined. As organization developed more indirect modes of supplying satisfactions it increased private and social overhead costs and so tended to increase people's normal disinclination to disturb familiar going relations. The same trend separated men further and further from felt connection to end results; this induced them the more readily to measure their social concerns by the limits of their immediate assignments in the division of labor. The law offered many examples of these tendencies by which absorption in technique pre-empted the field against re-examination of fundamentals. A notable instance was the contrast between the enormous investment of professional skill in details of legislation, administration, and adjudication surrounding the 20th century federal tax structure, and the want of investment by Congress in studies of the ground values of federal taxation commensurate in depth or breadth to the significance which the subject took on for the whole range of national life.

The functional imperatives which produced the most defined results on events were those which derived from the immediate operations of accepted social institutions. After disestablishment, a free church produced sectarian divisions, more lay participation in church policy, and the spread of denominational colleges. National political organizations rose outside formal constitutional structure; their operations enhanced the Presidency as a prize of power and promoted expression of sectional interests as politicians sought means to muster followers and voters against continental obstacles of distance and diversity. The role accorded the middle-class family in social order fostered emphasis upon closely restricted sex relations as the core of "morality," as it also through most of the 19th century encouraged local control of education and limited the demands made on government to care for children, sick people, or the aged. The institution whose functional needs and expressions had widest reflection in public policy was the market. The market required that men be able to deal within a framework of reasonably assured expectations; the law of contract and property thus naturally bulked large in a market-oriented community. The market required that labor and talent, money and other mobile capital flow freely in response to profit-making opportunities; in such a context the commerce clause naturally loomed large in the structure of federalism, and the presumption ran against requiring any official license for undertakings. The market counted by money and sought to achieve the most productive equilibrium of factors in an immediately given situation; public policy made in this context was slow to appraise resources used by a real (physical or psychological) calculus, or by a calculus which preferred future over present satisfactions. Tension between market and nonmarket factors was involved in more or less degree in the example cases discussed in this essay. The Wisconsin lead lands title case (*Smith* v. *Wood*) reflected the yielding of a federal lands reservation program before public demand to bring land into market; in *The Genesee Chief* the pressure of growing commerce prevailed over legal tradition; the Massachusetts automobile axle (*Doherty*) and railroad air whistle (*Libby*) cases reflected pulls and hauls upon law to determine how far and on what terms legal regulation should encourage the use of a new market-developed commodity, the motor car, in competition with older interests of property; the 1860-1911 Wisconsin sequence of industrial accident policy making turned about efforts to bring certain cost allocations out of the domain of simple market bargaining and under accounting rules defined by nonmarket criteria.[26]

Organized search for knowledge and organized communication and application of knowledge, basic and applied —but mainly of applied knowledge—grew into significant institutional life in this country from a point at least as early as the founding of the American Philosophical Society (1744). Among this operations-minded people the central functional demand of organized knowledge was that it find use; at this point this institution wove closely into the operation of the market, which our policy allowed to allocate resources with minimum legal hindrance in response to new information for manipulating the environment. It is relevant to recall the comments already made in this essay, on the pervasive influence of new types of machinery in creating problems of social adjustment brought to law. The organization and application of knowledge probably had its widest influence on social cause, however, not in a separate capacity but in the heightened pace which it contributed to other functional demands generated out of the operation of other institutions. Thus the influence of the machine was typically translated into accelerating force for change through market responses to new opportunities for novel mixture of factors of production. The scale of industrial and distribution operations expanded fast and enormously as men learned

[26] See Chapter 1, note 6, and in the present chapter notes 1, 6, 10-13 *supra.*

new techniques of organization; rapid transformation of the old real estate mortgage into the corporate trust indenture showed how much the pace of change could be stepped up even within a domain of tradition, when new knowledge of enlarged horizons worked on ambition; the rapid growth of a new law of labor relations within 20 years following 1935 bore witness to the quickening effects of a new technology not only of the machine but, more important, of human relations. Particular examples bring us back to a point noted earlier. We tended to value knowledge primarily for use. Hence if an accession to knowledge showed utility, this fact in itself tended to generate action. This suggested that organized knowledge might play a distinctive role among the various institutions which generated functional pressures upon events. I have noted that functional emphasis tended to run on means rather than ends, and therein to foster our native bent to concentrate only upon immediate operations. But insofar as the very possession of potentially useful knowledge tended to generate pressure for its use, there was here perhaps an uniquely favorable influence toward the examination and further definition of social values. We shall consider this in the next chapter.

This essay has emphasized types of influence which worked from outside the law with great effect upon the role of law in the growth of the United States. Likewise it has emphasized factors which tended to make massive change rather than stability the more common experience of the country, and elements which tended to make unpurposed drift or narrowly perceived function the source of influence upon social affairs, more potent than directed effort. I have described the social role of law as generally that of adding only a marginal increment—though in some ways a critically important marginal increment—to the sum of causes. All this puts a somewhat negative or at least dampening estimate upon the part legal order played in creating social order. Legal history should not yield to the vanity of exaggerating its own importance. Perhaps what this essay sketches sufficiently hedges against that danger. The following chapters will take a more positive line, as they emphasize positive contributions of law to the life of the United States.

III

Initiative and Response

1

In the United States of 1850 milk was food for babies or invalids; in 1950, with consumption of milk and cream at about 350 pounds annually for every man, woman and child in the country, milk had become a prime fuel and protector of the general life. The dynamics of this change derived from outside the law. Milk consumption increased with the upward curve of real incomes created by the machine and by invention of large-scale organization of industry and markets. It marched with the changes which science and technology wrought in dairy farming and milk handling. It spread with new popular notions of hygiene, diet and consumer satisfactions borne on the rising tide of production and the spread of new medical knowledge. But if law did not create the mass milk market, uses of law were inextricably woven into this market history. In 1934 in *Nebbia* v. *New York*[1] the Supreme Court of the United States saw this fact as the base line from which to appraise whether the New York legislature acted within the bounds of rational choice in imposing price regulation upon retail milk sales:

> Save the conduct of railroads, no business has been so thoroughly regimented and regulated by the State of

[1] 291 U.S. 502, 54 S. Ct. 505 (1934).

> New York as the milk industry. Legislation controlling it in the interest of the public health was adopted in 1862 and subsequent statutes [1893, 1909] have been carried into the general codification known as the Agriculture and Markets Law [1927]. A perusal of these statutes discloses that the milk industry has been progressively subjected to a larger measure of control. The producer or dairy farmer is in certain circumstances liable to have his herd quarantined against bovine tuberculosis; is limited in the importation of dairy cattle to those free from Bang's disease; is subject to rules governing the care and feeding of his cows and the care of the milk produced, the condition and surroundings of his barns and buildings used for production of milk, the utensils used, and the persons employed in milking. . . .Proprietors of milk-gathering-stations or processing plants are subject to regulation . . . , and persons in charge must operate under license and give bond to comply with the law and regulations; must keep records, pay promptly for milk purchased, abstain from false or misleading statements and from combinations to fix prices. . . .In addition there is a large volume of legislation intended to promote cleanliness and fair trade practices, affecting all who are engaged in the industry.[2]

In *Nebbia* the majority of the Court ruled that the legislature might add price regulation to the catalog of the law's concerns with the milk industry, where it appeared that this might reasonably be deemed necessary to check destructive and demoralizing competitive conditions which threatened

[2] *Id.* at 521-22, 54 S. Ct. at 509.

the flow of product from farm to city by reducing the farmer's income below costs of production.[3]

Regulation of food supplies to protect public health is as old as the rise of cities. However, there are distinctive features of the development of milk regulation from the early 19th century on in this country which make the story a pertinent introduction to the subjects of this and the following essay.

(1) This was a field of regulation developed by legislation. The common law of nuisance was built almost exclusively out of lawsuits relating to the use of land and provided no source of market regulation. In theory the consumer of impure or adulterated milk might have remedies for breach of contract or warranty of quality, or in tort for fraud or for damage caused by the seller's negligence; in practice the interest of private litigants proved insufficient to provide a pattern of regulation out of suits in contract or tort. Statutes gave form to the substance of public interest in this field.[4]

(2) The course of legislation showed alternations from broad to specific definition of the subjects and standards of regulation. Early statutes spoke of broad categories of goods and in terms so general as to carry little guidance for enforcement and little fear to wrongdoers. Thus the Statutes of the Territory of Wisconsin, 1839, and again the Wisconsin Revised Statutes of 1849 simply punished anyone who

[3] *Id.* at 530, 54 S. Ct. at 513.

[4] See Freund, STANDARDS OF AMERICAN LEGISLATION 20-22, 83-84 (1917); Horack and Cohen, "After the Nebbia Case: The Administration of Price Regulation," 8 U. CINC. L. REV. 219, 222-24 (1934); Horack, "The Common Law of Legislation," 23 IOWA L. REV. 41, 48 (1937).

"shall knowingly sell any kind of diseased, corrupted or unwholesome provisions, whether for meat or drink, without making the same fully known to the buyer." In 1883 the legislature specifically authorized the Milwaukee Common Council "to tax, license, regulate and restrain hawkers, peddlers and venders of milks . . ."—an authority which the Common Council did not use until 1887. In 1887 the Wisconsin legislature first specifically penalized "any person who shall with intent to defraud. . .sell for human food, any milk diluted with water or in any way adulterated, uncleanly and impure, or milk from which any cream has been taken. . . ." This was still a long way from regulation adequately adapted to the circumstances of the product. In 1889 the legislature created the office of dairy and food commissioner to enforce the statutory standards and began to spell out with increasing detail standards of nutritional value and cleanliness to govern the milk supply. Milk and other dairy products bulked so large in the Wisconsin economy from the turn of the century that the legislature jealously kept to itself the elaboration of quality and safety standards. Finally, however, in 1929 it granted general rule making authority to a new department of agriculture in which was incorporated the work formerly done by the dairy and food commissioner, and in 1939 it gave the department specific authority to set standards and make rules for inspecting, sampling, and testing milk and keeping test records. In dramatic contrast to the crude provision of Wisconsin Revised Statutes, 1849, the 54 sections of the department's General Order 124, of November 15, 1949, defined requirements for farm inspection, milk and cream transportation, standard test methods, cream grading, exclusion of producers from market, records and reports, departmental inspections, and identification of adulterated milk. The law had moved from a generality that approached ineffectual vagueness, to step-by-step specification, and then to general ordering of specifics into a reasonably integrated pattern.[5]

(3) In various aspects the growth of milk regulation showed the use of law to create leverage upon social situations. Scale of operations was relevant to social direction; when law organized social assets beyond a certain point, it became practical to set forces in motion which otherwise stayed at rest. Thus the early 19th century statutory pattern was to delegate to local government the definition and enforcement of quality and safety standards for foodstuffs, including milk. But the local units were slow to act; though general statutory warrant existed from as early as 1839, Milwaukee provided no milk inspection procedure until 1887. In small or medium-sized municipalities, there was commonly no effective milk regulation well into the 20th century; thus the Lynds could report that as late as 1935

[5] See Stat. Wis. Territory 1839, at 350; Wis. Rev. Stat. 1849, ch. 140, § 1; Wis. Laws 1883, ch. 308; Wis. Laws 1887, ch. 157; Wis. Laws 1889, chs. 425 and 452; Wis. Laws 1929, ch. 479; Wis. Laws 1939, ch. 492. For simplicity I have chosen fluid milk regulation as my example. In fact Wisconsin's dairy industry developed its earliest large-scale efforts in processing milk into other products, notably butter and cheese, and the fluid milk regulatory story is anticipated on most counts by previous growth of the law along similar lines regarding such processed commodities. For example, rule-making power was given the dairy and food commissioner regarding butter and cheese makers as early as Wis. Laws 1915, ch. 597. On the growth of Wisconsin dairy food regulation generally see Abrahamson, "Quality Control of Dairy Products in Wisconsin" (unpublished manuscript in University of Wisconsin Law Library, 1957); Beuscher, FARM LAW IN WISCONSIN 205-08 (1951); Laurent, PRODUCTION AND MARKETING REGULATION FOR MILK AND MILK PRODUCTS IN WISCONSIN (1957); Still, MILWAUKEE: THE HISTORY OF A CITY 385-86, 555 (1948).

in "Middletown" (Indiana) the city council refused to pass an ordinance to limit sales to pasteurized milk, the state Board of Health reported the condition of Middletown's milk supply as "serious" and local newspapers advised boiling milk before giving it to babies. The first response to inadequate local regulation was a trend to define standards by state regulation, and to provide some measure of state enforcement. Then the growth of metropolitan areas brought development of more specialized local government, and from this eventually came fresh impetus for milk regulation; thus, when Milwaukee finally enacted a milk inspection ordinance in 1887, this followed pioneering agitation by an energetic city Health Commissioner, whose office had been set up in 1878. In form, state and metropolitan action presented contrasts of central and local approach to the problem, but they had in common that out of a larger investment in social overhead capital they generated more initiative for action.[6] Specialization of function was a second mode by which legal arrangements created leverage for action, as indicated by the contributions of specialized state and metropolitan administrative officers. The development of milk regulation showed a third, immensely important leverage effect of law, in the facility it offered to bring into effect advances in scientific and technical knowledge. The Wisconsin legislature first adopted a butterfat criterion against adulterated milk in 1889, hard on the publication of the first workable butterfat content tests, and regulatory effort against adulteration

[6] See Lynd and Lynd, MIDDLETOWN 450 (1929); ———, MIDDLETOWN IN TRANSITION 399 (1937); Schlesinger, THE RISE OF THE CITY, 1878-1898, at 133-34 (1938); Still, *supra* note 5, at 385. The governing officers of towns, villages, and cities and the justices of the peace were given broad authority to take measures to protect public health as early as Stat. Wis. Territory 1839, at 125.

gained real momentum after the devising of the Babcock test in 1890. Earlier state statutes emphasized adulteration. In the late 19th century the work of Pasteur, Lister, and Koch provided information about bacteria; in 1892 the first bacterial count of milk was made in this country; in short order—for example, in Wisconsin statutes of 1899 and 1903—regulation turned to new emphasis upon cleanliness in milk production and distribution.[7]

These, then, are significant features of the law's regulatory relation to the milk industry. But this was only part of the story. We should not equate law with regulation, nor should we equate regulation with restriction. As we examine relations of law to men's efforts to direct their affairs we must note that the law's largest effects on the milk industry were promotional rather than restrictive; its Yea was more than its Nay. The promotional effects of law were felt mainly through its capacity to provide procedures for organizing action, both attracting purpose and furnishing it with facilities. The milk industry's growth proceeded by educating farmers and processors to wider ambitions for their product. In Wisconsin this was helped by the favor the law showed to associations of farmers and processors, providing them corporate status, sanctioning their initiative in sponsoring fairs, educational activities and marketing

[7] On adulteration control and the butterfat-content tests, compare the specific three per cent criterion under Wis. Laws 1889, ch. 425, with the general ban under Wis. Laws 1887, ch. 157, and the vaguely hopeful authorization in ch. 157 to make proof of adulteration "by a disinterested competent person with such standard tests and lactometers as are used to determine the quality of milk, or by chemical analysis. . . ." See Glover, FARM AND COLLEGE 118-20 (1952). Legal acknowledgment of germ theories of disease may be seen in Wis. Laws 1899, ch. 313, and Wis. Laws 1903, ch. 67. See, generally, Curti, THE GROWTH OF AMERICAN THOUGHT 539-40 (2d ed. 1943); Freund, *supra* note 4, at 83.

programs, and supplying public subsidies and exempting their property from taxation. This was public support by indirection.[8] The state also offered direct encouragement to fresh venture and contrivance in the dairy industry. Two forms of direct support were especially influential. One was through the state university. The extension activities of the university were at least as effective as its on-campus instruction in persuading Wisconsin farmers and processors to adopt the quality and sanitary standards that were necessary to win wider markets. The state of dairy science and technology was the ultimate source of the industry's growth, and the university's research activity represented the state government's contribution to this source of initiative; it was at the university in 1890 that Professor S. M. Babcock devised what was to become the standard test for the butterfat content of milk. The second principal form of direct state governmental impetus toward new directions for the milk industry was road building. Roads rivaled schools in the state's budget after the turn of the century. Of special relevance to the milk industry was the fact that public money was to be had, under energetic local pressure, to develop the all-weather secondary road system which became the framework of industry operations as the motor truck took over milk transport.[9] Finally we must note that the availability

[8] *E.g.,* Wis. Gen. Acts 1853, ch. 5 (incorporating the Wisconsin State Agricultural Society); Wis. Laws 1870, ch. 95 (tax exemption for associations to promote agriculture); Wis. Laws 1880, ch. 17 (appropriation in aid of Wisconsin State Dairymen's Association). See, generally, Mills, "Government Fiscal Aid to Private Enterprise in Wisconsin: A Quantitative Approach," 1956 WIS. L. REV. 110, 113, 119, 124-27.

[9] See Glover, *supra* note 7, especially chs. 5 and 10, and p. 119; Schafer, A HISTORY OF AGRICULTURE IN WISCONSIN 159-61 (1922); Wisconsin State Highway Commission, A HISTORY OF WISCONSIN HIGHWAY DEVELOPMENT, 1835-1945, ch. III (1947).

of the law to provide a regulatory framework for the industry had significance not just to police against wrongdoers but, even more important, to make possible the industry's expansion into markets of large, impersonal reach.[10]

Many of these items of legal regulation or promotion have relevance to more than one role of law regarding social change and stability. In one view, we see law encouraging and helping men to take deliberate initiative to steer their affairs; in another aspect the same legal activity—perhaps at a later point of time—has meaning more as a factor to sustain established lines of action than to help initiate new ones. This duality provides the distinction between the subjects of this essay and that which follows. The distinction may be pointed up, for example, in terms of legal regulation of quality and safety standards for milk. Once a workable pattern of regulation was established it became an indispensable sustaining influence to enable the milk industry to supply wide markets on terms that were functionally acceptable, given the needs and hazards of close-knit urban living. On the other hand, the fact that a legal order existed which made it possible to create such a framework of action was, at the outset, an influence which stimulated the imagination and will of a handful of leaders—in Wisconsin, Stephen Faville, William Dempster Hoard, Chester Hazen, for example—to organize and obtain the kind of regulatory setting within which the industry could grow.[11]

[10] See Schafer, *supra* note 9, at 149-51, 157. The positive, market-sustaining function of legal regulation of commodity standards was an old one in our legal history. See Handlin and Handlin, COMMONWEALTH: MASSACHUSETTS, 1774-1861, at 67-72 (1947).

[11] That dairy industry leaders saw legal regulation as an opportunity to develop and sustain the market, and that the availability of the law's facilities acted as a spur to leadership, are symbolized in the fact that

I have begun with this sketch of the law's relation to the growth of the milk industry—and, indeed, it is only the broadest outline of a most complicated story—as preface to some more general ideas. These general ideas concern uses of law to foster men's initiative. What follows must be more abstract. I hope that the milk example may help relate some general propositions to the rich particulars of the country's growth.

2

Man's primary problem as man, has been to make some sense for himself out of experience. Of course survival is prerequisite to anything else. But in this respect man merely shares the fate of all creatures. What made him distinctive in the evolution of life was his uncommon development of brain. This meant an uncommon development of intelligence —the capacity to translate the infinite particulars of immediate experience into ideas of relationships which could be used to manipulate experience. It meant an uncommon development of memory, learning, and communication, so that intelligence could store up and transmit its product of ideas, to pyramid its effect. It meant an uncommon development of emotion, enlarging the objects of emotion, expanding sympathies, and perhaps most important, interweaving with intelligence to create sustained, self-conscious, and disciplined feeling. Out of these special capacities of intelligence, knowledge, and sustained emotion developed the

for many years the office of Food and Dairy Commissioner was administered with great vigor and integrity by J. Q. Emery, a past president of the Wisconsin Dairymen's Association. Note the tribute paid Commissioner Emery in the opinion of the Wisconsin Supreme Court in John F. Jelke Co. v. Emery, 193 Wis. 311, 318, 214 N.W. 369, 371 (1927).

sense of self, which consisted in conscious selection and integration of experience, so that it was man's nature to impose his own order on circumstance, at least to the extent of achieving his own identity.

Man's problem is that though the course of evolution has left him with these peculiar capacities, all other phenomena are indifferent or hostile to them. The earth, the heavens, other forms of life show no care whether he survives, let alone whether he realizes his distinctive potential. The infinite variety, quantity, and detail of things and events threaten to confound his understanding and dismay his will. The more he learns, the more his learning is fragmented into specialties. His knowledge grows by reason, but his drives are from feeling, and his recurrent vision of the immensity of the uncaring universe and the measureless welter of detail from which he alone can make meaning keeps him close either to frustrating fear or despair or to apathy about all save his most private concerns. In a measure man's own creative capacity works to raise barriers to its further expression; the weight of cumulation, context, and pace in the growth of culture multiplies the factors with which mind and will must deal and thus adds social inertia or drift to the inertia and drift of physical and biological processes. So far as man does not impose conscious direction —or at least awareness—upon events, his life is shaped by chance or by the mindless trend of things, denying its human quality.

Man's efforts to make life meaningful in his terms present the central secular theme of his history. The fact that most of what has happened to him has happened without his willing or wanting it or even being aware of it, poses the central secular challenge to his development. To this theme all else is secondary. Measured against the sweep of drift and inertia, and the unpurposed results of narrow strivings, conscious conflict and contrivance seem grossly exaggerated when, as typically, they are made the prime subjects of general or of legal history. What law has done or failed to do in enlarging rational direction and responsible emotion in individual and social life provides the frame which lends such ultimate meaning as there may be in other uses of law. This seems so at least of the role of law in the growth of the United States. For here the cultural character of law—its preoccupation with constitutional ordering of power relations, with procedural regularity and with resources allocation—emphasized the imposition of man's calculated will upon events, whether through the state's direct action or its support and scrutiny of the action of private persons.

Of course drift and inertia would pose no challenge were they completely in command, along with nature's cyclical regularities. We need no theological postulate of free will to give man his own history. But we do need the possibility of unique, noncyclical development—to which, the previous essay noted, the record testifies—plus real availability of alternatives or options upon which he may exercise his peculiar capacities of mind and feeling. This reality base for man's conscious direction of affairs exists.

Admitting that the odds favor chaos or mindless cumulation, we should be realistically modest but certainly not despairing about what we have shown we can do. One form of fatalism argues that "you can't change human nature." Beyond its most obvious truth—which is that some changes take a very long time to occur—the proposition is of little help in defining the range of practical choice. The persistence of the human organism is a fact. But its biological continuity and homeostatic or feedback processes for automatic response to environmental change at best offer literary analogies for characterizing social process; the biologically functional needs of man do not much confine his capacity to invent adaptations to his earthly environment. The unique quality of the human brain has proved to be its capacity for general and flexible rather than specialized adaptation; so far the record shows no discernible limit to man's ability to devise new ways of life.

Most striking has been his demonstrated capacity to grow in competence. This is the immense positive force of culture, which thus far we have noted chiefly in its negative aspects. Man has shown himself able to cumulate not only reasoned knowledge but ordered discipline of feeling, transmitted as felt values and respected traditions. Man's rational capacity is innate, but his ideas of purpose and morals are not; these express the result of social experience and social pressure generated out of long social experience. By cumulation of knowledge and ordered feeling man has lifted himself to new levels of capacity to control himself and his environment. This is certainly not a subject for complacency; the record amply testifies that there is no natural law of cultural progress; there have been retreats as well as advances. But the positive increase of creative capacity out of culture is a massive fact of general history. Civilization has grown, though in physical terms man's brain capacity does not appear to have changed significantly in 40,000 years—or, at least, if brain has grown, it seems that the change must have been by selective pressure of developing culture upon genetic variations. Primitive people appear no less talented intrinsically than civilized people. But primitive societies offer few outlets for creativity; because primitives have so limited ability to manipulate environment, they have fewer objects of attention and hence enjoy fewer stimuli to mental development. Recorded culture expanded man's options. His competence grew particularly by the development of urban life, which put a premium upon dealing with men more than with nature, and upon flexible and matter-of-fact rather than customed-based or emotionally rooted relations.

As much as cultural cumulation, cultural variety attests that man is malleable and educable and has in fact possessed a significant range of choice for growth. The evidence proves no single-line or recapitulatory course ordained by nature for cultural development. All cultures serve certain common needs of human life—such as for minimal security and communication—but these common needs are too general in their demands to explain the rich diversity of cultural content. There has been wide variation in forms and in the substantial uses made of like forms. Back of the surface regularity of social forms always hides a considerable range of individual variation, out of which time has brought institutional innovation. Of course men did not deliberately invent or legislate the bulk and diversity of culture, the immensity of which can only remind us how far drift and inertia have provided life's context. Nonetheless the cumulative power of culture and the striking extent of variation it displays testify also that man has opportunity to exert leverage upon circumstance. Civilization has consisted in using this leverage.

Civilized man learned to make his cultural environment

relatively more important, his physical environment relatively less important, in determining the quality of life. He learned to convert physical and vital energy into cultural institutions. He learned under the spur of strife and competition. But he scored his greatest advances by showing capacity for cooperative action and by steadily enlarging the variety and scale of peaceful concert. Increasingly successful science and technology bred habits of mind which compounded the trend toward more rational control. In particular the greater use of machines, with the accompanying systematic calculus of operations, made more common a matter-of-fact, manipulative approach to life. Modern man invented invention. Not the least of his new techniques of social invention was a new style of law. Men invented forms and procedures of social relations—market techniques, private associations, constitutional law, national and federated sovereignty, for example—which more efficiently mobilized and directed scarce natural and human resources. Beyond this growth in contrivance, the development of the emotional content of culture provided dynamic for the rational faculties. The evolution of Judeo-Christian ideas led men to value the individual person and to see the life of men and their societies not as a closed cycle but as unique growth toward ever enlarging meaning. The Christian concept of divine order and the secular confidence developed by Greek logic and philosophy and the technical skills of artisans helped build the will and faith which men needed to embolden their reason to seek meaning in the universe. Individualism, belief in evolution and in life's potential for meaning generated demands upon life and criteria of morals which shaped concepts of legal order. *The Federalist* papers—and Marx and Freud—teach us to doubt that cultural values represent absolute truth or error. But to recognize that values and procedures are relative to interests and social context does not deny that culture shows continuity and order and opportunities for creative choice.

On the facts of genetic and cultural development which gave man increasing opportunity to exercise direction over his life, we can erect some secular values. These are relative values, relative to the fuller realization of the distinctive potentials of human nature. Their validity derives from the fact that they proved functional for human life, enriching its content, expanding its energies. If they lack the finality of divine ordinance, at least they are relevant to worldly experience.

First, to define purposes for himself and means to their achievement was good for man since the universe tendered him no meaning other than he perceived for himself. As a corollary, it was valuable that he cultivate awareness of himself as separate but in relation to things and other life. Awareness was functional even if it brought realization of weakness, for man was in fact weak save as he discerned usable relations in physical, biological, and social phenomena that existed apart from his will. Second, it was good that man grow in the range and complexity of his own formed purposes and means and in both the reason and the disciplined feeling required for such growth. If life was good, such growth was good, because it was the only meaningful notion within man's own grasp of how he might enlarge life; life consisted in organization imposed on matter, and human life consisted in accomplishing this with maximum awareness. Inorganic nature tended to the slow loss of energy. The special quality in the emergence of human life was that mind, by making order out of responses to experience, could make life renew itself and refresh itself with the stimulus of constant novelty, so that it constituted not a closed but an open system of energy. Third, it was good that man cultivate his will, his capacity to make decisions. Here especially the discipline of emotion supplemented the training of reason. The infinity of the universe condemns man, if he is to attempt direction at all, again and again to act on imperfect knowledge. Passivity does not suit his nature, is not what has advanced the species; if respect for reason counselled against action unless all relevant factors were known and measurable, it would stultify rather than fulfill man's distinctive character. To take responsible decision on imperfect knowledge required poise and courage, which could grow only on exercise.

These values, focused on the individual, had counterparts for social context. Man's particular qualities of reason and feeling required communication for their full unfolding. Thus if man needed to create purpose for himself, he needed no less to strive for purpose in his social arrangements. Likewise his development required that his relationships grow in content and variety of directed effort. Society would probably always include more unpurposed than purposeful elements, but the latter measured the opportunity for increase of distinctively human satisfactions. There were also involved factors relevant to social strength and indeed to survival. We confronted always the challenge of mindless circumstance. But circumstance opposed us with no positive purpose of its own; general drift and inertia frustrated weak or ill-directed effort, but there was infinite variety in things and events, and hence there was a premium upon flexibility and diversity in men's social efforts, that there be the largest chance of capitalizing on a favorable conjunction of circumstance and purpose. Moreover, the social value in directed effort grew as men devised more elaborate divisions of labor, increased the size of public and private overhead capital commitments, and became more and more dependent upon intangibles of organization for the flow of satisfactions. This elaboration of social contrivance exposed society to a wider range of variables, made it more liable to dangerous disruption at key points, increased the risks of irreparable damage where commitments were so great. Thus the logic of social growth made it a function of all formal organization, not least of law, to cultivate capacity for responsible decision and well calculated innovation.

If the facts of man's development suggested such definitions of the good, they suggested also the nature of evil, or at least of that in experience which was most hostile to human quality. The evil was what denied fruitful purpose or destroyed sensible relations of means to ends, or—second only to the first—what gathered the creation of purpose and the determination of means into closed, tight monopoly. Such was the evil of selfishness. Such was the evil of totalitarian government, as of all political movements which sought expression for irrational fear and hate in racial, religious, or class war. It was not accidental that political reaction often cloaked itself in dogmatic distrust of mankind's capacity to govern itself by reason and tolerance, or in despairing prophecy that experience moved only in closed cycles or marched along a prescribed line to a foredestined end.

The facts likewise suggest what may be deemed dangerously false, if not evil. Thus failure to estimate man's problem as that of achieving self direction, or failure realistically to measure the preponderant tendency to drift and default, may be the most dangerous, because the most subtly concealed surrender to meaninglessness. Again, in the first enthusiasm to draw social doctrine from biological analogy, men read into natural selection values which were not there. Natural selection in fact showed itself a high-cost and inefficient process for developing species. It favored survival of characters most useful under the immediate pressures of the present without reserve for future contingencies. It produced only that degree of adaptation necessary to survival in given circumstances, without impetus to perfection beyond the minimum for marginal success. It operated only negatively, denying development to unfavorable variations but containing no inner drive to creative innovation. In all these respects natural selection fostered change along lines of dangerously rigid and specialized growth, doomed to rapid failure before drastic change of circumstance, so that it is not surprising that almost all species of life which have come into being under this regime have also disappeared. In all these respects natural selection was irrelevant to the distinctive qualities of man and offered little useful analogy for his problem solving.

That the facts offered men opportunity to extend their direction of life, and that these facts implied values, did not of course mean that in any given time or place men would realize their opportunities or adopt these values. This presents a matter critical for legal history. The attitudes a people hold toward the possibility and worth of responsible effort to shape their affairs will materially affect their resort to law.

The prevailing middle-class temper in the United States combined general ideals of personal dignity and advancement and social progress with a continuing preoccupation with practical operations. It was not a temper favorable to the close articulation of subtle or consistent philosophy. However, the place and the time favored the development of a remarkable consensus on the nature of man and individual and social values derived from his nature, such as to emphasize purpose, growth in purpose, and exercise of will in creating and pursuing purpose. These were attitudes fundamental to the role of law in social change and stability in the growth of the United States.

Hector St. John de Crevecoeur romanticized the "American farmer" citizen of the late 18th century. But Crevecoeur truly caught the prevailing national spirit of enterprising decision and responsibility. It is significant, too, that he found this temper intimately bound up with the law of real property and of free contracting status: "Europe contains hardly any other distinctions but lords and tenants; this fair country alone is settled by freeholders, the possessors of the soil they cultivate, members of the government they obey, and the framers of their own laws, by means of their representatives. . . . A European, when he first arrives, seems limited in his intentions, as well as in his views; but he very suddenly alters his scale; two hundred miles formerly appeared a very great distance, it is now but a trifle; he no sooner breathes our air than he forms schemes, and embarks in designs he never would have thought of in his own country. There the plentitude of society confines many useful ideas, and often extinguishes the most laudable schemes which here ripen into maturity. Thus Europeans become Americans."[12] About 1830, when the national spirit was well formed, Tocqueville was impressed, further, by the people's confident readiness to enlarge their individual effort by associated action, public and private. Here, he found, "the citizens enjoy unlimited freedom of association for political purposes"—he wrote as the full tide of national growth had brought the rise of a new style and vigor of popular parties—and here, likewise, was "the only [country] . . . in the world where the continual exercise of the right of association has been introduced into civil life and where all the advantages which civilization can confer are procured by means of it."[13]

The people who by 1830 had set the model of working belief and faith in the United States saw man as by nature a maker and a doer. They symbolized this attitude in the steady extension of the suffrage, as the basis for participation in public decision. They expressed the value they put on private decision-making in the prominence they assigned the law of contract and property. They held no mystical notions of "the state" or "the people" as living entities possessing claims or rights. They believed that the ultimate unit of rights, duties and creative capacity was the individual human being, "born equally free and independent" with all others, possessing "certain inherent rights; among these are life, liberty, and the pursuit of happiness," to secure which governments were instituted, "deriving their just powers from the consent of the governed." As appropriate tribute to formative tradition, in 1848 Wisconsin's Yankee constitution

[12] Crèvecoeur, LETTERS FROM AN AMERICAN FARMER 55, 58 (Blake ed. 1912).

[13] Tocqueville, 2 DEMOCRACY IN AMERICA 115 (Bradley ed. 1945).

makers adopted the honored words as the first section of their charter for a new state which would soon be settled mainly by Germans and Scandinavians. The concept of individuality itself inherently stressed responsible self direction. What constituted an individual was awareness of a separate self, in relation to an environment over which one wielded some measure of control. The law contributed to the creation of individuality. Law likewise attested the value we put upon this individuality. Law did so in favor shown education which would cultivate awareness, in rights of contract and property which implemented control, in constitutional guarantees of person and possessions which protected the privacy which was the valuable part of separateness. On the other hand, confronting this untamed continent, we knew better than to adopt a doctrinaire individualism. Man, we saw, was by nature a doer and maker in company as well as alone. The prime symbol of this acknowledgment was the classic generation of constitution making, from 1765 to 1800, and second only to this the procedure best known through the Northwest Ordinance of 1787 for orderly creation of new states out of a wilderness. This pertained to the deliberate making of public order. Public policy put no less emphasis on the creative possibilities in private association. A generation of Jacksonian polemic against special privilege did not in fact prevent legislatures from chartering by the hundreds academies, colleges, hospitals, churches, banks, insurance companies, transport companies, and industrial concerns—Wisconsin's legislature granted over 1100 special charters to business firms alone from 1848-1871—and by the 1870's general incorporation statutes had stilled the old argument, and policy had formally witnessed private association as a constituent element of the society.[14] In any case, whether in individual or associated action, we busied ourselves with contriving new relations of men to things and of men with men. This was a society that prided itself on being practical. Its special character, however, was to express its practicality in devising increasingly elaborate patterns of intangible relations. In such a society the law naturally emphasized the constitutional order of power, procedure and the allocation of resources to provide an assured framework within which interdependent relations might develop.

Closely related to the value we put on purposeful action was the notion that man fully realized his nature only if he grew in competence. Growth was a natural preoccupation of a people who confronted our opportunities for continental expansion. Natural, too, was a considerable amount of naive confidence that progress was the proper course of life in this rich, unexploited setting. But, for all our naivete, after the first disappointments we did not expect to get rich without hard work. However, we measured the worth and relevance of work by the expectation that we would get steadily better at what we did and would reap a steady increase of product

[14] Wis. Const. art. I, § 1, embodies the quoted propositions of the Declaration of Independence. On the elements of individuality as reflected in law, compare Wis. Const. art. X (Education), art. I, §§ 2, 9, 12-16 (rights of contract and property), and art. I, §§ 2, 3, 11, 17-19 (rights of privacy). See also Brown, "The Making of the Wisconsin Constitution," 1952 WIS. L. REV. 23, 24-25, 54, 57-60. Constitution making, the admission of new states, and the development of policy toward incorporation of private associations are discussed in Hurst, LAW AND THE CONDITIONS OF FREEDOM IN THE NINETEENTH-CENTURY UNITED STATES 15-18, 40-41 (1956). For the Wisconsin period of special charters for business associations, see Kuehnl, THE WISCONSIN BUSINESS CORPORATION 143 (1959).

for what we put out. These attitudes had profound effect upon our uses of law. They provided much of the impetus which gave contract the high position it occupied in our arrangements of power. They explain why in practice we were never as tender toward vested interest as the contract clause of the Federal Constitution formally declared us to be. We respected property and contract rights, but primarily for their utility in keeping affairs in productive motion; where men sought merely to hold onto an established position athwart promising new growth, we were likely to find doctrinal means to shunt them aside.[15] We accepted growth as the norm also in public affairs. From the beginning of our national life we provided orderly procedures for admitting new states to our union. No political dogma kept us from using the law affirmatively to advance community development wherever we saw practical chance to do so. Thus Wisconsin's Governor Fairchild appealed both to the criterion of individual and community growth when in 1867 he urged that the legislature create a state agency to promote immigration:

> Almost without exception these people bring with them habits of honest industry; most of them bring moderate amounts of capital, many are skilled in the mechanic arts, and all are moved by a strong desire to better their condition, and to secure for themselves homes and comfortable surroundings. Immediate steps should be taken to induce as many as possible of their number to settle within the borders of this state. Our countless acres of uncultivated land, our numerous water-privileges unimproved, our almost inexhaustible store of mineral wealth yet hidden in the earth, together

[15] See Hurst, *supra* note 14, at 23-29.

> with our easy access to the markets of the world, offer to the immigrant advantages scarcely to be found elsewhere.[16]

In this buoyant atmosphere growth was not just an opportunity, it was a moral imperative. The point held good to a most sophisticated observer of this society in 1900. For Mr. Justice Holmes,

> Life is action, the use of one's powers. As to use them to their height is our joy and duty, so it is the one end that justifies itself. Until lately the best thing that I was able to think of in favor of civilization, apart from blind acceptance of the order of the universe, was that it made possible the artist, the poet, the philosopher, and the man of science. But I think that is not the greatest thing. Now I believe that the greatest thing is a matter that comes directly home to us all. When it is said that we are too much occupied with the means of living to live, I answer that the chief worth of civilization is just that it makes the means of living more complex; that it calls for great and combined intellectual efforts, instead of simple, uncoordinated ones, in order that the crowd may be fed and clothed and housed and moved from place to place. Because more complex and intense intellectual efforts mean a fuller and richer life. They mean more life. Life is an end in itself, and the

[16] General Message of Governor Fairchild, Jan. 10, 1867, WIS. SEN. J. 22 (20th Legislature, 1867). This emphasis upon growth as a self-evident value appeared regularly in Wisconsin legislative memorials to Congress, seeking bounties of federal lands in aid of settlement or transportation improvements. See, *e.g.,* Wis. Gen. Laws 1860, J. Res. no. I (homesteads); Wis. Gen. Laws 1864, Mem. No. 3 (speedier survey to advance settlement); Wis. Gen. Laws 1867, Mem. No. 15 (military road to open area to settlement) and Mem. No. 27 (aid lands for a railroad to speed general economic growth of north-central Wisconsin).

> only question as to whether it is worth living is whether you have enough of it.[17]

Two other points need be noted. First, there was an important area of ambiguity in this value pattern, regarding the relations between leaders and followers. To believe that man expressed his nature best as he strove to exercise responsible decision over his affairs might be fully consistent with egalitarian faith. But it might also subtly imply the value of an elite and the desirability of fostering it. This is a matter we must consider again later in this essay. Here it suffices to observe that to be a responsible follower requires conscious and responsible decision, too. Within the values of self direction there was room for disciplined response as well as for creative initiative. This was the insight on which Jeffersonian and Jacksonian faith erected the extension of the suffrage. ". . . [T]hough the will of the majority is in all cases to prevail, that will, to be rightful, must be reasonable; . . . the Minority possess their equal rights, which equal laws must protect, and to violate which would be oppression . . . . Some times it is said that man cannot be trusted with the government of himself. Can he, then, be trusted with the government of others? Or have we found angels in the forms of kings to govern him? Let history answer this question."[18] Second, it would caricature our history to equate our belief in the values of self direction with a simple faith in reason. Our political tradition included hardheaded recognition that man was a creature of

[17] Speech at a Dinner Given to Chief Justice Holmes by the Bar Association of Boston on March 7, 1900, in SPEECHES BY OLIVER WENDELL HOLMES 85-86 (1918).

[18] First Inaugural Address, March 4, 1801, in THE COMPLETE JEFFERSON 384-85 (Padover ed. 1943).

passions, in whom worked powerful motives of fear and self regard. The challenge to man's nature was as much to grow in discipline of feeling as in rational capacity. Men's ultimate values were rooted in their feelings. Emotion was not to be viewed simply as an obstacle to reason; reason was in the last resort an instrument to serve values whose dynamic lay in feeling. Public policy should protect men's ability to enlarge the range and depth of their emotional experience, for in this consisted life's quality. There was no higher symbol of our belief than the declarations of the Virginia Statute of Religious Liberty (1785), which found only "impious presumption" in the civil and ecclesiastical rulers "who being themselves but fallible and uninspired men, have assumed dominion over the faith of others," so that they had "established and maintained false religions over the greatest part of the world, and through all time . . . ."[19] But passion did lead men into doing wrong upon others, and men needed institutions to educate their will as well as their reason. Out of this realism No. 10 of *The Federalist* explained the importance of checks and balances in the arrangement of legal power. "[U]nited and actuated by some common impulse of passion, or of interest," majorities and minorities might seek what was against the legitimate interests of others or of the general community. This was a hazard inherent in the possession of liberty. Moreover, "as long as the connection subsists between [man's] . . . reason and his self-love, his opinions and his passions will have a reciprocal influence on each other,"[20] and the fallibility of reason and the diversity of faculties will

[19] Hening, 12 STATUTES AT LARGE OF VIRGINIA 84-85 (1823).
[20] THE FEDERALIST No. 10, at 52-53 (Lodge ed. 1888) (Madison).

provide diverse conceptions of interest to which self-regarding passions may attach. It would be vain to trust only to enlightened leadership. "Enlightened statesmen will not always be at the helm. Nor, in many cases, can such an adjustment [to subordinate clashing interests to public good] be made at all without taking into view indirect and remote considerations, which will rarely prevail over the immediate interests which one party may find in disregarding the rights of another or the good of the whole."[21] Therefore, Madison concluded, we need look to the controlling and educating effects of representative government and dispersed federalism to teach and enforce the growth of emotional discipline without which popular government must degenerate into tyranny.

The men and women who set the norms of achievement in this country did not wait upon philosophers to tell them that pragmatism was their working philosophy. Meaning lay in purposeful action, was defined and tested by purposeful action. We would learn by doing, and by doing we would enlarge our competence to do more.

We lived little by absolutes. Our habit was to take decisions relative to circumstances. We followed some general postulates, though not many. We believed that there was order in the universe, some of it divinely given, some left by Providence for us to make. So far as we acknowledged completed, revealed truth, we did so mainly in the realm of personal morals. Busy and stimulated by the challenge of the unopened continent we trusted to our own practical reason to discover the possibilities of social order. This was a pattern of attitudes we made visible in the separation of

[21] *Id.* at 55.

church and state. Time and again it found homely expression when, as in regulating the purity of the milk supply, we erected laws upon a broadening base of knowledge of the material world.

One other general postulate of our conduct was belief in the ultimate worth and creative potential of the individual human being. This was one of our few absolute articles of faith, though obviously it also drew conviction from experience of the options open to individuals in our time and place. Characteristically, we made our own translation of the practicing import of this belief in individuality. It is a misunderstanding to call ours a materialist culture. There is no doubt that we put our faith in material means to realize ideals. In this we were all Hamiltonians.[22] We believed that the unique opportunity in North America was to build a more self-respecting life for the individual out of the expanding options created by an ever mounting curve of material productivity. Material ambition is at least as dangerous as spiritual pride. Naive or calculated, our material ambitions spawned much greed, cruelty, waste and vulgarity. We did not want for critics to tell us so, particularly of our crude 19th century: Dickens, Mrs. Trollope, George Fitzhugh, Mark Twain, Henry George. Homely testimony to like effect abounds in the matter-of-fact language of the statutes; recall that Wisconsin's milk regulation began with the condemnation in the Territorial Statutes, 1839, of one who "shall knowingly sell any kind of diseased, corrupted or unwholesome provisions, whether for meat or

[22] See Hamilton, "Report on Manufactures, Dec. 5, 1791," in Hamilton, PAPERS ON PUBLIC CREDIT, COMMERCE AND FINANCE 175 (McKee ed. 1934); the "Report" is also reprinted as S. DOC. No. 172, 63rd Cong., 1st Sess. (1913).

drink, without making the same fully known to the buyer." Yet, though our production- and market-oriented way of life carried moral hazard, it also supported generous possibilities. At our worst we were not misers or hoarders; we did not want to possess things so much as to possess power to do with things. We visioned making a society of continental scope. We set ourselves constantly higher challenges of organized effort which depended upon our capacity to cooperate and to show mutual good faith and fidelity to the job. We resented the indignities and denials that circumstance inflicted on individual growth, and we used material means to overcome ignorance, disease, and poverty, to enlarge the content of life.

When it bred true, this pragmatism brought us to generous purposes, subtler knowledge, larger control of ourselves and our situation. However, philosophy conceived from interplay of thought and action was peculiarly subject to the wayward influence of circumstance. Out of our time and place we bred also a bastard pragmatism which warred with the truer strain. The social history of law in the United States consisted in very large part of the uses of law either to express or to combat this bastard pragmatism.

We prized intelligence and we trusted it—within limits. This could be the stance of wisdom, recognizing that man's drives and values find their ultimate sources in feeling and not in reason. Our preoccupation with immediate operations amid the thronging challenges of a raw new country inclined us, however, to vulgarize this insight. Popular attitudes translated respect for intelligence into respect for wit or shrewdness, or in its least attractive aspect, Yankee smartness. At best the cultural odds incline man to spend his limited energies upon improvising for current operations rather than upon long-term, multi-factored thinking; he has been experimenting with speculative reason for perhaps 2,500 years, but he has been living on his wits for 40,000. This cultural bias took strong reinforcement from the local situation. Short of labor as we were rich in natural abundance, we learned to prize the handy man. Short of talent relative to natural plenty and expanding markets, we saw large and often spectacular yields from management of resources, and hence assigned highest prestige to the entrepreneur. This, too, was a judgment of wisdom. In a society committed to dispersed decision, competence to organize means and to make responsible choice of purpose was a critical asset. Again, however, our situation inclined us to vulgarize a good insight. Natural riches and growing population in the 19th century allowed high yields to opportunistic boldness. Common opinion easily mistook opportunism for high-order management. Common opinion easily mistook being busy about affairs for being in command of affairs. The popular image of good managing intelligence tended to exaggerate the value of vigor and skill in short-run operations. Conversely, popular, "practical" judgment was impatient with, and distrusted a long-range, many-factored calculus which in its nature might favor a slower pace of development. There was no more remarkable evidence of twisted esteem for managerial talent than the naive self-righteousness of the 19th century farmer and the uncritical acceptance which general middle-class sentiment gave to the farmer as mainstay of sturdy republicanism. In fact the first and second generation farmers were not farmers, but soil miners and market speculators to whom land was not so much a continuing productive asset as a source of relatively short-term capital gains. This working attitude produced a pre-Civil War decade of boom and bust in Wisconsin wheat farming, ending with exhausted soil. Significantly, when Wisconsin's rural economy found a secure long-term base in diversified agriculture and especially in dairy farming, this was the result of long-range plans and education pressed only by an energetic minority among the native-born farmers and supported by enlistment of a new generation of German, Scandinavian, and Bohemian immigrants to whom the land was important for its production of goods and not of trading profits.[23]

Desire for equality was another factor of ambiguous influence upon our attitudes toward directed effort. We wanted a community of equals. This demand was real and shaped relations of power. But it could mean different things in expression, with different consequences. So far as equality meant "the equal protection of equal laws,"[24] or so far as it meant equal access to theatres for exercising talent, the demand invigorated the best pragmatic development of competence. This was the feature of egalitarian faith which Crevecoeur hymned for its release of individual energy and which Tocqueville saw as a creative force through freedom of association.[25] However, this restlessly mobile society fostered a high level of personal discontent—mirror reflection of ambition—and among socially mobile persons it was hard to find stable criteria of self-esteem and relative place. This was a remarkably open society, in ideals and in

[23] See Schafer, *supra* note 9, at 154-63.

[24] See Yick Wo v. Hopkins, 118 U.S. 356, 369, 6 S. Ct. 1064, 1070 (1886).

[25] See notes 12 and 13 *supra*.

practice. But strong cross currents of personal insecurity moved men also to want likeness rather than distinction in their fellows and to distrust special quality. Since those who achieved greater power did so by unusual drive of will or sharper bite of mind, popular distrust of difference expressed itself by valuing a middle range of talent and preaching the superiority of intuition over reason; more men could hit close to a mean of performance; differences in feeling usually had less visible results than differences in brains. Again, we confront an attitude which had wisdom in it. We sensibly used our abundance and our generous elbow room to launch a society of uncommon decency. Men did not burn their fellows out of religious conviction or follow a man on horseback to bloody glory. But we warped this wisdom by turning it to justify mediocrity. The influence of natural plenty and the surge of expanding population entered, too. In our buoyant 19th century growth many men could advance their position by middling exercise of will and intelligence; circumstance tinctured the century's competitiveness with underlying complacency which could see no virtue in special effort for long-term or broad-scale thinking when immediate returns were so good for those who did enough to ride the wave of the present.[26] Granted that other factors were at work, yet we can see the influence of this depreciation of quality in the loss of professional standards for training and admission to the bar that began with the Revolution and extended into the late 19th century. There was telling evidence also in the exaltation of rule of thumb that flooded state legislatures with three generations of

[26] Compare Marshall, I AUTOBIOGRAPHY OF ROUJET D. MARSHALL 5, 259, 288, 305, 326, 357, 359-60 (1923) for naively revealing discussion of 19th century measures of a successful professional career.

special and local laws before we could bring ourselves to sensible general provisions for chartering corporations, granting and administering utility franchises, and conferring home rule on local governments.[27]

Another trend which fostered a bastard pragmatism was that toward increasing neglect of the social context of action. This was another defect of quality—on the side of official policy a degeneration of local into parochial interest, on the nonofficial side disregard of the social overhead costs of rights of privacy. We settled this country on the flood tide of middle-class power in the western world. We gathered the sense of our own nationality within the political tradition set by the English Parliamentary Revolution. With this inheritance we believed that a healthy society—fostering individuality within a context of relations both tough-fibred and flexible—was a society in which all kinds of powers of decision were widely dispersed. We expressed this belief in the separation of powers and in federalism. We expressed it, too, by sanctioning broad delegation of powers to private will through the law of property, contract, and association, which left great initiative to nonofficial decision—as, for example, in the contributions which the dairymen's association made to developing effective standards of quality control in Wisconsin's milk industry.[28]

This was the positive side of the matter; the wide dispersion of decision making encouraged multiplication of purposeful effort in ever more diverse, intricate and challenging patterns of organization, so that we taught ourselves in-

[27] See Hurst, THE GROWTH OF AMERICAN LAW: THE LAW MAKERS 30, 66, 251, 277 (1950).

[28] See note 8 *supra*.

creasing competence. However, dispersed power appealed also to interests that narrowed the foci of ambition and taught us more ardency and perhaps more competence in restricted operations while draining off creative energy from larger areas of maneuver. Within the legal order this phenomenon took the form of an excessive localism. This localism tended to make Congress and the state legislatures less representatives of their whole sovereignties than ambassadors for districts. A similar influence was felt in judicial organization; well into mid-20th century, inertia or active resistance opposed efficient unification of court systems and tradition was that each locality should hold what amounted to a property right in the exclusive services of the home bench.[29]

In the sphere of private action the narrowing influence of dispersion policy was twofold. For one thing, within the law's protection the market became so engrossing a theatre of ambition that throughout the 19th century it lured away from public affairs the bulk of top managing talent; particularly this was so in the generation following the Civil War, when freedom of association invited men to focus their most creative energies on devising a new scale of private economic organization. The more and the longer that talent concentrated in the market, the more middle-class opinion learned to value this as the normal arena of talent. By the end of the 19th century we had developed a guilty conscience toward investing our best efforts in public programs. Within the domain of private endeavour itself, the unprecedented range of opportunities for private venture and quick and high return from investment of entrepre-

[29] See Hurst, *supra* note 27, at 39-41, 90-96.

neurial talent tended to narrow business decision to the closest main chance. Again, there is telling evidence of popular values in the self-righteous readiness with which the 19th century farmer mined the soil for capital gains on the sale of "improved" land. When this was the temper of the most respectable segment of the middle class, it is not surprising that public opinion was slow to object to the concealed social subsidies which larger operators got by not paying the full costs of the labor, timber, minerals, transport, and water supplies that went into their production.[30] The flexibility of the market's money calculus fostered a mobile, opportunistic style of operation.

There was some change of temper as the 20th century brought private organization, both of individual firms and of economic and social interest groups, to a scale where overhead costs and power and profit advantages of management and staff promoted more institutional continuity and hence attention to wider ranges of relations. However, these more institutionalized centers of nonofficial decision generated their own self-centered drives and greater power to press them. Public opinion was complacent toward this development. The people sensed that a prized standard of living had grown out of, or at least along with, bigger organization. Twentieth-century opinion tended more and more to accept the legitimacy of claims based on stated functional needs of groups and organizations. This could provide a favoring atmosphere for more directed effort. As large organizations bred their own bias of interest, however, this state of opinion permitted the spread of corroding

[30] Compare Adams, "A Chapter of Erie," in Adams and Adams, CHAPTERS OF ERIE 8 (1956); Tocqueville, *supra* note 13, at 156-57.

cynicism toward the reality of public interest. In our excessively localized politics this development also gave leeway to group veto power sufficient to threaten our capacity to make positive policy.

In another aspect abundance created attitudes which sapped the energies available for policy direction. The 19th century United States was production-minded. The 20th century United States turned attention more to consumer satisfactions. This could mean a healthy adjustment of balance between means and ends. It also carried the subtle attractions of concentrating upon close-at-hand, more understandable, and more immediately rewarding affairs of personal life, at the expense of apathy or resignation toward problems of the social context which made a more decent individual life possible.[31]

Public policy making in the United States could and did proceed at one or all of three levels—dealing (1) with the technical detail of legal doctrine and procedures, (2) with the allocation of initiative and discretion among major types of official and nonofficial decision makers, or (3) with the determinations of fact and choices of values by which life was translated into law. The quality of law and its penetration into general experience, were the products of the relative attention given to technique, the separation of powers, and the definition of values. These three levels of concern—with method, power, and purpose—existed not only in law but in all individual and group decision making. As in the law, so elsewhere, the relative balance among them expressed and helped shape individual or group character. It is, then, not

[31] See *e.g.,* Cantril and Strunk, PUBLIC OPINION 1935-1946, at 133, 335-36, 481 (1951).

surprising that the balance struck in law was influenced by the balance struck in other areas of life. Factors in general history and in the special circumstances of the growth of the United States favored using law to promote the development of men's competence to exercise broad-purposed direction of their affairs. So far as this was so, it meant that we did not spend all our energies elaborating the law's technical detail or using law simply as a tool for our most immediate business, but that through law we created arrangements of power and helped ourselves to the experience of new values which enlarged and enriched the content of life. In the context of this society these factors came to expression in a prevailing pragmatism. Other elements worked to produce an illegitimate pragmatism which warped or in important respects defeated achievement of greater control of circumstance. The expression in law of this tension between the true and the bastard pragmatism provides one of the organizing themes of the social history of law in the United States. Indeed, from the standpoint of law's relation to realizing man's distinctive quality as man, this is the most important theme of our legal history.

3

How tell of law's functions affecting purposeful initiative in the growth of this society? Probably there are many concepts by which we may orient materials to this theme. One way to look at the matter is to inquire what procedures of thought and action the law provided, to foster directed effort. Another way is to ask, not how it was done, but what was done. What were law's contributions or defaults in generating purpose and considered choice in various areas of life? This essay considers procedures; the next chapter considers results as well.

By inheritance from abroad and by development at home, ours was a legal order which emphasized procedural regularity and the constitutional (secularly responsible) nature of legitimate power. Given its procedural and constitutional character, this legal system contributed to increase purposeful initiative in the society because it fostered creative tension between form and substance and between generals and particulars. These are aspects of experience not peculiar to legal order. Ideas of form and substance and of generals and particulars and their relations to each other are tools of perception by which men have discovered or made meaning for themselves in all sectors of life. However, law provided its own distinctive resources for generating meaning from the interplay of form and substance and the general and the particular. So these offer useful concepts for organizing study of law's relation to directed effort. In different respects these concepts are useful, also, to examine law's sustaining, as distinguished from its initiating, functions in social order; this is a matter for the next essay. In either case legal history is concerned with "form and substance" and "generals and particulars" mainly as these terms express aspects of law in action, though so taken the concepts may lack the precision or depth which would satisfy professional philosophers.

Taken so with reference to legal operations, form means that the law provides its own prescribed procedures for (1) finding facts, (2) weighing the findings and the options for choice (values) relevant to facts found, (3) validating, and (4) explaining or justifying decisions to use the law's resources for purposes defined out of this consideration of facts and values. Aside from the important values for human decency that reside in fair procedure and which are the distinctive creation of law, its forms are more peculiar to the law than are the values it embodies, which range far into and draw their meaning typically from realms of experience outside law. In this context substance refers to the raw material of life outside the formal legal apparatus, on which the law is put to work. Some of this is raw material from any standpoint—ideas and feelings and responses to circumstances part perceived or felt as possible sources of satisfaction or trouble, but barely above the threshold of awareness and not yet organized into meaning by any criteria, legal or otherwise. Some of this is raw material only in the sense that it is nonlegal experience out of which legal product is yet to be fashioned; within some nonlegal context it may be experience which has already achieved form other than legal, belonging to ordered areas of feeling, or of scientific, or technological, or religious, or other organized basic or applied knowledge. In this latter instance the law's function for social direction is not to give first form to experience. Its role here is, rather, to add impetus to a direction of energies already shaped by purposeful initiative created in some nonlegal sector of men's activity, or to give such an initiative some added object defined through legal process. When Wisconsin began its regulation relevant to a safe milk supply, by the penalties which the Territorial Statutes of 1839 laid upon one who "shall knowingly sell any kind of diseased, corrupted or unwholesome provisions," the vague reach of the statute represented an elementary response in law to market imperfections as yet barely perceived, let alone defined. When statutes of 1883 and 1887 first singled out milk for special regulation, they gave legal form to now more definite practical knowledge of urban consumer problems. In 1889 statutory adoption of a butterfat measure of honest as against adulterated milk translated into legal form a still higher level of ordered experience from outside the law, created by the progress of dairy science and technology.[32]

Taken with reference to legal operations, generals and particulars both have importance for the definition of distinctive values. General aspects of experience are abstract and common, or shared. Yet perception of abstracted likenesses among phenomena of richly diverse content has produced the practical results of science and technology. Particular experience is concrete, immediate and unique, the felt matter of life as men live it with ever fresh novelty moment to moment or year to year. Yet out of the tangible and unique qualities of particular experience, western man has made the intangible and shared value which he ranks first among secular goods—the dignity and creative worth of the individual human being. For the value of individuality—as also its potential for dangerous error—lies in the fact that every man draws from life some ideas and feelings that he alone has, so that he holds the potentiality of some meaning which he alone can discover or make. This is the secular basis for the rights of privacy acknowledged by the Anglo-American tradition of constitutional (limited) government. It would be unrealistic, however, to treat the particular aspects of experience as of separatist effect only, or the general aspects of experience as without relation to

[32] See notes 5 and 7 *supra*.

the uniqueness of the individual. Man realizes his special capacities only through communication. He needs a healthy and growing social context. He has built this by generalizing out of his particular experience to make an increasingly productive and challenging social order within which individuality may achieve richer content. On the other hand, the grasp of reality in its multi-factored particularity can contribute to more functional and enduring social institutions. Behind the surface uniformities of custom and institutions exist infinite individual variations; from this particularity flows the invention and the testing by approach and withdrawal out of which stronger, because more flexible, generalizations are made. Thus there can be creative tension between particular and general perceptions of experience. This creative tension can exist in ascending levels, for man has increased his capacity to abstract from experience to form more intricate patterns of generalization. So he turns his generalizations of today into the particulars from which he abstracts further to make his generalizations of tomorrow. On the other hand, effective generalization means perception of manipulable relationships—the surer grasp of cause and effect. This should not be confused with generality. Vagueness is not generalization, it is ignorance. Effective generalization reduces confusing, apparently unrelated variety to statements of relative simplicity, yielding perception of relations that can be manipulated. However, translation of this insight into action typically involves orderly re-creation of variety, defining limited objectives and contriving specific means to realize the new knowledge in the context of varying circumstance. Such interplay of general (abstracted) and particular (undifferentiated) perceptions largely determined the quality as well as the content of United States legal history. This was especially so for law's relation to purposeful initiative.

The milk regulation story shows some features of this creative tension of general and particular perception. Men know illness and health, fear the one and value the other. They trust and distrust, know fair dealing and fraud, warm to the one, curse the other. These are total responses to total experience, reflecting the crudest perceptions of what goes on. But they serve to produce the first pressures upon law when social living passes some base line of complexity. Vague as it was, Wisconsin Territory's 1839 statute abstracted some elements from undifferentiated, concrete experience and so moved a step toward control of a situation. The 1839 statute recognized that there was special danger where one man pursued his own interest with intentional disregard of another's, and so it penalized the "knowing" seller of impure foodstuff; it singled out food supply as a concern specially relevant to health, concerning which imposition was peculiarly intolerable; it recognized that the market might function below a socially acceptable level because buyers might not be able to match the knowledge of sellers. We must not idealize the process; though law fostered directed effort to control a situation, it moved usually only under pressure of circumstances, and by trial and error. The Wisconsin food laws stayed in this elementary condition for a generation. But the '80's saw interplay resumed between concrete reality and generalizing action in law. First, the legislature determined that milk supply—differentiated from "provisions" in general—had such special importance to health and carried such peculiar hazards of contamination and adulteration that it should be regulated specifically; next, the laws began to reduce the broad notion of milk hazards to specifications and measures of ways in which milk might fall below socially acceptable standards; focused initiative then gained added impetus when the legislature created a specialized administrative office to implement standards. At this point another current of development enters the story, within the law's own institutional development. This regulatory history began in 1839 with the broadest, least differentiated legal response to the situation; the legislature took on itself the whole responsibility for defining standards of conduct, and committed to the public prosecutor and the courts the enforcement of these standards in detail. No less general was the contemporary legislation which entrusted concurrent regulatory power to municipalities. Again, the '80's brought significant further developments. The legislature authorized the Milwaukee city council to enact specific regulations to safeguard the milk supply, and—still more indicative of things to come—authorized the new preventive sanction of licensing. In 1889 the legislature brought into play preventive licensing and specialized enforcement to support state-wide standards, when it created the office of dairy and food commissioner. Through the following generation the legislature jealously held onto a monopoly in defining standards, and added to the detail of its definitions until the statute book spelled out a complex pattern of substantive regulation. The growth of new generalization was not ended, however. In 1929 and 1939 the legislature brought its own role back to that of broad surveillance when it committed to a new department of agriculture authority to make rules defining standards of milk quality as well as techniques of enforcement. This was not a retreat from closer analysis and control. It was a practical recognition that generalization out of particulars (abstraction of cause-effect relations) logically grows into specifications best handled by specialists. It was a development that implied a challenge to the legislature to redefine its own role, to realize effective superintendence of policy. Thus the pull and haul of generals and particulars yielded growth not only in substantive uses of law, but also in more effective division of labor among the branches of government.[33]

4

Let us come back to questions of the creative tension between form and substance. Our constitutional, procedure-oriented legal system defined processes for finding facts, discussing fact findings and choices of ends and means, deciding and justifying what choices should be backed by public power. By channeling into law's forms the flow of life's substance from outside the law we increased purposeful initiative in at least four ways: by attracting desire, cultivating awareness, economizing effort, and legitimating will. In all these respects the significant point was increase of conscious decision, whether for stability or change; it would be unwarrantably narrow to identify the notion of purposeful initiative with innovation alone. In all these respects we dealt with the generation of leadership. But it would be unrealistic to identify leadership solely with the captains

[33] *Ibid.* Compare Rosenberry, J., for the court in State *ex rel.* Wisconsin Inspection Bureau v. Whitman, 196 Wis. 472, 493-500, 506-07, 220 N.W. 929, 937-39, 941-42 (1928).

of policy. Effective initiative requires lieutenants as well as captains; cultivating the first supporting response is as necessary as cultivating the primary definitions of purpose, if directed effort is to make ground against drift and inertia.

The availability of formal legal resources energized will by providing it with realizable goals. To possess the powers of government was itself a prize of ambition. A constitutional legal order required that contestants for this prize justify themselves by programs. If the politician was more often a broker or customer for ideas than an inventor of them, his availability as broker or customer nonetheless was a law-created stimulus to those who had an idea or interest to realize. The rapid rise of parties in the first generation of our national history attested the attraction to purposed action exerted by the existence of formal instruments of power. Our favor for the principle of widely dispersed decision making multiplied attractions to planned venture. Large-scale organized activity came to bear primarily upon the legislature and the chief executive, for they held the power of the purse, the disposal of public property, and authority to lend or deny public force to private interest. Thus the public domain was a tremendous magnet drawing forth individual and group ambitions—for low-priced farms and free homesteads, for turnpike, canal, and railroad construction subsidies, for privileges to graze stock, cut timber, dig minerals, or exploit waterpower. The legislature was a target for purpose because it could create corporate franchises, give protected markets by public utility regulation or by tariffs, and—after we developed a more ample and flexible money supply and larger public revenues—grant cash subsidies or subsidies of government services to great interest groups. The availability of the courts was likewise an attraction to the formation of purpose and the manipulation of affairs, though in ways different from those fostered by the readiness of the legislative process. Mid-19th century egalitarianism made an elected judiciary standard in the states, but this development was followed by only episodic political attention to judicial elections. This was not because the courts were unimportant in defining and creating legal interests. From about 1810 to 1890 the courts made a vast body of common law in the United States. But they did so incident to exercise of judicial power which by constitutional tradition was limited to deciding suits between parties who presented specific legal and real interests focused in specific controversies. The specific focus of litigation made it a process ill adapted to stimulate presentation of purposes of large scope on the initiative of suitors. On the other hand, subject to the narrowed focus and limited means of particular suitors, the availability of litigation offered uncommon opportunity for individuals or small groups to press for policy definition. To obtain action from the legislature or from a chief executive usually required mobilizing substantial group effort; to obtain action from a court a litigant needed only his own courage and the means to retain counsel and pay other expenses of suit. The burdens on the litigant should not be minimized. Sometimes it was cheaper and easier to get a statute passed than to fight a law suit. Nonetheless by the availability of litigation the law stimulated initiative for defining public policy from a far wider range of sources than responded to the opportunities available through legislation. The judges lacked the authority or means to take such policy initiative as was open to the legislature and the chief executive. During the 19th century, however, through the opportunities presented by lawsuits they boldly declared the larger policy which they deemed to set the frame for particular problems tendered by litigants. The calculated dictum was a potent device of 19th century law making. Thus the judicial process allowed judges as well as litigants to add to the sum of purposed direction in affairs. The incentive which litigation offered to judicial law making and to individual or small group pressures for policy definition was peculiarly important because of John Marshall. On his precedent our tradition acknowledged the courts as normally the final interpreters of the large terms in which constitutions granted and limited official power, and it was mainly in lawsuits that detailed content was put into these standards. In the 20th century the great development of executive and administrative powers created new foci of attention to attract the initiative both of individuals and sometimes of large organized interests in obtaining definitions of policy, or the grant of licenses, or privileges, or the taking of other decisions which had value calculated to draw purpose and energy to bear upon obtaining them.

It would be a close question if we had to decide whether the availability of legal process contributed more to purposed initiative by energizing will or by sharpening perception. Circumstance and change present a baffling infinity of detail to man's mind. Cultural inheritance alone tenders such a range of stimuli as to confuse direction or induce surrender to habit; in its most purposeful energies, law can provide only marginal increments to the total factors that affect social life. Amid this distracting variety and press of experience, the range and acuteness of men's perception is critical to what they can do in discovering or making meaning out of the universe. Given the bewildering total of things and events, their perception depends upon what they think. They do not think about what they see; they see what they think about. The state of awareness is more fundamental than concert or conflict in determining how men direct affairs. They do not plan or venture, agree or fight until they perceive a choice or a problem. I observed earlier that historians exaggerate conflict; a measure of this exaggeration is the neglect to study how perception has determined purpose and action. As early as 1839 the Wisconsin statutes show concern about impure food, but at this point regulation dealt only with completed trouble, not with its causes; the law rested on no more complex observation than that individuals became sick from things they ate. Sanitary regulation of farms and dairies did not become an issue in the statutes until about the turn of the century, after the germ theory of disease had entered public awareness. Thereafter the story became more complicated; sanitary regulations in effect required greater capital investment by farmers and dairymen, therefore affected the margin of survival in the industry and encouraged trends toward concentration and the rise of co-operatives; in the name of sanitation particular segments of the industry sought to enlist the law to handicap competing products or protect local markets against distant suppliers. Thus in familiar fashion the pull and haul of contending interests entered the development of milk sanitation law.[34] But the opening of this new theatre of legal

[34] See note 7 *supra. Cf.* John F. Jelke Co. v. Emery, *supra* note 11; Dairy Queen of Wisconsin, Inc. v. McDowell, 260 Wis. 471, 51 N.W. 2d 34 (1952); Comment, "Perception of 'Special Interest' as a Factor in Statutory Interpretation—Judicial Reaction to the Farm Lobby," 1957 WIS. L. REV. 456.

action depended in the first instance on awareness that facts and relations existed that had relevance to life and private and social well-being. New awareness sometimes generated fears or tensions not theretofore known. It also generated constructive purpose. Moreover, under the scrutiny of reason and disciplined feeling, fear or tension were not in themselves bad; indeed, they were reactions by which we preserved and increased life, as individuals and in society.

The formality of legal process tended to increase the span of awareness, first, by insisting on definition as the necessary condition of obtaining things men wanted from law; a bill must be drawn before a statute could be passed, pleadings must be filed and evidence presented before a judgment could be had; cause must be shown, forms filled out, compliance with license conditions proved, before executive or administrative action. Herein the effect of the law's formality was similar to that of the law's insistence on generalizing (abstracting) from particulars. In both respects the availability of legal process encouraged men to increase their awareness of relationships among things and events and thereby to sharpen their eyes to the existence of gains and costs and the sources of gain or cost. This sharpening of vision was inherent to the use of formal procedures, which could not be worked without attention to details as these were relevant to larger ends. Knowledge grows by taking meaningful distinctions among things that are different; to classify phenomena is no substitute for studying their dynamic relations, but just as an orderly classification of forms of life was prerequisite to recognizing let alone understanding evolution, so some classification is prerequisite to discerning factors that must be managed or accommodated in a situation of social control. Classification can also be a dangerously attractive resting place for thought; there is a nice balance to be kept between giving names to things or events and moving on to study their working relations. Thus the concept "public utility" or "business affected with a public interest" was useful to focus attention upon the social importance of organization and key points in organization, as this society grew into tighter interlock and dependence of processes. But the concept obstructed perception of social interests when it was allowed to become a closed formula to measure the limits within which the legislature might regulate access to market and terms and conditions of service. So in *Nebbia* v. *New York* the United States Supreme Court wisely let dynamic analysis prevail over static classification.[35] There was no closed category of businesses that might be subjected to regulation. The issue must always be treated pragmatically: the question was whether there was reason to discern a public interest to warrant a given legal intervention. There appeared to be such a public interest in promoting regular supply of milk; if this made the milk business so far a "public utility," so be it, though this departed from prior classifications.

The formality of legal process also increased men's awareness because it enforced on their attention the existence of the political dimension of life in addition to relationships brought to focus in the market or through informal association. Values which failed of expression because their proponents lacked market power, for example, could make themselves visible through efforts to obtain legislation or to fight lawsuits, as the milk consumer's interest found

[35] See notes 1 and 4 *supra*.

expression in the statutes which it could not find in the market.[36] Because law insisted on its own procedures and declared all forms of secular power subject to its scrutiny, the availability of legal process invited men to more awareness of the power implications of their relations. How important was this feature of legal order became especially clear where the forms of law lagged behind social development so that they did not stimulate perception and grasp of emerging power problems. Nowhere was this more painfully apparent in the mid-20th century United States than in failure to order the rapid, sprawling growth of urban living, largely for want of effective forms of metropolitan legal organization.

A third way in which the forms of law increased men's awareness of emergent fact, relation, opportunity, and tension was by providing legitimate, and sometimes obligatory means of communication or exchange among persons or groups otherwise separated by social space or by ignorance of each other's existence or points of view. The largest example of this was the development of national political parties as forms to align diverse interests to capture the Presidency. Every time a legislature convened, its halls and committee rooms provided trading areas for sharper definition and accommodation of a great range of nonofficial interests many of which had no other place of exchange, not even the market. Sometimes, as under mid-20th century labor relations statutes, the law required interests to talk with each other in good faith, to bring to light bases of mutual accommodation which might be lost in combat.

The availability of formal legal process increased pur-

[36] See notes 4, 5, and 7 *supra*.

poseful initiative by encouraging more efficient use of imagination and will. This is important because men confront the bewildering detail of life with only limited energies to organize it. Since management competence is scarce, it is necessary to contrive an economy of competence; the law's forms helped maximize output of purpose. This estimate runs counter to familiar criticisms of formalism or formal procedures. By crusted habit and overhead costs of unwarranted detail, formal proceedings can slow or block sensible adjustment of affairs. These criticisms had validity in United States legal history, particularly for the costs of outmoded judicial structures and procedures. Form can be made by contrivance or by custom. Whatever its source, form does tend to become an end in itself out of the feelings of security or the technical preoccupation which attend its continuance. These things are so, but they are not the whole of the matter. For want of form efficiently strong and adapted to function, intelligence and disciplined feeling were wasted also in aimless, diffused motion. The problem was something like that of bringing water from a pond to play on a burning barn. An unorganized crowd with buckets would splash to little effect; a bucket brigade would stand a better chance; most effective would be a pumper which, through an intake pipe dropped into the pond, and protected by a strainer to sieve out dirt and weeds, would draw water, channel it into a hose, and so bring it to bear with force and direction where it was useful. Such were uses of the legislative process. By its availability to make decisions and set up procedures, the legislature tended to draw to itself—as the pumper the pond water—ideas and emotions, worries and hopes, affirmations and denials churning about in the general life. There must be bills introduced, hearings held, committee reports made, differences debated, legislators informed and argued with and put under pressures of political reward or penalty; these necessities tended to strain out casual, irresponsible or unworkable elements in the influences pressing upon the law from without. By the difficulties it posed as well as the opportunities it afforded, formal legislative process thus offered means to register the acceleration or cumulation of thought and will about some new focus of social interest. This was important, because it was acceleration or cumulation rather than regular flow that tended to create problems of adjustment in social relations. Man's laziness or the fact that he is tired incline him to regard time as a uniform motion of regular units of measure; formal processes which would disturb his illusion were needful to his safety. This sieving process in policy consideration sometimes went on for years in the legislative process, while purpose was generated and brought to useful focus. Much major national legislation of the 1930's had a history of bills introduced and hearings held in Congress running back nearly a generation, relating to labor relations, regulation of finance and credit, and provision of fair labor standards. Wisconsin's pioneering unemployment compensation act of 1932 had origins in state legislative proceedings dating from 1915.[37] It was especially important at the emergence of a new area of awareness—when data was lacking, ideas undefined, emotion not yet enlisted—that procedures existed by which men troubled or challenged by the first perception of opportunity or

[37] See Chamberlain, THE PRESIDENT, CONGRESS AND LEGISLATION 18, 23, 453, 459, 463 (1946); Haferbecker, WISCONSIN LABOR LAWS 122-27 (1958).

tension could bring the matter over the threshold of attention. Channeled into legitimate inspection, even poor ideas might be turned to account in defining more constructive notions. So the Townsend Plan agitation of the 1930's contributed to consideration of a workable social security system. There were features of our culture which created special need that the law's forms contribute to creative purpose. Two of these features are implicit in examples just cited. Strong elements of our tradition were hostile to imposing form on fluid events; the Puritan element opposed religious forms; Jacksonian democracy exalted the superiority of spontaneous impulse and intuition over cultivated reason. Where formal process was kept under scrutiny so that it served social functions, it helped curb the tendency of a bastard pragmatism to foster loose thinking and undisciplined emotion. The pace of social change in the 19th and 20th century United States lent additional function to the law's insistence on formal process. Illegitimate pragmatism encouraged a naive faith in action which tempted us to justify means by uncritical devotion to ill-defined ends; it was therefore desirable to promote purposeful initiative through processes that emphasized the decency of deliberate and responsible procedure. This was the more so because the pace of change this country experienced meant that its institutions were relatively young and its people under continuing tension between ideals and action.

The availability of the law's forms also fostered purposeful initiative by providing insignia of legitimacy for will. Few of the problems of accommodating individual and group interests could be decided in town meeting. The initiative of individuals or small groups originated most proposals for public action; consideration and decision almost always had to proceed by delegation to relatively small numbers of men. As the country grew larger and relations within it more impersonal it was a functional necessity of its growth that law provide accepted tokens of authority—in regular procedures and in statutes, court judgments and opinions and executive orders. This was basic to the confident exercise of directing will.

Accepted forms of law did more. Decisions to let things stand were usually the easier to make, carrying the security of the familiar. But decisions must be taken also for change, and this was more apt to puzzle the will. The law's formal processes abided, however. So long as change moved within established forms—by fresh interpretation of the large terms of constitutions and through the regular procedures of legislation and adjudication—the psychological costs of initiating change were lessened and the chances for launching rational adjustment to reality increased. The fashion in which the Supreme Court restored flexibility to the concept of substantive due process of law in *Nebbia* v. *New York* is a case in point.[38] Another example is the Court's many-sided development of that clause of the United States Constitution which forbids any state to pass any law impairing the obligation of contracts. Extensively construed by Marshall to protect grants and charters, this apparently rigid formula was subsequently adapted to preserve legislative power to meet change; no commitment by an earlier body could prevent a later legislature from acting to protect public morals or from employing the power of taxation; if creditors' substantive rights were unimpaired, the state might change

[38] See notes 1 and 4 *supra*.

procedures for enforcing debts where change might reasonably be deemed in the public interest, so that the legislature might decree a mortgage moratorium, where spiraling foreclosures amid general depression threatened collapse of property institutions.[39]

The infinite variety of minds, wills, and circumstance insured that there would always be more elasticity in practice than would appear from the formal face of law. Moreover, the inherited advantage of practical over speculative reason meant that men more readily adopted change in material techniques and in everyday practice than in their forms of organization. Of course the contrasts of form and practice could involve hypocrisy or shirked responsibility; gaps between the law's declarations and its enforcement provided disquieting histories, as in morals regulations or the administration of divorce. Yet the legitimating shelter of form also allowed constructive variations to develop. Men have no recourse but to learn a good deal of policy by trial and error. This requires opportunity to be inconsistent, which has often been furnished by the breadth of formal doctrine; a conspicuous 19th century instance is the court's use of fictions to experiment in allocating costs of unintended damage under formulae of agency and imputed negligence.[40] Form may also shelter the growth of a new perception of value emerging in a climate of hostile or distrustful opinion. So the courts justified advanced zoning regulations as protections of morals or property, before the judges were ready

[39] See the discussion as well as the demonstration of this doctrinal development in Home Building & Loan Ass'n v. Blaisdell, 290 U.S. 398, 427-37, 442-44, 54 S. Ct. 231, 235-40, 241-42 (1934).

[40] See *e.g.*, Wedgwood v. Chicago & Northwestern Ry. Co., 41 Wis. 478 (1877).

to declare that aesthetic considerations warranted land use controls.[41]

In all these respects—by attracting desire, cultivating awareness, economizing effort, and legitimizing will—the formality of law helped generate purposeful initiative. In light of the argument made earlier in this essay, I take this to be prima facie a good outcome. Of course purposeful initiative may be for evil or mistaken decisions; in any given area of policy, legal history must follow the story farther than our present concern carries us. However, the possibility of abuse was generally not treated as impugning the values this society put on purposeful initiative.

> Those who won our independence believed that the final end of the State was to make men free to develop their faculties; and that in its government the deliberative forces should prevail over the arbitrary. They valued liberty both as an end and as a means. They believed liberty to be the secret of happiness and courage to be the secret of liberty.[42]

But there is another aspect of the matter besides the possibility of abusing freedom. Law's insistence on form could stifle as well as foster purposeful initiative. I have already noted some reasons why the law's formality tended to make law itself a source of inertia or drift. Let me conclude by noting others of these cross currents.

[41] See Village of Euclid v. Ambler Realty Co., 272 U.S. 365, 47 S. Ct. 114 (1926); General Outdoor Advertising Co. v. Department of Public Works, 289 Mass. 149, 193 N.E. 799 (1935); Cream City Bill Posting Co. v. City of Milwaukee, 158 Wis. 86, 147 N.W. 25 (1914). *Cf.* Wis. Stat. 1957 § 31.06.

[42] Brandeis, J., concurring, in Whitney v. California, 274 U.S. 357, 375, 47 S. Ct. 641, 648 (1927).

Particularly where the spending of public money was concerned, the law's processes looked to preventive and constructive action. But the most visible and dramatic forms of law were those which provided ordered procedures of combat. In this respect the law's forms helped fasten our attention unduly on conflict at the cost of talent diverted from more positive functions. One sign of this was the relatively late development and continued under-estimation of the creative possibilities of legislative investigation. This formal exaggeration of conflict likewise detracted from policy leadership because it pandered to the common taste for melodrama and for estimating situations in terms of good men against bad men, rather than by rational weighing of will and circumstance. Within the legal apparatus itself, emphasis on form tended to generate unthinking habit and custom and an emotional unreadiness to acknowledge changing facts. In their preoccupation with formal process, lawmen tended to create a sense of vested interest in their specialized technical knowledge, to elaborate detail for its own sake, and to adopt a real or professed neutrality toward the values which their techniques might serve. Moreover, legal forms were in large part word forms, because it was so much the function of law to define uses of power. This character of legal formality helped import into law the drift and inertia of custom which build most language. So far as law contrived its own words of art—"fee simple," for example—if the formulations proved useful, their success tended by habit to reify them and they became statements of self-evident values, substitutes for fresh thought. These were defects of formality which characterized the bar and the judicial branch and routine administration on the executive side more than the legislature. Though inertia protected its internal procedures and structure, the legislature was closer than most other lawmen to the rough and tumble of general interest conflict and the flow of changing circumstance outside the law. Measured over time, substantive legislative activity was less subject to the cramping effect of the law's formality than most other processes of law making or administration. Taken in all its aspects, however, with the many avenues which judicial and executive as well as legislative processes opened to expression of the wants, fears, hopes, and insights springing from the general life, the law's formality contributed far more impetus to purposeful initiative than to drift or inertia in the growth of the United States.

5

The creative tension which legal processes maintained in perception and valuation between the general (abstracted) and the particular (concrete) aspects of experience was a prime contribution to considered initiative. This interplay of general and particular in law was a special instance of the interplay of form and substance.

The formal structure of legal agencies and doctrine governing the forms of exercise of legal power—the emphasis of this legal system upon procedure and upon constitutionalism—promoted continuing, ordered competition between general and particular insights and general and particular values. From the Parliamentary Revolution we inherited and developed a positive concept of legislative authority to deal with the large framework of social living. This was implicit in the legislature's power of the purse, its power to investigate matters of common concern and to provide for the good order of relationships on which the common life depended ("the police power"). However, we steadily broadened the elective base of the legislature and set short terms of office in the more numerous chamber. Out of early difficulties of travel and communication our tradition became hard-set that legislators be elected from and be residents of relatively confined districts. These were factors that made the legislative branch sensitive to the pressures of individuals and, especially, of groups. Indeed, by mid-20th century, legislative sensitivity to particular views and wills seemed built into the structure to an extent that imperilled its capacity to produce generalization adequate to the times. As this appeared, the generalizing function became more dependent upon second chambers and chief executives, to whom the protection of broader constituencies and longer terms allowed initiative for broader purpose. The "judicial power" with which our constitutions invested courts in practice included authority to generalize, to declare and apply values which reached beyond the immediate lawsuit. If announced philosophy lagged behind the reality, yet 19th century appellate judges in fact generalized broadly and in depth under the spur and opportunity of the specific trouble cases brought to them. However, their constitutional function typically limited them to making law within the bounds of the record in particular litigation. Litigious stress on particulars helps account for much of the tough-fibred generalization that went into common-law growth. It helps account, too, for the unduly narrow interest calculus by which issues were often weighed, to the neglect especially of social costs—for example, in the assumption of risk doctrine in industrial tort, or the inadequate curbs which the concepts of "nuisance" and "waste" could put upon destruction of natural resources. The increased functions of the executive branch, including the administrative arm, spelled the most striking structural development in law after about 1905. This shift presented mingled emphases on generals and particulars on which at mid-century it was still difficult to strike a balance. The consolidation of a policy leadership role in the office of President, the tendency of state governors to seize more programming initiative, the wide delegation of rule making power to administrators within broad limits of substance and procedure set by the legislature or the courts, were elements which fostered purposeful initiative over drift of policy. The nature of much executive and administrative work also brought it closer to particulars than any other legal operation save that of the trial courts. The executive and administrative processes, however, lacked the guiding and confining traditions within which courts made common law from particular instances. Thus after some 50 years of broadened executive-administrative activity, initiation of policy by interplay of generals and particulars had yielded much ill-defined, often unrecorded administrative product, and, indeed, had stimulated unease over proprieties of the process. Structure and function here seemed clearly still in growth.

Constitutional doctrine also set standards which legitimated competition of generals and particulars under criteria which pressed men to think and to discipline feeling for responsible decision. Constitutional legal order inherently favored purposeful initiative over drift. Constitutionalism meant that the ends and means of government were limited;

power must be used only for legitimate ends and by legitimate means. Constitutionalism thus stood for ideals of rationality and emotional self-restraint in conducting affairs. There is little evidence how firm was the loyalty of general opinion to these ideals. There is enough evidence of excesses in our history to suggest that, under stress, the working effectiveness of constitutional ideas derived from the understanding and conviction of relatively small numbers of the people and that the faithful minorities were differently constituted according to interests and areas of concern. Nonetheless appeal to constitutional principle proved a potent instrument to mobilize political opinion, and with the leverage afforded by formal legal structure the devoted minorities likewise had effect.

The central constitutional doctrine that pressed men to justify official decision by grounding it in general policy was the insistence that power be used "reasonably"—which meant that official action bear rational relation to valid ends. Late 19th century development of the substantive meaning of the due process and equal protection clauses of the 14th Amendment gave this criterion of reasonableness high visibility. But it had in fact been framework doctrine for this legal order at least from the establishment of national government, implicit in the ways in which we hammered out concepts of state police power and federal commerce or fiscal authority. Power should be validated by showing that it fit into a legitimate general context. Classic early instances of this approach were the opposing opinions which Jefferson and Hamilton tendered President Washington on the constitutionality of a national bank, and Marshall's later opinion in *McCulloch* v. *Maryland*.[43] The bad name which special and local legislation acquired in mid-19th century, reflected in the limitations on such forms of legislating then commonly written into state constitutions, testified further that our central tradition trusted to generalization as a criterion of proper direction of public policy.

Analogous though less sharply identified emphasis on generalization marked the development of judge-made law. Thus the Bench readily followed the lead of Kent and Marshall in making written opinions a major obligation of the judicial job, at least on appeal. The development both of stare decisis and of careful devices of distinction and fiction to introduce flexibility, attested the judges' concern that their work fit into general patterns. Given the high value put on market freedom and dispersed power, it was striking how cautiously judges reserved power to test the legality of contracts by their conformity to "public policy." Of like import was the courts' insistence on objective measures of prudent conduct and reasonable expectations, in determining liability in tort or contract. Thus even where policy favored maximum delegation of discretion for private decision—and, hence, a large indulgence of particular variation—doctrine pressed men to determine action by fitting particulars into functional general relationships.

However, formal legal structure and doctrine also gave weight to particulars as well as to generals—to whole ex-

[43] 17 U.S. (4 Wheat.) 315 (1819). For the opinions on the national bank submitted to President Washington by Jefferson on Feb. 15, and by Hamilton on Feb. 23, 1791, see, respectively, "Opinion Against The Constitutionality of a National Bank," in THE COMPLETE JEFFERSON 342 (Padover ed. 1943); and "Opinion as to the Constitutionality of the Bank of the United States," in Hamilton, PAPERS ON PUBLIC CREDIT, COMMERCE AND FINANCE 100 (McKee ed. 1934).

perience as men encounter it in pattern and unique context. The key proposition of our constitutionalism was that law existed to serve individual life, or the ultimate in human particularity. We embodied this proposition in constitutional guarantees of fair trial to the criminal accused, of free speech and religion, of private property. When we gave constitutional definition to the highest crime against the political community—treason—we hedged it with protections for individuals and minorities by limiting the kinds of conduct which might be punished as treason (only levying war or aiding enemies) and requiring that proof be made by two witnesses to an overt act. Constitutional guarantees apart, the broad sweep offered to private will by the ordinary law of contract, property, and tort invited realization of infinitely numerous particular perceptions of life. Legislation was typically the field of generalization, but the power of legislative investigation provided means to draw into consideration of general policy making the full rich variety of particular life. The procedural rules of legislative houses aimed primarily to facilitate proper majority action, but also protected the privileges and opportunities of expression of individual members and minorities. Given its constitutional function of deciding controversies between parties presenting focused factual and legal interests, the judicial branch provided the most distinctive forum in law for expression of particularized wants and desires. This was especially true of trial courts, most of whose time went into the exacting business of superintending examination of facts of more or less unique situations. By its nature the executive branch was continually immersed in dealings with the full-dimensioned event, the concrete happening; thus from President to policeman executive attention to general policy was regularly conditioned by relentless exposure to special circumstance. This carried peculiar danger of arbitrary action in the administration of law; hence judicial review of administrative action was a sensitive area of legal growth as the 20th century witnessed its vast expansion of executive business. Conversely, where administrators met the infinite details of their task with responsible alertness to broad implications, this immersion in detail equipped them to enrich the content and strengthen the operation of general policy. The courts recognized this in interpreting ambiguous statutory language when they gave weight to the construction of the language evidenced by the uniform, long continued, consistent practice of its administrators. "The practice has peculiar weight," Mr. Justice Cardozo pointed out, "when it involves a contemporaneous construction of a statute by the men charged with the responsibility of setting its machinery in motion, of making the parts work efficiently and smoothly while they are yet untried and new."[44]

The linking of general and particular in law, I suggested earlier, is a special case of the connection of form and substance. Of the several ways in which the law's relation of form and substance fostered conscious direction as against drift and inertia, two seem specially to operate through creative tension generated between generals and particulars. The interplay of general and particular aspects of experience in law tended to increase purposeful initiative (1) by cultivating awareness and (2) by legitimating will.

The competition of general and particular insights and

[44] Norwegian Nitrogen Products Co. v. United States, 288 U.S. 294, 315, 53 S. Ct. 350, 358 (1933).

interests which the law facilitated had many and complex effects upon men's perceptions of their situation. There were cross currents and confusions. However, on balance the effect seems to have been to increase the extent of considered direction given to affairs. The matter deserves examination by major fields of policy, for it is apparent that there were marked variations in courses of policy growth according to time, context, and subject matter. Thus policy concerning the quality and safety of the milk supply developed with increasing emphasis upon generalizing the value implications of new scientific and technological knowledge and the regulatory potential of new styles of preventive law administration. In contrast, antitrust policy developed largely out of the pressures of dealing with the distinctive context of particular industries or markets. The difference stemmed partly from reactions of legal process to different types of knowledge. From the late '80's on, the effort to shape general policy regarding the milk supply was helped because science provided relevant biological generalizations translatable into legal regulation. As late as mid-20th century we had no comparable body of scientific generalization on which to erect comparably definite generalizations of antitrust policy. For want of a better way, in antitrust law we proceeded largely by teachings of particular experience. Since this better fitted the style of judicial than of legislative policy making, there was a relatively larger component of judge-made law in the field of antitrust than in the field of milk controls. The milk regulation and antitrust law examples have in common that they both show use of legal process for the constructive work of bringing social variables into relation. At best this is an imprecise operation because our knowledge is imprecise. Yet there is some rationality in most social situations, some functional relation of aspects or processes, and hence room for useful contribution by law in helping bring known factors into pattern.

The interplay of generals and particulars in legal process enlarged perception especially by making men more aware that they acted always in a field of relations. Because of those elements of legal structure and doctrine which invited efforts to generalize choices and which measured the legitimacy of decisions by their rational relation to general ends and procedures, legal process made men more conscious of cause-effect relationships, both closer and more remote. Legal process thus also made men more aware of the sources and the extent of gains and costs in alternative courses of behavior, and hence aware of a wider range of factors relevant in attaching legal responsibility to behavior. For we deal here with enlarging awareness in two different areas; to identify cause and to assign responsibility in law are different matters. The milk regulation history, for example, expressed growth in perception on both these fronts, out of law's generalizing response to what was at first only ill-defined concern for hazards and frictions of an increasingly impersonal urban-market-governed way of life. Milk regulation moved from response only to the fact of harm—the sale of impure product for consumption—to more searching attention to preventing the causes of harm, by fixing and enforcing sanitary standards in farm and dairy operation. So law's invitation to frame general policy encouraged a subtler attention to causes. Implicit in this shift of attention was also a new calculus of gain and cost. It was a calculus at once more closely defined than before and embracing more elements. Tighter regulations in effect redefined what constituted a socially acceptable minimum value of milk. Moreover, by affecting the levels of investment involved in doing business according to sanitary standards, law in effect redefined minimum capital requirements and minimum operating costs for a socially acceptable dairy industry. Thus by its invitation to generalize policy, law tended to cultivate awareness of the logic of social functions or relations. It was a service to perception especially valuable in this society, where men's restless busy-ness and preoccupation with current operations inclined them either to settle for unhelpfully large abstractions ("the public good"), or moral melodrama (good men versus bad men), or to exhaust their energies in detail. It fostered that desirable sophistication which supplants gross generalizations (at once unduly elaborate and unduly vague) with simpler statements of relationships; so we abandon the impossible attempt to comprehend multiple causes and whole outcomes for the manageable enterprise of distinguishing differences and devising and relating specific programs. Sharpened perception of relations took on greater human significance because this society developed a technical apparatus which was largely indifferent to the uses made of it, whose elaboration threatened to make its operations ends in themselves and whose specialization was dangerously divisive of immediate interests; we needed all the help we could get in defining values which would keep technique in its place and hold men in the sense of broader community. As the homely example of sanitation policy suggests, men did enlarge their reach of values by rational pursuit of understanding of the context of life. They enlarged their perception of feeling as well as of reason. In this society, Bryce observed, greater even than what scientific progress taught of the things that could be done by collective effort was "the influence of a quickened moral sensitiveness and philanthropic sympathy. The sight of preventable evil is painful, and is felt as a reproach."[45] So, for example, the uses of law for combating racial prejudice lay only marginally in compulsion, mainly in exposing the illegitimate bases in fear, greed, or hatred on which discrimination rested.

General propositions are necessary instruments to make sense of particular experience and to cultivate judgment and emotional poise in meeting it. But they are not the only kind of dependable knowledge. Indeed, they may do harm, where they tempt men to treat useful abstractions or fictions as if they were full-dimensioned, existent entities. The immediate perception of experience is always particular. Perception of the particular provides not only raw material for generalization but the sharp sense of differences out of which generalization is born and the means for checking its utility. Man has a history only because he has found unique aspects in reality; it would be a naive naturalism which saw reality only in general, regularly recurring phenomena. Legal process thus contributed to purposeful initiative as it provided procedures which brought particular interests and particular events sharply into focus in adjustments of social relations.

I have noted trends in this society which created a bastard pragmatism at odds with a healthy pragmatic impetus toward conscious direction and control. Because of this fac-

[45] Bryce, 2 THE AMERICAN COMMONWEALTH 591 (New and rev. ed. 1914).

tor, it is peculiarly difficult to strike a balance on law's accommodations to the pressure of particulars, in measuring its contributions to purposeful initiative. With this caution in mind, let me suggest some ways in which legal processes brought particulars into creative relation to policy.

This constitutional legal order put its highest value on the individual life. In this context it was always relevant to hold means in rational subordination to this end. The multiplying of functionally organized, special-focus interests increased the value of legal processes—notably litigation—which brought the operation of social apparatus under the test of its service to the whole man. The size and internal discipline of great organizing institutions tended in practice to make any but institutional norms irrelevant in large areas of life as criteria of action; this tendency underlined the constructive importance of procedures by which the law might permit or even protect a measure of rebellion against institutional codes, that growth in moral perception not end or lose touch with the values of individuality.

Moreover, where social arrangements so emphasized dispersion of power and scope for individual experience, the logic of the structure invited knowledge and responsible feeling to grow by dialectic out of the interplay of individual and group variation, cooperation, and competition. All elements of law which facilitated expression of particular interest and experience promoted this natural dialectic of growth. In this aspect law's contribution fitted a 20th century tendency in the growth of knowledge, by which division of labor between basic and applied knowledge became less sharp than earlier in Western culture, and men advanced learning by freer movement back and forth between these emphases. The pressure of particular interest, particular hope or fear, gain or hurt, was typically the first response to change of circumstance. By providing legitimate channels for expressing this response, the law's forms sharpened men's perception of shifting fact and thus fostered that awareness which is prerequisite to debate or decision. This function gained importance as the increased complexity of social organization increased the number of points at which damaging malfunction or maladjustment might occur. The pressure of particular variations in interest and of particular conjunctions of circumstance also taught a salutary sense of the large element of uncertainty in affairs—man's incompetence to grasp all the variables in his situation, which he calls chance—and this offered useful curbs against pride of reason or feeling.

The urgent expression which particular interest or particular situation might find through legal process—whether in a legislative investigation, a lawsuit or an executive order—could also contribute to assessment of social gain and cost. Most often it was pursuit of generalization which advanced social accounting. But social change is a line projected into infinity, not a circle. Men make many irrevocable choices in their individual and collective lives. The irrevocable is particular, unique, and in handling it the law for better or worse affected our perception of social gain and cost. No function of legal process was more important than the help it might give to bringing into clearer focus and under responsible consideration the occasions of irrevocable decision. Such were, for example, the Declaration of Independence, the Louisiana Purchase, Lincoln's refusal to accept secession, Wilson's choice to arm our merchant ships,

Roosevelt's decision to lend-lease destroyers to Britain. Irrevocable choices were not only made in great single strokes. They were made also in courses of action over time, as in the pattern of policy which accepted destruction of the Lake States forest in exchange for a generation's faster development of the prairie and plains economy. The examples suggest that there is much useful work that needs doing, to assess the quality of law's performance in this regard, area by area.

The interaction of generals and particulars through law promoted purposeful initiative not only by its effects on perception but also by its effects on will. This is of high practical importance; realism requires that we guard against over-rationalizing political processes, as if they were logically derived from established principles of objective reality. Belief and action rest ultimately on feeling. By exercising their minds and disciplining their emotions within law's procedures men gained confidence to act despite their ignorance. Here were means by which they could seek workable generalizations of their relationships, held accountable to the ends of a decent life by the legitimated pressure of particular interests and points of view, and held close to reality by the check of particular experience. Thus men legitimated not merely the will to act, but—what was essential to realizing their concept of human dignity—the will to act responsibly. Legal process contributed to life functions because herein it promoted growth of competence, in reason and feeling; in this the law entered deep into our way of life, for we believed that growth was the proper nature of man. Let me recall what I said earlier, that leadership requires lieutenants as well as captains. To become a moving factor in the common life, creative initiative depends upon mustering early response of understanding and devotion to a new idea or a new-felt value. Critical to enlisting this core support or response is a framework of legitimacy for growth of fresh perception and new objects of will. Law may help here by its own positive action. Thus by its support for the state university, Wisconsin's legislature stamped with legitimacy one source of leadership toward a new dairy industry. More often perhaps the law helped by indirection, by legitimating growth of initiative and response through nonofficial activity. This approach fitted closely into our general favor for dispersing power and multiplying sources of creative energy. Thus a handful of talented men of vision were better able to enlist supporters for new standards of milk supply because law validated their enterprise by chartering private associations such as the state dairymen's association.

Interplay of generals and particulars on law worked in many ways to legitimize will. Before the infinity of the sensible world men despair, unless they have means to select and organize data according to generalizations which they can test against the tough particulars of independent reality. In this society especially we needed formal processes which gave scope for abstracting thought from will, intermediate to action, because the engrossing pressures of opening up a new continent so biased will toward preoccupation with particular objects. Because law dealt mainly with relations of interests and processes outside law, at almost every level government offered training for the generalizing competence that was peculiarly important amid increasing division of labor. Likewise, because growing specialization of interest and function inclined men to narrow their active concerns, it was important that law provided procedures for bringing into focus the broader context of affairs. The more men comprehended patterns of interests, motives, bias, or functional relations, the more likely they were to feel responsibility for what went on. By providing general processes within which particular interest could legitimately seek expression or particular events or experience be brought to awareness, law encouraged men to risk the inconsistency necessary to experimental increase of knowledge and competence. By providing regular means of criticism and contest over affairs, legal process brought particular trouble or malfunction into view and helped overcome men's unwillingness to acknowledge mistakes or inefficiency. Similarly, as legal process promoted continuing adjustment of general policy to tests of particular experience, it cultivated a desirable matter-of-factness toward the means we used. So we lessened the likelihood that by unchallenged usage means would take on the sanctity of ends. In many fashions thus the press and tug of general and particular in law encouraged us to try to command circumstance.

IV

Leverage and Support

1

The General Acts of the Wisconsin legislature, 1853—a little book of 142 pages, containing 112 principal "chapters" —offers examples to introduce two themes useful for understanding how law gave positive impetus to processes of stability and change in the life of the United States.[1] These themes concern leverage and support functions of law; they refer to use of law's compulsion or of means assembled by law to give a push toward action, either in new directions or along already established lines of motion. In the preceding chapter we dealt with ways in which law fostered perception; here and in the next chapter we deal with ways in which law guided will. I go back to the 1850's in Wiscon-

[1] As in other years before an 1871 amendment to the Wisconsin Constitution put an end to the practice, the legislature's output was also contained in a much larger volume, the Wis. Private and Local Acts, 1853. The nearly 900 pages of this cumbersome book, with its 409 chapters, contain mainly (1) acts setting up units of local government or amending previous acts of this character, (2) charters of business corporations or nonprofit associations of an eleemosynary nature, and (3) grants of franchises or licenses to private parties to build dams or otherwise "improve" navigable waters. The existence of such a volume of statutes points to certain distinctive features of the mid-19th century legislative process, notably to the want of either plan or tradition to channel general business into legislative and more particular business into executive or administrative consideration. At appropriate points in the present essay I shall take some note of these distinctive aspects of special and local legislation. However, a survey of the General Acts,

sin because it is useful to show these legal functions operative in a relatively simple social context, though in a context which reveals main currents of national growth. The year 1853 is far enough behind us to lend perspective; it is advanced enough in our chronology to present problems and attitudes which suggest hopes and tensions of maturity. I take my examples from Wisconsin statutes rather than from the Wisconsin Reports because the form and methods of legislation exemplify more boldly than most judicial opinions the law's contributions to creative initiative and to general social structure.[2]

1853, serves the purposes of this introductory section; for the broad themes or definitions here developed, the material from the Private and Local Acts would be mostly cumulative, dividing also into leverage and support legislation. The one peculiarity relevant to this introduction is that the number of special corporate charters, quantitatively considered, would much increase the ratio of leverage to support laws. This quantitative factor would seem misleading, taken at face value, however, for these special charters tend to fall as much into type as if many of them had been issued under a lenient general incorporation statute; the reason why businessmen sought special charters was less to fulfill peculiarly individual wants, than to obtain rather standard terms more favorable to management than those given under existing general incorporation acts. See Kuehnl, THE WISCONSIN BUSINESS CORPORATION ch. 12 (1959).

[2] The Reports reflect the leverage and support functions of law also, but for reasons later explored the examples of leverage in the Reports are far fewer than in the statute books. The overwhelming bulk of reported cases in a state appellate court deal with administration of social framework or the structuring of the general social situation. See, *e.g.,* Hutchinson v. McClellan, 2 Wis. 16 (1853) (judicial procedure); Gardiner v. Tisdale, *id.,* at 153 (1853) (interests in real estate); Sumner v. Bowen, *id.,* at 523 (1853) (promissory note); Attorney General *ex rel.* Turner v. Fitzpatrick, *id.*, at 542 (1853) (county government). The only clear-cut instance of leverage doctrine in the first two volumes of Wisconsin Reports seems to be Richards v. Sperry, 2 Wis. 214 (1853), establishing for Wisconsin that an actor causing damage will not be held liable at law ordinarily unless the complainant sustains the burden of showing want of ordinary care. *Cf.* French v. Owen, *id.,* at 249 (1853) (reflecting the mill dam law).

The 1853 Wisconsin General Acts show important aspects of the order to which law contributed. (1) Order was a condition made by affirmative action, not merely a given condition preserved by command or penalty. (2) Order consisted in a moving series of adjustments or fresh-made equilibria. Through these adjustments we sought to make change meaningful by keeping it within a framework of stability. Through them we also attempted some accounting—if only a crude accounting—of gains and costs of change and stability, to help us show a net balance in real satisfactions for individuals from life in society. (3) At any given time and place—as in the 1853 legislative session in Wisconsin—most legal action concerned continuing adjustment of relations within existing, accepted patterns of organization and values. Even in this society of fast, wide-ranging change, most of the thought, feeling and effort that made legal history were invested in sustaining the vitality and continuity of existing social processes. This estimate must be read in light of the two propositions which precede it. This devotion to continuity did not mean we stood pat or tried to turn back the clock. We sought stability through change, through practical adjustment or administration responsive to fact. That we would adjust did not, on the other hand, mean that we submitted tamely to circumstance or to anyone's arbitrary will to power. The statute books reflect that we believed in constitutional (responsible) power, in regular procedure, and in the legitimate claim of law to oversee all arrangements of power in the society. In these aspects our statute books told that we were conservatives. Also, however, we were ready to use the resources we could mobilize through law—tax moneys, public property, creation of public franchises, the use of public force—to structure positively the directions and conditions of social continuity. In this we were liberals. (4) The emphasis on values of social continuity was qualitatively as well as quantitatively important, but it did not sum up the whole creative use of law. The statute books record decisions and devices favorable to creative innovation. These items had significance far greater than their relatively small number might suggest. They represented resort to legal process to obtain leverage for calculated, constructive change toward large objectives. Thus they expressed our most direct challenge to all the forces that worked to make drift or inertia predominate in shaping our lives.

There are 112 chapters in the General Acts of 1853.[3] Thirteen of these provided means to create leverage for purposeful initiative in affairs; 99 of them developed or supported existing patterns of social organization and values. This one to nine ratio probably represented a higher proportion of leverage acts than would appear in most legislative sessions in Wisconsin or elsewhere. High as it may be, the figure is yet small enough to point up that leverage uses of law formed a relatively small part of legal activity. However,

[3] Wis. Gen. Acts 1853, also includes ten pages of "Memorials" addressed by the legislature to the federal government. Of the 24 "chapters" here contained, 21 dealt with petitions for improved mail service, one asked an additional appropriation to improve a Lake Michigan harbor, one sought an appropriation for pay and expenses of members of the 1842 territorial legislature, and one asked that Congress pay a Wisconsin sheriff the expenses of keeping a federal prisoner. This was a less demanding list of requests upon Congress than many other Wisconsin statutory volumes would show; in later years particularly, many more memorials typically petitioned for federal lands or funds to aid transport developments. Wis. Gen. Acts 1853, pp. 124-31 also includes notation of particular appropriations from the general fund, chiefly for routine operations of the legislative and executive branches.

their small number was offset by their character, which was to use legal resources where they promised multiplier effects in stimulating further awareness and further deliberate creation of purpose and purposed means.

The 13 leverage statutes in the General Acts of 1853 show some, though not all, of the important uses of law to multiply purposeful initiative. Chapter 5 incorporated the Wisconsin State Agricultural Society, "to promote and improve the condition of agriculture, horticulture, and the mechanical, manufacturing and household arts"; in addition, Chapter 5 gave the society free use of space in the state Capitol, and Chapter 70 made an appropriation of state money in its support. Chapter 17 incorporated the State Historical Society of Wisconsin, to collect and preserve a library and, among other objects, "to exhibit faithfully the antiquities, and the past and present condition, and resources of Wisconsin." Chapters 34, 53, and 56 continued and expanded provision first made in 1852 for state immigrant agents, charged to promote movement of settlers into Wisconsin.[4] Chapter 47 provided for appointment of a state geologist with an appropriation to support his work in conducting a continuing "thorough geological and mineralogical survey of this state." Chapters 43 and 96 provided original authority for disposition of state-owned lands; Chapter 43 provided for appraisal and offering at public auction for benefit of the school and university funds of any yet unappraised and unsold state lands held in trust for those educational purposes under federal grants and under stipulations of the state constitution; Chapter 96

[4] See Wis. Gen. Acts 1852, ch. 432. Compare Chapter III, note 16, *supra.*

granted unqualified authority to the state commissioners of school and university lands to grant to any railroad company any such lands which might be needed for the purposes of their road, on such terms as the commissioners and the railroad might agree upon.[5] Chapter 68 was a general incorporation act, authorizing any number of persons not less than three by written articles to form a joint stock company "for . . . carrying on any kind of manufacturing, mechanical, mining or quarr[y]ing business, or any other lawful business."[6] Implementing the Revised Statutes of 1849,[7] Chapter 88 of General Acts, 1853, redefined part of the form for incorporating any religious society. Chapter 98 incorporated the Fox and Wisconsin Improvement Company, a private corporation, to take over a state project to connect and improve the Fox and Wisconsin rivers to allow navigation between the Great Lakes and the Mississippi.[8] Finally, Chapter 112 provided the terms and procedures by which the boards of supervisors of several towns in Walworth and Jefferson counties might issue town bonds, to buy stock in or make construction loans to any railroad company authorized to build a railroad through the towns.

I do not want to stop here to explore the full meaning which these examples have as legal leverage for new purposes and fresh programs. This subject calls for a broader treatment than seems appropriate to our immediate examples, and will be the focus of later portions of this essay. Here let me briefly note that these 1853 examples have in common three points which suggest broad themes in United States

[5] See, generally, Wis. Rev. Stat. 1849, ch. 24.
[6] Compare Wis. Rev. Stat. 1849, ch. 51.
[7] Wis. Rev. Stat. 1849, ch. 47.
[8] Compare Wis. Laws 1848, at 58.

legal history. First, eight of the 13 statutes (Chapters 5, 17, 34, 47, 56, 68, 88, and 98) had a constitutive function; they set up or authorized the creation of agencies or franchises for fresh action. This common character was probably more significant than the fact that some of these agencies were public (like the Commissioner of Emigration or the State Geological Survey) and some private (like the State Agricultural Society, the Fox and Wisconsin Improvement Company, or the joint stock companies authorized under Chapter 68). Second, nine of the 13 statutes (Chapters 5, 43, 47, 53, 56, 70, 96, 98, and 112) put at the service of these law-sanctioned (if not altogether law-made) agencies economic means held in the disposition of law (public lands, public buildings, public money, public credit). Third, implicit in all 13 statutes was another endowment bestowed by law apart either from the creation of office or organization or the grant of law-controlled economic means. All 13 statutes contemplated or even directed action by someone to initiate purposes and programs not then in existence, at least not then in existence in the forms here sanctioned. The last is the point. All 13 statutes in effect—some of them explicitly—conferred legitimacy upon these new centers of initiative, stamped them as desirable and consistent with the good life, and protected against legal complaint or private aggression the activities they might launch. These three features are aspects of legal action of prime significance for the balance between awareness and purposeful initiative on the one hand and drift and inertia on the other, in shaping affairs.

Of the 112 chapters in the Wisconsin General Acts of 1853, 99 dealt primarily with the continuity of the general life. These statutes supported or by adjustment sought to render more effective organizations or values which were part of the sustaining framework of social life. A point of form evidenced this focus on institutional continuity. Of the total 112 chapters, 42 expressly or by clear implication amended prior acts. Two of the 13 leverage acts (Chapters 34 and 88) amended prior leverage legislation; 40 of the amending acts thus fell among the 99 statutes whose function I classify as support rather than leverage. For a community only in its fifth year of statehood this was a considerable percentage of tinkering with policy already laid out. On their face some of these amendments attest no more than want of craftsmanship in the originals, requiring patchwork; others indicated that even in a simple community undergoing rapid change there was much business in adjusting relationships to growth and experience. Of the 99 statutes relating to social framework, 76 concerned the organization or procedures of formal legal process; 32 of these dealt with the organization and procedures of courts, 20 with the organization and support of the legislature and executive agencies and operations, 20 with the organization and operation of local units of government, and four with levy and collection of taxes. Five other acts dealt with details under existing programs for disposition of state-owned lands; in one view these might be counted to raise to 81 the total of the acts dealing with the law's own household, but in another they belong to the category of economic affairs. Two acts particularly remind us that Wisconsin belonged to a federal union; they ceded lighthouse sites to the United States. Sixteen of the 99 social-framework statutes dealt primarily with the status, activities, or interests of private persons in relation to social interests. Of these 16 statutes, three dealt with creation of interests in real property, three with intangible property claims, five with provision or regulation of transport facilities (by road, stream or railroad), and two with conservation of fish and game; thus 13 of these 16 acts defined or sustained terms of private dealings with economic resources and market procedures. Three acts concerned personal status and moral standards: one providing a procedure for adoption of children, one abolishing the death penalty for murder, one arranging a referendum on enactment of a prohibitory liquor law.

Again, without stopping for detailed comment, let me note for future reference some key features of this body of social-framework legislation. Most obvious is the high relative proportion of attention to the organization and operation of formal legal process itself. Most of the 76 statutes of this type dealt with the internal housekeeping of government; only a small number was primarily concerned with rights or duties of private persons as these were directly defined by official procedures. Thus of the 32 acts dealing with courts, four organized courts, eight set terms of court, seven concerned matters of internal administration of the judicial system and seven defined general procedures; six acts of the 32 set out procedures which in effect entered directly into the practical scope and effectiveness of property titles or creditors' rights. Second, the influence of the federal system is reflected in these statutes mainly by indirection—directly, only in the cession of lighthouse sites, indirectly in laws which dispose of federal lands granted in aid of the Fox-Wisconsin rivers improvement (here we reach back into the leverage acts), and in laws which add details regarding the sale of state lands derived from federal grants. Taking these two points together, the Wisconsin General Acts, 1853, suggest that men here treated law as an important part of social-framework, but tended to exhaust their attention in close-to-hand detail. Third, the rest of this social-framework legislation dealt mainly with economic conditions of the common life, notably with the economic bases on which an infinite variety of particular economic activity might proceed—the provision of transport, market procedures and conservation of natural resources. These statutes, finally, are studded with references which remind us of the high value this society put on widely dispersed power—references to contract, private property, corporations, the speedy transfer of public land to private ownership, the stress on local government. Given this bias of policy, and the early stage of development of the state, there is here, nonetheless, striking assertion of law's proper concern with structuring the general situation in which men found themselves. Thus Chapters 28 and 87 fixed limits on taking game birds and fish; Chapter 44 set procedures for locating and establishing state roads; Chapter 38 defined terms on which railroads might build across or along public ways and waters; Chapter 72 redefined the requirement that a permit be obtained from the legislature to build a dam or bridge in or over any navigable stream. Such legislation implicitly affirmed that law was legitimately used not only to support the existing fabric and going processes of society, but to enlarge the loom and help fashion the design.

These comments invoke the Wisconsin General Acts, 1853, only for examples to introduce the law's functions of leverage and support in relation to social stability and change. That the statutes exemplify these leverage and support functions does not mean that we developed these uses of law fully or effectively. Our vision was often narrow and limited, our execution often a failure or fumbling. Among the leverage acts, for example, the geological survey was understaffed, pinched for funds, and recurrently hampered by partisan politics, personal disagreements among its administrators, and pressures from mining interests to color reports to promote investment.[9] Again, the Fox-Wisconsin rivers improvement wound a tortuous course through a generation of Wisconsin politics, ultimately to fail.[10] Among the social-framework statutes of 1853, the acts to conserve fish and game and to safeguard public rights on highways and navigable waters, for their time and place were remarkable acknowledgments of commonwealth interests. But none of them created a procedure adequate to enforce the principles it witnessed.[11] To identify functions of leverage and support locates organizing themes for studying law's roles in United States history, but the substance of the matter remains to be weighed in any given area of policy.

2

The central concern of these essays is with concepts useful in telling how law helped or hindered men's awareness and their will to exert purposeful direction for stability or change in the growth of the United States. The previous

[9] See Lake, "Legal Profile of the Mining Industry—Part II," 1955 WIS. L. REV. 566, 575-82.

[10] See Raney, WISCONSIN 109-10 (1940).

[11] *Cf.* Hurst, THE GROWTH OF AMERICAN LAW: THE LAW MAKERS 381 (1950).

essay examined how the law's formality, or the interplay of form and substance in legal process, contributed to these ends. The forms of law expressed the value we put on constitutional (responsible) power and on regular procedures; the creative tension which legal process generated between general and particular aspects of experience dramatized the interplay of form and substance in one fashion especially important for promoting purposeful initiative. However, this legal order provided not only forms to shape thought and feeling, but it provided also means to give impetus for action. Our people used law to validate the distribution of all forms of secular power; in the last analysis this meant that law held the legitimate monopoly of violence in the society, and hence at second remove, the authority to say what other forms of power might exist and in whom. Our people also accepted as proper that law be used to muster and dispose of parts of their economic and moral resources to help structure the common life. These were features as integral to this legal order as its constitutionalism and procedural emphasis. They, too, were aspects of law relevant to helping or hindering men's awareness and their will to exert purposeful direction of affairs.

However, there were differences in modes of expression of the constituent elements of this legal order. Constitutionalism and procedural regularity found expression primarily in the forms of law, and especially in law's manipulation of generals and particulars. The law's functions of validating distributions of power and allocating resources to shape social structure found expression in the law's use of force or compulsion upon men's wills. This summary statement requires elaboration and qualification which it is the business of this and the next essay to provide.

Law rested on force, but in this naked simplicity the statement would lead to the most unreal hypotheses about law's role in United States history. The prime qualification one must make is that law's force or compulsion represented only marginal increments to the sum of factors influencing affairs and derived only from marginal increments in the total means available for action in the society. In part this marginality of law was not peculiar to United States legal history; in both simple and complex societies the variety of experience and the number of points of contact between individuals and environment and between natural and social environment are such that law cannot encompass the whole. In part, however, this marginality of law existed in our legal order as a product of deeply felt and quite explicit principle. Here the constitutional and the force elements of this legal order wove together. It was basic in our values that law should not directly control the principal resources of the society, and that while law should hold accountable all power allocations, law itself should be accountable. The practical basis on which men could call law to account was that they did not depend on law for all the sources of their moral and material strength, but that in fact they commanded resources not held at the arbitrary discretion of government. This was the constitutional significance of the emphasis our legal-social values put on privacy, individuality, private property and contract, private association, and the separation of official powers. That law worked only by marginal increments is, then, the main qualification to make when we explore how law used compulsion. I said also that it was necessary to elaborate as well as to qualify emphasis on law's use of force. To elaborate means to note that law's force made itself felt mostly by indirection. The next essay examines the relative place that direct use of legal force had in the history of the United States. In this essay, when we consider leverage and support uses of law there is always in the background the possibility of force—the sheriff may levy for taxes, the army may enforce government's control of public lands, a court may jail for contempt subordinate officials who persist in acting under a state statute held to violate the federal Constitution—but typically we deal with subtler legal influences, where law made itself felt by initiative taken in the face of apathy, by persuasion or inducements to cooperation by regulated persons, by structuring power so that one course of action was easier to take than another. The indirect use of compulsion offers one of the rich themes of United States legal history.

We are experimenting with ideas for their utility in organizing data. We should treat these ideas as instruments and not as dogmas. I have suggested that the constitutional and procedural emphases in our law found expression primarily in form and in the creative tension of generals and particulars, and that the power-validating and resources-allocation uses of law found expression primarily in the direct and indirect use of compulsion. The distinction usefully directs attention to differing modes of legal influence. But it does not define rigid categories of difference. The effectiveness of the law's forms and the law's practical capacity to bring general and particular experience into fruitful interplay depended, in a showdown, on law's capacity to make itself felt. Conversely, the attitudes and responses taught by formal process helped make more effective the marginal force which law could bring to bear on situations, reducing the need overtly to invoke compulsion and narrowing the issues on which compulsion must be used. We should remember the criss-cross of influence among these factors of form, generals and particulars, and compulsion, as we examine the leverage and support uses of law.

3

The legal history of milk sketched in the previous essay shows characteristic leverage and support functions of law in the United States, and characteristic relations between the two. Support came first here, and this was typical. To employ law to sustain values already formed from the accretion of social experience was less demanding on mind and will than to employ law to help create new knowledge or purpose. In penalizing knowing sale of unwholesome foodstuffs to unwary buyers, the Statutes of Wisconsin Territory, 1839, lent law's help to maintaining both the biological requisites of life and the service requisites of an acceptable market. To define and exact minimum behavior necessary for health and useful exchange of goods was to help sustain an already existing frame of relations within which life in society was at the least possible and at best might gain in quality. To define and support general terms and processes within which life could go on and yield men satisfactions continued to engross the principal attention of law in this field, through specification of standards and development of preventive licensing in the statutes of the 1880's to elaboration of a milk code by administrators under legislative delegation in the second quarter of the 20th century. Nor did the support function appear only through regulation. When the motor truck made possible more flexible, wide-reaching, and economical distribution procedures, the legislature's generous response to local pressures provided funds which made possible a network of hard-surfaced secondary roads essential to growth of the dairy industry.[12]

The milk story also shows characteristic uses of law to give leverage for developing fresh perception of relations and of the gains, costs, and possibilities of manipulation involved in them, and hence creating impetus for action. Law had leverage effect, first, because the legislature set up specialized official agencies or authorized the formation of specialized private agencies to gather information and initiate plans relevant to improving milk supply and quality. The legislature accomplished this initiative directly by authorizing specialized municipal health authorities, and by providing the state university, the office of food and dairy commissioner, and a department of agriculture; it worked indirectly to this effect by incorporating the state agricultural society and the dairymen's association. Second, the legislature used public money and public property to shelter and promote the work of these specialized agencies. Thus, in its resource-allocations role, backed by its power to tax, law helped arm the will to act upon new awareness of purpose.[13]

Leverage and support uses of law might both work to build particular policy, as in the milk story. In a broader sense, however, leverage and support belonged together as functions of law in this society. The use of law to create leverage for growth of fresh awareness and purposed will

[12] See Chapter III, notes 5, 7, and 9, *supra.*

[13] See Chapter III, notes 5, 7, 8, and 11, *supra.*

was itself part of our social structure. This was so whether the immediate issue was of directed effort for stability or for change. In either case, as the previous essay observed, we valued awareness and purposed will because these were constituent elements of individuality, and because a society of increasingly high organization and large commitments could not survive save by sophisticated knowledge of where it stood in a constantly shifting situation and by disciplined nerve for decisions that must be made on imperfect knowledge within limits of circumstance.[14] Even so, the lines of force did not all run one way. Leverage use of law to promote perception and purposed initiative ran counter to all the influences which favored drift and inertia; for the reasons explored in the second of these essays, the bias of man's total situation is against insight and enterprise; man had to work hard against odds to enlarge his life, and the margin between success and possible relapse into savagery was never wide. These were elements inherent in the human situation.[15] They were compounded by the tendencies in North American culture toward a mental set which the previous essay characterized as bastard pragmatism. We deceived ourselves by our busy-ness into thinking that we commanded the situation more than we did. Preoccupied with immediate operations, we tended to deny or defeat more creative uses of law by applying its leverage only to objects closest to hand and most readily seen. The 1869 legislative session in Wisconsin provides a symbol; on the one hand, the legislature found funds to hire field agents to protect against theft the valuable pine on public lands

[14] See Chapter III, section 2, *supra.*
[15] See Chapter II, section 4, *supra.*

held in aid of railroad construction; but, on grounds of economy, it declined to appropriate for a second printing of a legislative report "on the disastrous effects of the destruction of forest trees . . . in Wisconsin."[16]

Thus there were reasons why tension and conflict of values centered upon leverage roles of law. Throughout our national existence there was never question of the legitimacy of law's leverage uses, taken generally. It was natural to the setting and the temper of the people that this should be so, with a continent to be occupied by men borne on the surge of striving and contriving middle-class ambition. The legitimacy of using legal process to enlarge perception and considered decision was written plain in formal definition. We based legal order on written constitutions. These defined stable, presumably long-term arrangements of power. Also, however, they regularized procedures for their amendment, and they contained such guarantees of free speech and press, free religion, and peaceable assembly and petition as were calculated to favor growth and spread of knowledge and discussion and to promote more conscious decision making. The state legislatures, by inheritance from the House of Commons, and Congress, by grant of the Federal Constitution, possessed the power of the purse, which held enormous leverage potential. By our own peculiar condition, the United States possessed a vast public domain available for disposition in ways that might multiply purposeful initiative. By English inheritance the state legislatures, and by Hamiltonian interpretation Congress possessed authority to constitute corporations which might become generating centers

[16] Compare Wis. Gen. Laws 1869, ch. 46 and Report of the Senate Committee on Agriculture, 22d Legislature, WIS. SEN. J. 387 (Feb. 24, 1869). See also Chapter III, section 2, *supra*.

of new plans and purposed decisions. As a legacy from troubles with England, the first state constitutions set a pattern of a weak executive; but the federal constitution makers deliberately created a Presidential office of large capacity for fresh programming and bold initiative. Our constitutional tradition committed broad initiative to private will through the law of private property and contract; by this delegation alone, the law created leverage for fashioning numberless new perceptions of experience and numberless new targets of purpose. "[W]hat most astonishes me in the United States," Tocqueville reported in 1835, "is not so much the marvelous grandeur of some undertakings as the innumerable multitude of small ones."[17]

If the large pattern of formally declared values was thus clear, there were nonetheless ambiguities and unresolved conflicts behind this front. Let me note two areas of difficulty. One involves the market as an institution to accomplish social adjustments. The other involves ideas of equality, the constitutional responsibility of government, and the legitimacy of leadership.

Rights of contract, property, and private association gave leverage for shaping and implementing an infinite variety of fresh perception and purpose. It was partly in the nature of this kind of delegation of power, and partly due to 19th century scarcity of fluid capital (money, labor, and managing talent) relative to real resources and opportunities, that up to about 1870 this frame of policy promoted great dispersion of action and fragmenting of plan and will into countless private projects of closely limited focus and time span. Representative of this pattern was the rapid spread of family

[17] Tocqueville, 2 DEMOCRACY IN AMERICA 157 (Bradley ed. 1945).

farms through the central United States, and the typical small or modest scale of mining and lumbering operations in Wisconsin of 1850 through 1880. With little examination or challenge, we accepted the market as a procedure to relate and adjust the energies which the leverage of contract, property, and association provided on so many limited fronts. Taken as units, dealings in market represented relatively rationalized decisions. Taken in aggregates, market transactions yielded conditions upon which reasoned decisions could be made for further unit transactions, or even for broader planned operations of the sort which promoted the late 19th century trend toward mergers and consolidations and loose-knit combinations to limit competition. But as men undertook to concert broader plans for market operations, they threatened to subvert the market itself. On the other hand, so far as we left adjustment to the market without closely appraising the scope or adequacy of the process, we fell into paradox. We created great leverage for fragmented perception and purpose. But the market created no leverage for fashioning knowledge or programs to deal with interests which were in fact at stake but did not receive market consideration because they were not within the calculations which market discipline enforced upon private dealers.

Thus, for example, by allowing full play to the pressure of the Midwest lumber market upon the Lake States pinery, we exchanged depletion of the forests for more rapid growth of the prairie town-and-farm economy. Under the discipline of overhead costs, the need to meet short-term bankers' loans, and the attractions of recurrent boom, lumbermen pressed for maximum short-term production. Their decisions were rational, in a given market context, for private decision makers. It is more debatable whether it was rational to use the Lake States forest in ways which substantially destroyed it as a continuing major source of saw timber for the Midwest market. For the Lake States the event meant long-term reduction of the tax and industrial base and creation of submarginal areas which for generations could not pay their way. For Mississippi Valley industry and consumers the costs included loss of future economic flexibility and indefinite imposition of a heavy transport tax to move in timber from the South and West. For the nation the outcome involved imbalance in sectional economies and imposed manpower and capital costs of continuing lumber supply to the Central States which hampered our ability to meet such a national emergency as World War II. These are difficult calculations on which to strike a balance. They involve too large problems of social structure and process to allow any easy answer such as condemning "robber barons." The point here relevant, however, is not this striking of accounts. The point is that a great decision of social economy was taken in this matter largely by default, without material awareness or discussion, because we resigned decision to the limited calculus of the market.

We did not do so altogether by default. As original owners of the Lake States forest the United States, and the states as its grantees, held the basic responsibility for allocating this resource. By the 1850's, when substantial Lake States lumbering began, popular pressure to create a republic of family farms in the Central States area had shaped public lands policy. Government should speed transfer of land from public to private fee simple ownership;

public land should be made a marketable good as rapidly as possible. It was a program that made sense for prairie regions, although soil mining by farmer speculators taught us eventually that market processes did not enforce adequate social cost accounting even for a small farms economy. The implicit assumptions of the policy thus set by 1850 did not in fact apply to lands primarily suitable for growing saw timber. Facts thus posed a typical challenge for creative leverage use of law, to define a new situation and bring to discussion and decision a new program. Nineteenth century legal process proved inadequate to the challenge. The United States had long since disposed of the bulk of its Lake States holdings when, in 1876, Congress first seriously examined the peculiar problems of public timberlands in discussing the future of the southern pinery.[18] No Wisconsin governor or legislature posed the question, whether forest economics differed from prairie economics, until the Wisconsin forest had passed the point of irreversible depletion as a continuing producer of saw logs.[19] Had alternatives been fully explored, we might likely still have done what we did. But, again, this is not the point here relevant. Within our ideals of legal order—the scrutiny of power, the enforcement of responsible (constitutional) use of power through regular procedures, and the creative use of law's resource-allocating capacities—it was a central function of law to help insure that major decisions not be taken by default. Law's leverage function failed of fulfillment in the pinery story. It is a

[18] See Ise, THE UNITED STATES FOREST POLICY 50-52 (1920).

[19] Contrast remarks in the General Messages of Governor Upham, 42d Legislature WIS. ASSEM. J. 21, 23 (Jan. 10, 1895) and of Governor Davidson, 49th Legislature, WIS. ASSEM. J. 47-48 (Jan. 14, 1909).

type of problem the assessment of which should bulk large in telling United States legal history.

We must not fall into the fallacy of reifying "the market" as villain. We are concerned less with man's selfishness than with the limits of his imagination and energy of will, which it is the function of law's leverage to help surmount. Even when we deliberately wrote social cost accounting into legal regulation, the support functions of law could combine in impact with market pressures to produce decisions by default. Consider, again, the milk regulation history. Out of the growth of scientific and technical knowledge and the response of public opinion to what it learned of preventable evil, grew an expanding body of legal and practical regulation of the purity and quality of milk supply. Pasteurization, bottling, refrigeration, all required expensive additions to the investment needed for handling milk. In practice, thus, the combination of public opinion and sanitary regulation set investment requirements for entry or continuance in the business which tended to eliminate small dealers and thus to foster such economic concentration as was a prime concern of another area of public policy, embodied in the antitrust laws. The development of cooperatives might have offered a larger continuing role for smaller dealers. But such help as the law brought to this end proved too slow to affect the course of milk distribution.[20] The point for us is not the substantive merits of the outcome. Again, the point is that there was significant decision by default—in this instance the more striking because it was the unpurposed result of two deliberate courses of public policy concerning sanitation and

[20] See Till, "Milk—The Politics of an Industry," in Hamilton, PRICE AND PRICE POLICIES 431, 450-52 (1938).

economic concentration. We could not escape the mounting challenge of our own growth. From original exaggerated dependence on market calculus, we learned its limitations. But as we supplemented market calculus with accounting defined in law, we increased the factors at work in our situation, hence the likelihood that we would generate results our imagination or will did not encompass. The more we invoked law for support, the more we needed it for leverage to create awareness of where we were and what we were doing and to foster will for fresh decisions upon our new awareness.

When we used law to give leverage for perception and initiative, in effect we used law to help develop leaders. This was the nature or end of the leverage function. We did not find the notion of leadership inconsistent with our democratic faith. Common sense taught that we needed leaders; our ideal of man as one who should grow in competence as maker and doer implied the legitimacy of leaders who would teach growth. Politics bore witness to these beliefs, in the emotional as well as reasoning support that great numbers gave in their time to Washington, Jefferson, Jackson, Clay, Webster, the two Roosevelts. Private affairs did not lend themselves to mustering mass support about individuals in this fashion. To the contrary, given our belief in dispersed power, it is not surprising that when men of private affairs achieved such power as to stand out as individuals—Nicholas Biddle, or the elder Rockefeller or Morgan, in the 19th century, or John L. Lewis or James Hoffa in the 20th—prevailing middle-class opinion regarded them with distrust. The realm of private affairs was not without its acknowledgment of the legitimacy of leadership.

However—and here the theme of leadership significantly weaves into that of the market—the acknowledgment was of the legitimacy of a type, the 19th century businessman or the 20th century business administrator. Assignment of legitimacy to the type, but not to the outstandingly powerful individual, was consistent with our inclination of resigning responsibility to impersonal market processes to work necessary adjustments among the infinite variety of perception and purpose given leverage by the law of contract, property, and association. That majority opinion assigned legitimacy only to those powerful individuals whose office was from and in the law was implicit acknowledgment that the growth and health of society required a broader calculus than the market could supply.

However, there were strong crosscurrents of feeling that created distinctive problems for emergence of policy leadership in the United States. These attitudes derived from the broad base of participation in this society, and from the large scale of its operations. Out of our middle-class heritage our faith was egalitarian and our preoccupation was with current operations; we extended the suffrage, and the event proved right those Jeffersonian and Jacksonian prophecies that a large electorate was slow and conservative in movement; we expanded our markets on the base of a successful mass production technology and a successful federal structure, and witnessed both the education and the dominance of mass buying power; we developed the size and intricacy of both public and private organization, and learned to prize efficiency and administrative continuity. These were factors of ambiguous import for the role of creative perception and purpose. They were factors that entered into making a more humane and decent life for more individuals. They were also factors that fostered the dominance of mass taste and imagination and will, threatening inventive variation and bold contrivance, holding back adjustment to shifting circumstance, strengthening the negative more than the positive elements in the common life. Those very different political philosophers, John C. Calhoun and Henry David Thoreau, warned that a community in which the majority ruled risked moral complacency and the tyranny of transient combinations of narrow interests.[21] Constructive leadership meant the entrance into affairs of more rational insight, more subtle feeling, more dynamic will. But the elements of bastard pragmatism whose roots sank deep in our 19th century life distrusted qualitative differences in reason or feeling. Men may be known by the epithets they keep. It is significant that we tended to convert into terms of depreciation the words "political" (favorable opposite: "businesslike") and "theoretical" (favorable opposite: "practical")—as if a constitutional republic could operate other than by political direction, and as if our prized individuality did not consist in enlarging the self by greater knowledge of cause and effect, which is all that good theory consists of. A community in which a wide political electorate might freely cast its ballots and a wide consuming electorate "vote" its dollars needed law's leverage functions to preserve it from self satisfaction and narrowly private involvement. Breadth of participation tended to establish a middle range of value and aspiration as the norm. There was good in this bias of affairs.

[21] See Thoreau, "On Civil Disobedience," in 1 THE PEOPLE SHALL JUDGE 646, 650, 652, 656 (Univ. of Chic. ed. 1949), and Calhoun, "The True Nature of Constitutional Government," (from "Disquisition on Government") in *id.* at 676, 678, 681, 684.

It cultivated decent restraint and tolerance as against pride of reason, interest or righteousness. There was peril in this bias of affairs, too. For it cultivated complacence or fear of quality in times when man's own advance in command of environment increased his ignorance and the hazards of irrevocable decisions.

Law's leverage function in the United States found four main expressions. Two of these inhered in our legal order at least from the start of our national existence. Law created leverage for awareness and purposed decision (1) by legitimating and arming men with capacity to make choices of action, and (2) by legitimating, and to some extent subsidizing, sources of dissent and criticism. Law created leverage thus by delegating power and by sanctioning difference. These approaches particularly cultivated the will to act. It fitted the temper of the times that they developed first and especially in the bustling 19th century. Time developed two other leverage uses of law which were in a measure special developments of the two basic modes, but carried more emphasis upon awareness than upon will; these ways of leverage had little use before the late 19th century and became substantial influences on policy only in the 20th. In these later developed forms law created leverage for awareness and purposed decision (3) by helping advance knowledge and exploiting the generative effects of knowledge, and (4) by providing means for more rationalized law making.

Prevailing opinion accepted as proper roles of law in this country that it should review allocation of all forms of secular power, and that it should enforce and be itself within the concept that all power must be constitutional. Within these roles it was the proper business of law to confer authority of decision upon individuals and small numbers of men. We did this when we created legislative, executive and judicial authority, when we created a working federalism, and when we sanctioned initiative of decision through the law of contract, property and private association. Such constitutive actions of law were the heart of its leverage function; so far as mankind enlarged the content and quality of life, it did so only through the initiative of individuals and relatively small groups; leverage for individual and group decision might work for better or worse, but it was a necessary condition of man's growth.

Delegated power developed leadership. A heartening lesson of our experience was that men could grow in competence in public office and become better Presidents, wiser judges, more principled experts in legislative compromise than we would have forecast. The contriving of the modern business corporation and its techniques of finance and large-scale production and marketing attested that the challenge of delegated private power evoked inventive response; the problem of our growth here was not to stimulate creative decision but how to legitimize it. Where concentrated private power was needed to perform services integral to the operation of the economy, we recognized its legitimacy but expressed our unease through controlled licensing. This was the field of public utilities, where the importance of the subject matter highlighted the mingling of the law's leverage (franchise-giving) and support (operations-regulating) functions. From the late 19th century on we responded to increasing interlock of social processes by expanding the public utility type of legal intervention in the economy. These expansions were typically launched on a wave of crusading enthusiasm. But by mid-20th century there was perceptible cooling, and largely because of concern that the law's support function could not become so prominent in an area of action without seriously limiting the leverage which law might provide for fresh ideas and fresh venture. The facts of social interlock remained; there must be legal regulations that realistically acknowledged these facts in order to sustain a highly productive but easily disrupted division-of-labor economy. The central issue in the delegation of power to private hands remained how to legitimize the creation of fresh awareness and creative initiative born of it in the conduct of great business corporations or corporations growing to greatness.

Our system distributed decision-making authority among various official agencies. Basic were the electorate and those to whom were committed constitution-making authority. Once past the classic generation, 1765-1800, the roles of electorate and constitution makers pertained more to the support of social institutions than to creating leverage for new perception and purpose. These were primarily organs of the balance of power, to ratify or veto initiatives that originated elsewhere. This seems no less a realistic appraisal of the working significance of the Progressive procedural changes of early 20th century—the direct primary, and the initiative, referendum and recall—than of the 19th century expansion of the suffrage.

Federalism was sometimes praised as an arrangement of power calculated to produce creative initiative; the states would be experimental laboratories of public policy. There were some examples of the prophecy fulfilled; Wisconsin of

1905-1915 and of the early 1930's may rank as one example. On the whole this side of the record was disappointing. Because Congress held so large a purse and had so many avenues to the varied experience of the country, because the President had patronage, commanded a national forum and based his tenure on a national constituency, and because the organization of the economy did not follow state lines and private economic power overmatched state power, the central government proved the more fruitful, continuing source of policy initiative.

Within the three-part division of authority in state government, the possibility of leverage for creative will lay originally with the legislature, which held the purse, the power to ask questions, the authority to constitute agencies. The outstanding fact through the 19th century—and in most states well into the 20th—was the failure of the state legislature to realize its potential for policy leadership. This was due to no want of formal authority, but to inexperience compounded by short and shifting tenure and want of tradition, and to the costly effects of a narrowly operational point of view which could not see beyond the business of the current session to the need for adequate legislative committee organization and staffing. At best the turbulent rush of the country's growth would have tried legislative capacity, but the state legislatures floated with the current.

These defaults reacted on the leadership potential of the state executive. Typically weak in constitutional endowment, the state executive branch had to depend on the legislature to arm it for vigorous programming. Well into the 20th century, however, the legislature not only saw economy in slender provision for executive offices, but typically showed jealousy of executive initiative. A characteristic expression of the mingled constitutional and legislative limits put on the state executive was the excessive assignment of *ex officio* duties to overburdened officers. Though the state lands were the greatest resource and leverage instrument held by the new state of Wisconsin, the Wisconsin constitution makers in 1848 committed their administration to the secretary of state, attorney general and state treasurer, as *ex officio* commissioners of public lands. Since, with the governor, these three officials constituted about all the executive establishment the state had during the critical years of its land dispositions, it was not surprising that they found no energy to devise a program for the lands, nor even to furnish the legislature with useful data on their handling. The legislature might have armed the commissioners with a staff to free them from detail and to help them survey the implications of statelands uses. But the legislature provided the commissioners only with minimum clerical staff. Not until 1897, after the state had disposed of most of its lands and so lost its prime leverage on the situation, did the legislature take the first step to create a commission to study broad questions of land use in Wisconsin.[22]

The state courts were vested with power to decide controversies, and this grant both gave and limited their op-

[22] See Wis. Const. art. X, § 7; Wis. Laws 1897, ch. 229. The want of programming adequate to the land-use problems of a fast-growing state was underlined by the one abortive effort at large-scale conservation planning in the study of wasteful cutting of trees under Wis. Gen. Laws 1867, ch. 36, and the inadequate response thereto in a program of agricultural tree-belt maintenance supposed to be fostered by Wis. Gen. Laws 1868, ch. 102. For a rare criticism of the wasteful economy of committing state lands policy to busy *ex officio* commissioners, see Biennial Report, State Superintendent of Public Instruction, 41st Legislature (Dec. 10, 1892), in 1 PUBLIC DOCUMENTS 141 (Wis. 1893).

portunities for policy leadership. Through the 19th century they made a good deal of common law, particularly for the market. In most states most of this common law, like most state legislation, was borrowed and expressed more the support functions of the law in providing institutional continuity and administrative detail than law's leverage for fresh appraisal of choice. There were sharp inherent limits to the leverage the judicial process could give for cultivating new awareness and purposed initiative. Reported appellate cases were the courts' main means for shaping doctrine; we need studies to show how far the controversies that reached appellate courts presented issues in typical rather than abnormal context. The courts could pass only on issues relevant to matters that the interests of litigants brought to them; one need only check the Reports to see that in major areas of law shaped primarily by legislation—concerning public lands disposition, education, public utility regulation, for example—court cases presented a scattering and random array of the range of issues actually present.

In the national government as in the states, it was the legislative branch whose history showed the most disappointing failure to realize its leverage potential. This is not to say that we should realistically expect policy leadership from any legislative assembly, taken as a whole. Mill's comment holds good as well in mid-20th century as for 19th century experience: "[I]n legislation . . . the only task to which a representative assembly can possibly be competent is not that of doing the work, but of causing it to be done."[23] However, consistent with this realism Congress might have developed its own specialized agencies for programming. There were

[23] Mill, REPRESENTATIVE GOVERNMENT 40 (Peoples ed. 1876).

promising beginnings. In the Fourth Congress Gallatin launched a movement to put power in standing committees. By 1815 Clay had consolidated the position of the standing committees as the centers of Congressional power over policy. The Third Congress (1793-1795) had named at least 350 select committees to handle its business, but the Thirteenth Congress (1813-1815) named only 70; the number of standing committees rose from half a dozen in 1795 to 20 by 1815, to 45 by 1867, to about 50 by the end of the century, while the number of select committees became negligible. These developments carried promise of such focus, continuity and cumulation of energy as might give Congress leverage to initiate new decisions of scope rather than merely to ratify or veto.[24] However, through the 19th century Congress failed to pursue its opportunity and allowed itself to become engrossed in the "practical" details of rivers and harbors and pensions bills and the particulars of tariff schedules. It did not use its purse to staff its committees for more than attention to current operations. Not until it set up the Industrial Commission of 1898 did it experiment with *ad hoc* programming agencies of its own; the Commission's careful work came to little, largely for want of a continuing center of initiative in Congress to make something of its work.[25]

Other causes contributed to the rise of the Presidency in policy leadership, but Congressional default facilitated the trend. The increased effectiveness of the federal executive in providing leverage for creative decision was the most

[24] See Luce, LEGISLATIVE PROCEDURE 100-102 (1922).

[25] *Cf.* Current, PINE LOGS AND POLITICS: A LIFE OF PHILETUS SAWYER, 1816-1900, at 199 (1950); Hurst, THE GROWTH OF AMERICAN LAW 414.

striking change in the processes of the national government in the 20th century. An early instance was the new direction given conservation policy by the combination of an imaginative, strong-willed President and a devoted executive specialist; Theodore Roosevelt and Gifford Pinchot together did more to fashion an integrated program for use of the public domain than had all the 19th century Congresses.[26] However, we must not romanticize executive leadership. As in the states, so in the federal government the legislature spent grudgingly to enlarge the programming competence of executive offices. In national and state government the growth of the independent administrative agencies added new sources of policy initiation, but at the same time tended to fragment planning for want of coordination either in the legislative branch or in the chief executive.

Thanks to the direction given by Marshall, the United States Supreme Court matched the executive in striking development of a leverage role for policy initiative. Marshall's characteristic approach was to open more than one avenue to future growth. In *Gibbons* v. *Ogden,* for example, he invited Congress to use the flexible device of the license as instrument to fashion a code of relations between national and state commercial regulation.[27] The suggestion was bolder perhaps than the ideas of the times would support. It was typical of Congress' ineptitude for shaping its own means of leverage that for over 100 years Congress not only made no substantial use of Marshall's invitation but also made no effective exploration of its possibilities. It was

[26] See Pinchot, BREAKING NEW GROUND 382-87 (1947).

[27] 22 U.S. (9 Wheat.) 1, 195, 214-15 (1824). On the significance of the Court's role under the commerce clause, see Frankfurter, THE COMMERCE CLAUSE UNDER MARSHALL, TANEY AND WAITE, ch. I (1937).

by the Court's exploitation of Marshall's alternative idea, through judicial enforcement of the negative implications of the commerce clause, that we built such a code of adjustment for federal-state commercial regulation as we achieved. Litigation had severe limits as a process for launching new policy, but it also gave great leverage for limited resources; it took only one determined appellant to provide the Court its opportunity to redefine the admiralty jurisdiction in *The Genesee Chief*.[28] Law's leverage consisted largely in bringing choice of values and means to awareness and to definition, and then in providing legitimate channels by which a small number of informed and responsible persons might initiate decision. For these ends there was great influence in the authority which the Court held to interpret the broad standards of constitutional grants and limitations, within processes set in motion by particular litigants. The school segregation cases of 1954 showed what purchase this leverage might give.[29]

Law created leverage for the direction of affairs not only by conferring authority of decision upon individuals and groups, but also by making special allocations of means for action at key points. I do not refer to the spending of public funds to pay for the regular operations of official agencies of decision; this belongs to the general support functions of law. I refer to the spending of public lands or the investment of public funds to subsidize road, canal and railroad building, the lending of the tax power to protect the growth of domestic industry against foreign competition, the use of federal authority and federal moneys to consummate the

[28] See Chapter II, notes 5 and 6, *supra*.

[29] Brown v. Board of Education of Topeka, 349 U.S. 294, 75 S. Ct. 753 (1954).

Louisiana Purchase, the gift or low-priced sales of federal and state lands to foster a family farm economy in the Mississippi and Missouri valleys. We used law to put capital to work at points where it promised to have a booster effect on the general economy and to generate productive results multiplied many times over. In its classic declaration this was, again, Hamiltonian philosophy. But the examples show that in action all major parties had faith in this booster or multiplier use of law-mobilized resources. In the 19th century this working philosophy had point primarily for the faster settlement of the continent and expansion of the scale of economic operations. In the 20th century the most notable expressions of the same attitude were in public support of basic and applied research, and public spending and fiscal controls as devices to moderate downswings of the business cycle. This kind of leverage use of law relates closely thus to those support functions of law that concerned the productive capacity of the society.

Law created leverage for awareness and purposed decision also by legitimating, and to some extent subsidizing, sources of dissent and criticism. We built this leverage into formal legal processes. We gave our chief executives a veto and a forum from which to address a wider constituency than any other elected officer. We made the two-chamber legislature our standard, guaranteed unusual tenure to United States Senators, and by legislative practice and rule safeguarded rights of individual members and blocs to have their say and to curb precipitate majorities. We hedged judges about with tenure, protected pay and civil immunity, gave constitutional status to the right to counsel, and through bar and bench provided means by which individuals or small groups could require authority to justify itself. We chartered religious and educational institutions whose normal function was to foster examination of the quality and defect of our life; in a community still crude and new, the Wisconsin General Acts, 1853, Chapter 17 incorporated the State Historical Society "to exhibit faithfully . . . the past and present condition, and resources of Wisconsin." Out of the inheritance of the middle-class revolution of 17th century England and the value our own situation taught us to put on individualism, we desired that men have the courage of independent means, that they might hold law to account. Hence we put great store on contract and property and despite our muddled philosophy groped our way (as by Chapter 68 of Wisconsin's General Acts of 1853) toward making readily available for private association the convenience and power of the corporate form. Nor did this exhaust our inventiveness in association. As Chapter 5 of the 1853 General Acts chartered a state agricultural society, so generally we facilitated the organization of groups united by common interests which fell between religious or educational associations on the one hand and profit-making associations on the other. It became increasingly important that law foster institutions of criticism and dissent, as the society took on a higher degree of closely interdependent organization. This organization produced so unprecedented a level of creature comfort for so many people that claims made in the name of organizational stability, continuity, and familiar routine appealed more and more strongly to general feeling. Not the least subtle of our problems, moreover, was the tendency of our specialized associations to develop their own vested interest and excessive zeal; as associations developed tighter internal discipline and selfhood, we confronted new dangers of fragmented outlook and the tendency for the number of vetoes in a given situation always to outweigh the votes for a new integration of values. This bias of events spelled new, continuing need of law's leverage toward wider awareness and broader purpose.

Even in the relatively simple condition of mid-19th century Wisconsin in an atmosphere charged with attention to most immediate and practical operations, 200 years of western scientific and technical development had written themselves deep in general opinion. Of the 13 leverage statutes in the Wisconsin General Acts, 1853, three created agencies to develop knowledge—those acts which chartered the state agricultural and historical societies and set up the official geological survey—and a fourth dealt with realizing fresh funds for the state university. Integral to the true pragmatic strain in our values was the belief that knowledge was an asset for controlling environment; when a substantial opinion became convinced that we possessed reliable new knowledge on which we might better our situation, opinion demanded that we act on what we knew. Thus there was a core of readiness to use law's leverage to advance knowledge, in the expectation that knowledge would generate decision and mobilize will. The illegitimate strain in our pragmatism set up opposing currents of attitude here. Prevailing opinion on what were "practical" objects of public or private expenditure had as much to do with limiting the range of orderly inquiry at any given time as did physical obstacles or the limitations of knowledge or research procedures. These tensions produced some ironies; "practical" men sometimes staved off action by deflecting it into "study," only to find as did the conservatives who let Theodore Roosevelt have his Bureau of Corporations in 1903, that fact gathering and analysis generated new impetus to action.[30] Inquiry and analysis could cultivate new awareness of relations, gains and costs; from this awareness might come new motives of interest or reinforcement of motive or purpose hitherto only part formed, or the courage to act where before action was thought useless.

No attitudes better showed the leverage which new knowledge or beliefs about knowledge could effect than the pattern of ideas concerning the role of will in directing the general course of the economy. Through the 19th century men accepted the swings of the business cycle as phenomena of nature, dictated by immutable laws of supply and demand. However, by the investigations conducted in 1912 by the (Pujo) subcommittee of the House Committee on Banking and Currency and by the creation and operation of the Federal Reserve System, government taught public opinion the notion that there could be some management of the economy through fiscal controls. Other factors entered the picture. Nonetheless, knowledge and belief generated by 20 years' venture in fiscal regulation helped shape the prevailing opinion which in the 1930's renounced resignation before immutable economic laws and required that the national government tax, spend and maneuver to moderate the downswing of the business cycle. The 1950's began to write another chapter in this story. By controversy and compromise among the Treasury and the Federal Reserve Board, the Congress and the President, legal process provided lever-

[30] See Stocking and Watkins, MONOPOLY AND FREE ENTERPRISE 35, 353 n. 23 (1951).

age for creating a public opinion more sophisticated to dangers of inflation and the need to use fiscal controls to moderate the upcurve as well as the downcurve of general economic activity.[31]

With its powers of purse and investigation the legislative branch should have led in effective leverage by generating knowledge and opinion. Examples of legislative potential were not lacking, such as the work of the Pujo committee. Until the 1930's, however, Congress focused its inquiries mainly on the internal housekeeping of government. This was a significant part of the check-and-balance pattern within the national government, hence a significant support function, but it contributed only indirectly to substantive policy. Tensions of depression, war and cold war produced sharp-felt needs for self examination which from about 1930 on led to unprecedented emphasis upon the investigatory role of Congress. After some twenty-five years the pattern of development here still lacked desirable definition. In part Congress had permitted misuse of the investigatory power for support (policing) rather than leverage purposes; investigations too often became trials of individuals before a court of opinion. In part Congress had not broken free from the undue emphasis our bastard pragmatism put on current operations; despite the unusual attention given the investigatory function, it had yet to win merited priority upon the best talents and energies of the House and Senate.

In the states, legislative investigation typically remained almost wholly in the domain of internal housekeeping. The

[31] Compare with Carey, 3 PRINCIPLES OF POLITICAL ECONOMY 255 (1840), Roosevelt, "The Commonwealth Club Address, 1932," in 2 THE PEOPLE SHALL JUDGE 449 (Univ. of Chic. ed. 1949); The Employment Act of 1946, 60 Stat. 23 (1946), 15 U.S.C. ch. 21 (1958).

second essay pointed to the forecast of new needs and the first, limited responses in Wisconsin, where in 1901 the legislature set up a legislative reference library and in 1909 created five joint interim committees to lay foundations for major breakthroughs in legislative policy.[32] At mid-20th century there were promising state developments of "legislative councils" or other forms of staffed and continuing interim committees to pursue data and plans for broader legislative programming.

Partly by legislative default, partly by deliberate delegation, the national and state executive branches showed the more substantial record of generating knowledge and opinion out of which might proceed fresh initiative of decision. Wisconsin's pioneer geological survey law of 1853 stood at the beginning of a trend. Chapter II noted the contributions made to unfolding new policy toward industrial accidents in Wisconsin between 1905 and 1911 by the Bureau of Labor and Industrial Statistics and by John R. Commons' seminar at the university.[33] A contemporary example of like trends in the federal government was the impact which Forester Gifford Pinchot had upon the formation of an influential body of opinion to support fresh policy on conservation of natural resources.[34]

[32] See Chapter II, note 11 *supra.* An interesting and rare criticism of the crudity of the first measures taken by the legislature for developing broad programs of policy is contained in the Special Message of Wisconsin's Governor McGovern (Aug. 6, 1913), vetoing Bill 5038, 51st Legislature, which was to create an interim legislative committee to study accident and health insurance; see WIS. SEN. J. 1285-87 (Aug. 7, 1913).

[33] See Chapter II, note 11 *supra.*

[34] See Blum, THE REPUBLICAN ROOSEVELT 112 (1954); Gulick, AMERICAN FOREST POLICY 20, 26, 40, 58 (1951).

As usual, the currents did not all flow one way. As the executive apparatus grew larger and its business more specialized, possession of inside information or particular operational skill became a means of power which might be hoarded against competing power holders or used to outmaneuver less well-informed legislators or members of the public. It was a development which made more serious the failure of the legislative branch to realize the potential of its investigative role.

The courts and the bar contributed also to the leverage which law exerted by generating and publicizing knowledge and belief. However, because courts generally may act only upon matters brought to them by the initiative of litigants, this leverage effect was typically a by-product or incident of judicial work rather than a contrived product as it could be in the operations of legislators or executive officers. The main impact of the judicial process in this aspect was not by general organization and analysis of data for action but by giving dramatic form to issues which might help bring them into public awareness. Characteristic was the effect of particular hardship cases in the Wisconsin Supreme Court, and the Court's opinions pointing to need of legislative change, in fostering support for enacting a workmen's compensation act in 1911.[35]

Another useful way to appraise law's leverage function in its effects upon the state of knowledge and belief may be in terms of different types of knowledge. Some knowledge develops by ordered cumulation, of which science and technology provide the clear examples; here the law did leverage

[35] See Marshall, 2 AUTOBIOGRAPHY OF ROUJET D. MARSHALL 53-63 (1931).

service best by providing out of public money and organization the bases on which there could be means and continuity for growth. With all the frailties that marked its course, the Wisconsin geological survey, starting with the act of 1853, represents this type of leverage help for knowledge. Only the tax resources of law could meet the overhead costs of much of the accession of data needed to advance social order; the unique role of the federal Bureau of the Census provides the oldest sustained example in our experience. The law's shelter for cumulating knowledge was especially important where the objectives were too diffuse in effect or too long-term in reach to be provided for by the more sharply focused, typically short-term calculus of the market. Some knowledge develops by dialectic, by give and take of different, if not opposing interests; here the law did leverage service best by providing legitimated procedures for exploring and deciding new issues and holding conflict within bounds which kept it from destroying the possibility of experiment. Wisconsin's 1853 legislature accomplished a measure of this sort when it chartered a state agricultural society, within whose framework both venturesome and conventional farmers argued out workable terms for shifting the state's agricultural economy from wheat to dairying and animal feed crops. John R. Commons envisaged this leverage use of law when he maneuvered the inclusion in Wisconsin's new industrial laws of advisory committees of management, labor, and public representatives to promote definition of more efficient standards of health and safety in factory operations.[36] Some knowledge develops by speculation; here, as in the support of a state university, the law gave leverage

[36] See Commons, MYSELF 95, 96, 154-58 (1934).

by allowing some separation of reason from operational responsibility, so that the insistent pressure of current practice might not preclude the growth of understanding. Some knowledge develops by exposing the inner logic of large organizing ideas or feelings, that men may see more clearly what their objectives require of them; this is the nature of the arts, but it has its place also in the achievement of social order. The most familiar type of this leverage use of law was the appellate court opinion which, like that in *Doherty v. Inhabitants of Ayer* in the first essay (the case of the broken auto axle), undertook to define the assumptions of fact and judgments of value implicit in existing policy in order to measure their relevance to changed circumstances.[37] In a less precise way the legislative process contributed much to this development of knowledge by explication. Behind most major legislation, as for example the labor relations laws passed by the Congress in the second quarter of the 20th century, was a long history of introduced bills, committee hearings and reports, most of which in their time yielded no affirmative result, but which in total served to define interests and courses of action in a fashion essential to workable decisions in complicated areas.[38]

Closely related to the law's function in providing leverage for gaining the knowledge or cultivating the opinion which might generate fresh initiative was the development of processes for more rationalized law making. This, too, was a development which ran into conflict with the bastard pragmatic strain in our thinking and feeling. The Field code effort of mid-19th century was too ambitious and merited

[37] See Chapter I, note 6 *supra.*

[38] *Cf.* Chapter III, note 37 *supra.*

opposition on rational grounds. But the Field code controversy was conducted with an emotional heat which revealed that the proposal to make law by highly planned effort offended the "practical" sense of men who believed that society grew organically and only by dealing with the concrete instance at hand.[39] This was the familiar climate of common law growth. It was not accidental that with so little distrust of the adequacy of the process we fashioned great areas of 19th century policy through the common law process. The wasteful duplication and multiplying of needless detail in 19th century special and local legislation reflected our instinctive indifference toward more studied decision making.

Where choice touched matters of great substance, it would be naive to expect that decision would ever move simply according to reasoned plan; in proportion as issues moved men deeply the law's leverage was more effective in promoting knowledge and opinion formation than in channeling action within the reasoned programs of specialists. However, this society of increasingly complex organization had many needs of ordered procedure and definition of secondary values, which must be met if the society were to live, and should be met competently if the society were to realize its potential. It was in such matters, primarily of institutional order, that our impatient bent for improvising and for narrowly practical action was most costly.

General opinion typically had little interest in problems of institutional function. Hence in these areas of social order custom, drift and inertia had the easier sway unless

[39] See Patterson, JURISPRUDENCE: MEN AND IDEAS OF THE LAW 421-25 (1953).

the law provided leverage for sophisticated review and appraisal and initiation of action for useful change. The creation of the Conference of Commissioners on Uniform State Laws (1892) stands to the credit of the American Bar Association as a pioneer step toward more rationalized law making in this realm of institutional function. Beginning in the 1920's, states began to create judicial and legislative councils as continuing bodies to bring a new depth of investigation and a broader, longer reach of planning to the growth of policy. From 1923 on, the American Law Institute's "restatements" brought to the review of policy and doctrine in areas primarily of judge-made law an intensity of analysis and debate by qualified scholars, judges and practitioners such as common-law development had never known. Rule making by administrative agencies tended toward more formal patterns of investigation and debate; this trend of practice was sanctioned, for example, with provisions for notice and hearings and the use of advisory committees in the Wisconsin administrative procedure act of 1955.[40] As private organization of industrial production, marketing, and finance grew in size and specialization of function, more rationalized rule making tended to enter large areas of life in which law delegated the creation of order to nonofficial decision makers. Trade associations provided procedures by which industries could standardize measures of quantity and quality of goods. Large corporation programming moved into a period of increased dependence on committee processes. Collective-bargaining contracts between management and labor in great firms took shape in

[40] Wis. Stat. ch. 227 (1957).

what amounted to small statute books for ordering human relations in the conduct of production.

In a pragmatic sense which Coke probably would not have accepted, there was a legitimate artificial reason of the law, or of law making. When law created leverage for more rational processes of framing and initiating rules of behavior or allocating resources, it pressed events in a direction which the highly organized character of this society required. This judgment need imply no naive or dangerous exaggeration of reason. Men's ultimate values would continue to spring, as always, from feeling. But even at this ultimate level, the record showed moral growth as men applied their minds to discipline feeling. For example, in a more and more impersonal urban style of life there was need to stir emotion about symbols of party and interest groups, to give the minimum cohesion necessary for group decisions. However, the scale of organization in 20th century society involved great commitments and hazards of irrevocable choice. In this situation it was functionally important that issues be submitted to the most rational handling possible before they became the stuff of partisanship. There was little risk here that reason would run riot into ideological tyranny. The 20th century United States was a big country of great internal diversity; its cultural fault was an impatience with thought rather than an excess of it; its intricate division of labor meant that functional interlock imposed salutary checks upon excess zeal for any one program or value, however imperative its apparent logic, for no sizeable group could long stay unaware of how much it depended on the co-operation and good will of other groups. More rationalized policy planning thus did not risk the excesses which might be wreaked by programmatic enthusiasms in a simpler society where there was less check from the internal logic of a complex social system. On the other hand, because of its size, the pressure of a fast-growing, complicated cultural heritage and the functional demands of its intricate organization, our society needed all the leverage that law could give toward more awareness of relations, and more energy and courage for deliberated decision.

4

Chapter 79, Wisconsin General Acts, 1853, provided that when any bill of exchange, draft, promissory note, or other negotiable paper by its terms became due and payable on a Sunday or legal holiday, it should be due and payable on the next succeeding day of regular business. Chapter 84 in the same volume required county supervisors to levy and collect, for 1853, a state tax of six mills on the dollar valuation of the taxable property in their respective counties. The two acts reflect two aspects of law's function in supporting institutions necessary or useful to sustaining the commonwealth.[41] The state tax law provided for the overhead

[41] I have simplified the statement of the two statutes for the purposes of my main text. Chapter 84, levying the state tax for 1853, provided for a levy of five and 3/5 mills "in addition to the two-fifths of one mill on the dollar valuation, by law to be collected for the purpose of paying the interest on the state loans. . . ." *Cf.* Wis. Const. art. VIII, §§ 5 and 6; Wis. Acts and Resolves 1852, ch. 341; Wis. Gen. Acts 1853, ch. 55. Chapter 79, defining the effective maturity of negotiable paper, was drawn with the clumsy particularity characteristic of the times; it did not speak of paper maturing on a legal holiday, but of such instruments as in terms becoming due and payable "on either New-Year's Day, Sunday, Christmas, fourth of July, or the day of the year which shall be designated by the governor as a day of thanksgiving. . . ." Mid-nineteenth century legislative draftsmanship proceeded by trial and error. The legislature moved toward a better statement in Wis. Gen.

costs of legal order; of the 99 support statutes in the 1853 volume it belongs with the 76 which concerned the maintenance of formal legal processes. Obviously a great deal of the law's support went to support the law itself. The fact implied both the importance of the law and the need to turn a wary eye upon its claims. The next essay deals with the creation and control of legal force as a distinct element in social order. Our present concern is with law's support of other institutions than itself. In clarifying the due date of negotiable commercial paper, Chapter 79 fixed in position one more piece of a framework of rule and doctrine promoting the predictability, precision, and assurance needed to sustain market operations on credit. Law had not legislated into being the market, the credit conduct of economic exchanges, or the idea of negotiable paper; these were all primarily the product of desires, contrivances, and experience which originated outside formal legal process in the conduct of production, exchange, and wealth-getting. On the other hand, by 1853 what was "negotiable" and what consequences attached when an instrument was "due and payable" were ideas that included a large technical legal content, formed by the activity of lawyers, judges and statute makers in helping implement and administer transactions in market. The economic institutions had become so dependent in operation on terms and procedures defined and sanctioned by law that their content and effect could not be measured apart from their legal element.

Laws 1861, ch. 243, and the matter was at last handled in workmanlike fashion by Wis. Rev. Stat. 1878, §§ 1684 and 2577. *Cf.* "Report and Explanatory Notes of the Revisers of the Statutes," p. 132 (1878). That Chapter 79 of the General Acts of 1853 added a detail to an existing, substantial body of technical doctrine and rule, see Wis. Rev. Stat. 1849, chs. 44 and 98, and Brewster v. Arnold, 1 Wis. 229 (1853).

There should be no implication that we speak of the lesser uses of law when we distinguish support from leverage functions. The distinction is taken to help analysis, not as reflecting an order of nature; as I pointed out earlier, the use of law to provide leverage for creative initiative was itself a means by which law supported the values of an open society. Whether law's effect was leverage or support might depend not on the type of legal action but which stage of its results one appraised. Leverage refers to the help law gave to creative innovation or purposeful awareness in decisions that tended to reconstitute the frame of behavior; support refers to the help law gave to keep social processes in operation, whether these processes be the promising products of new awareness and fresh decision, or the familiar products of old institutions.

The record does not show that events moved only within a simple two-step sequence, from leverage to support uses of law. The distinction of leverage and support was sometimes one of phase, a distinction among successive types of applied human energy. Successful leverage use of law tended to pass into support use of law, which in turn might provide that surplus of confidence, detachment, and means out of which men contrived leverage for new purposes or new means. So, in breaking New York's attempt to grant statutory monopolies in steamboat transport, *Gibbons* v. *Ogden* provided legal leverage for wide venture in this new means of commerce. Being once firmly set, the role which that decision created for the United States Supreme Court in protecting national trade against parochial interest then had meaning primarily as providing continuing support for stable patterns of interstate marketing; yet, the succession of phases was not exhausted, for new circumstances created occasion for new leverage, as the Court, for example, adapted its role to the rise of rail, then motortruck, then air transport, and the relation of these to state regulation.[42] Again, as the business corporation became more common in the late 19th century, statutes authorizing incorporation (like Chapter 68, Wisconsin General Acts, 1853) in large measure served the routine conduct of the market; but the corporate form also facilitated such massing of capital and enlarging of organization as reshaped not only the purposes and products of industry and finance but also the types and allocations of power in the society at large.[43]

On the other hand, there was law which had operational meaning mainly by leverage, and law which had effect mainly as support. Support of orderly market processes was the prime function of those aspects of contract law that dealt with performance, breach, and damages. In contrast, leverage for creative innovation was the prime function of the rule which presumed the validity of agreements and cast on an objector the burden of proving that the parties' arrangements so offended public policy that courts should deny them enforcement. Leverage for action was the prime function of the tort rule which generally cast on the injured person the burden of showing why the actor should pay for harm

[42] *Cf.* Gibbons v. Ogden, *supra* note 27; Houston, East and West Texas Ry. Co. v. United States, 234 U.S. 342, 34 S. Ct. 833 (1914); Northwest Airlines, Inc., v. Minnesota, 322 U.S. 292, 64 S. Ct. 950 (1944).

[43] See the remarks of Mr. Chief Justice Ryan on the significance of the corporation for the concentration of economic power in "Address by Hon. Edward G. Ryan Delivered before the Wisconsin Law School" (1873); see also "Address by the Hon. Matthew H. Carpenter Delivered before the Columbian Law School, Aug. 20, 1870," 2 ALBANY L. J. 121 (1870).

caused by what he did; support of continued functional capacity was the prime function of the rules which defined particular items of recoverable damages. Law had leverage meaning where it fostered new awareness of purpose and relations and invention of means or will to implement such new awareness or such inventions. The leverage function was thus likely to be prominent where the law's business was with providing legitimated forms or means of initiating decision (as in the incorporation statutes or the contract or tort doctrines favoring fresh action). The support function was prominent where the prime need was to maintain morale (enforcing reasonable expectations arising in market, family, or other social relations), to interpret action (determining the particular content of agreed relations), or to adjust gains or costs consequent upon action already taken (appraising contract performance, enforcing a trust, determining damages for personal injury).

Whether we measure by historic patterns or by social functions, there seems no sense in trying to assign relative importance between law's leverage and support functions. Because of the factors making for drift and conformity to the functional demands of going social processes, men found it harder to create leverage than support uses of law. Thus the support function tended to bulk larger in the simpler years of the society. However, neither the leverage or the support function had meaning without the other. This was because together they expressed constituent elements of the distinctive nature of man—his capacity not only to grow in reason and emotion but also to pattern and discipline the products of mind and feeling. Man's competence was not comprised within a set of instincts or even habits; his mind was capable of enlarging his awareness of the relations in which he stood, and thereby enlarging his purposes and his means. This competence led him to seek leverage upon his situation. But experience pressed infinite detail upon him. The complexity of life's detail was compounded by constant, open-ended, irreversible change generated largely from man's own cultural accumulations. His limited energies of imagination and will would be overwhelmed and his competence for creative growth stultified, unless he could find or contrive some stability of ideas, feelings, and behavior amid this flux and variety. Where law supported the emergence or continuance of useful patterns of values, expectations, or procedures, it contributed not only to maintaining life in society, but to the conditions of stability prerequisite to creative change.

One way to tell of the law's support functions would be in terms of law's relation to principal non-legal institutions within which men patterned their lives. Thus we might tell the legal history of the market and occupations, the church, the school, the family, and social and welfare associations. Or we might somewhat change the emphasis, though not the general frame of reference, by considering how law supported or sustained major life objectives or fields of interest about which non-legal institutions gathered—men's concern with earning a living and achieving command of economic resources, with creating families and rearing children, with their relation to God or to such ethical ideals as they erected to give meaning to life beyond the daily round. These are useful approaches to organizing materials that are bewildering in mass and variety. I have three reasons for not taking such a line of analysis here. First, this inquiry by particular institutions or life objectives would be too extended for these survey essays. Second, emphasis upon institutions or institutionalized values tends to slight law's relation to the structure of individual lives. This bias undervalues the effects which the emotional drives and rational efforts of individuals had upon conditions of social change and stability. Moreover, it is not consistent with the working value this culture put on individuality. True, within our constitutional traditions of limited government and legally protected privacy law's proper concern was only with men's relationships, never with their aloneness. It follows that the main matter of legal history concerns institutions, that is, organized or at least patterned overt behavior. Nonetheless man's history can have meaning for him only in the terms on which he individually experiences the universe; thus we must read his institutional record with attention to what it meant for the course and structure of the individual life. Third, there were large themes of form and process which determined the content of social and individual life, which run through all particular institutional stories, but which may be lost to view if we focus only upon particular institutions. I shall sketch four such themes—the maintenance in the individual and in the social life of continuity, productivity, context and community.

Before I pass to these four more general themes, however, I must recur to one feature which dominates the record of law's support of the great non-legal institutions of social order. The catalog of Wisconsin General Acts, 1853, showed that, so far as the legislature was not concerned with the support of the law's own institutions, its preoccupation was with the economy; of 16 general support function statutes,

13 dealt with the framework of economic activity. If we look ahead 100 years, to the Wisconsin session laws of 1953, proportions have shifted somewhat, but not so as to alter the large pattern. Of general support acts passed in 1953, about 60 per cent related to the social framework of economic activity (compared with 80 per cent in 1853). The most marked change between the catalogs of the 1853 and 1953 session laws was the increase in legislation concerning dependent persons, persons who for reasons of age, ill health or mental or moral incompetence needed outside support to bulwark failing life structures. The 112 chapters of the 1853 statutes included one act on adoption procedures and, among laws pertaining to government housekeeping, three regarding support of schools. In contrast, about 21 per cent of the 1953 general support acts (i.e., other than acts on government's own housekeeping) concerned care of dependent classes apart from provision for ordinary public education of minors; if one includes the acts on public schools and purely housekeeping measures on dependents' institutions, 20 per cent of the total 1953 acts related to provision for dependent persons. The internal housekeeping of government bulked larger than any other single category of statutes in 1953 Wisconsin, as in 1853—a little over 50 per cent of the total 1953 acts fell in this category if one includes purely fiscal provisions for schools and other institutions for dependent persons, about 40 per cent if one excludes these dependents' measures—but (compared with the 75 per cent ratio in the 1853 General Acts) this category considerably diminished relative to legislative attention to adjustment of social relations in the community at large.

In summary:

Percentage Classifications of "Support" Legislation
Wisconsin Session Laws, 1853 and 1953

	All "Support" Laws		"Support" Laws on Matters Other than Government Housekeeping		
	Government Housekeeping	Other	Economics	Dependents	Other
1853	84%	16%	80%	7%	13%
1953	53%	47%	60%	21%	19%

An inventory of the total flow of business through the principal court of general trial jurisdiction in a Wisconsin county, 1855-1954, shows related patterns. Over this span about 70 per cent of civil actions filed concerned the working of economic institutions, and about 35 per cent of criminal cases involved crimes against property. Because it is the distinctive business of courts to make final scrutiny of the application of public policy to private persons, this trial court inventory naturally showed much lower proportions than the statutory inventories of business primarily focused on public administration; about 10 per cent of this century of trial court business concerned the criminal law, only a little over one per cent of the total civil actions concerned government administration. By the most liberal count, no more than 20 per cent of the criminal cases and no more than ten per cent of the civil actions in this 100-year trial court inventory directly concerned the family or matters of sexual regularity or dependent status.[44]

[44] The catalogs of the contents of the 1853 and 1953 Wisconsin session laws are my own. See notes 1-3 *supra* on aspects of the 1853 catalog. For the general comparisons made at this point in the text I did not undertake to distinguish among the 687 chapters of Wisconsin Laws,

The middle-class values which dominated United States history emphasized what men could bring about in this world. We sought life's fulfillment in contriving ends and means within a context of social relations which constantly grew in range and density. We early read the lesson of our unique situation on this rich, unexploited continent: here men might use material means to add new dimensions to life. It was a point of view which could easily, and often did lead into crass and vulgar pursuits. Yet we did also seek an ideal of a more humane, self-respecting life. Our core faith was not materialistic, though our faith in means was in large measure so. We believed that we could build a freer life for more men from a steadily rising material productivity, and we bent public policy largely to this purpose. In this respect we were all Hamiltonians. It accorded with the culture that here law's support functions related more to the economy than to any other non-legal institution. Economic means were our main reliance for fashioning new

1953, between those which might be deemed primarily of a leverage and those primarily of a support character; this problem of classification becomes much more subtle in the complex legislative patterns of mid-20th century, and justification of the distinctions taken would require treatment too full for this survey essay. I believe that perhaps about five per cent of the 687 1953 chapters might be argued to be primarily of leverage character, and that in any case the figure would be small enough not to affect the relationships discussed in the text. Different classifiers would inevitably differ on the categories to which to assign particular statutes, but within the broad headings I chose—the internal affairs of government, regulation or support of economic activity, care of dependent persons (other than school finance), and health, morals, and ordinary police regulations—I believe that there would likely be serious difference over classifying no more than two or three per cent of the acts, and that the differences would not affect the text generalizations. My classification of the 687 1953 chapters counted 366 as pertaining to the internal affairs of government (or 292, if one classes as "dependent persons" legislation 59 acts regarding educational finance and 15 regarding finance of institu-

ways of life. Science and technology (including the invention not only of machines, but also of new relationships in production, finance and marketing) impelled our economy to an increasingly complex organization. We made of organization itself a major productive asset. The features this culture assigned to law—its concern with the distribution of power, with constitutionalism and procedural regularity, with allocations of resources—meant that law's prime business was with the ordering of social relations. Through our 19th and early 20th century development, nowhere did relational patterns grow more exuberantly or with greater consequences for the location of power, than in the economy. The rush and scale of our economic growth made all forms of power specially dependent upon economic development; law thus naturally concerned itself largely with economic power. Social order here became peculiarly dependent upon economic order; in proportion as we used law to sustain social framework, we thus used law largely to support economic

tions for care of dependent persons); 200 of the 687 chapters I counted as relating to the framework of economic activity, 69 as relating to the status or care of dependent persons (or 143 chapters, if one adds under this heading the 74 acts concerning finance of education and of dependents' institutions), 20 as relating to health and morals, and 32 as relating to ordinary police (mostly regarding automobile traffic problems, but including a major revision of the state's criminal code). The data from the inventory of a century of business in a Wisconsin trial court is from the tables in Francis W. Laurent, THE BUSINESS OF A TRIAL COURT: A census of the actions and special proceedings in the Circuit Court for Chippewa County, Wisconsin, 1855-1954 (Madison, 1959). From 1921-1954 in the general period of the Laurent inventory the county court shared important areas of jurisdiction with the circuit court. There were reasons of administration and the local setting why the distribution of this county court business varied somewhat from that of the circuit court—most notable was a much higher per cent of domestic relations cases in the county court—but these differences do not alter the general patterns of legal order relevant to the present discussion.

processes. The marked increase in law's attention to dependent persons was related to the central position of the economy. More than any other factor, the growth in the scope, size, and functional discipline of economic processes made men less self-sufficient as individuals (or, equally relevant, less confident of their self-sufficiency), and exposed them to new tensions of life linked to market competition, the division of labor and the impersonality of the city. If economic growth had human costs, it worked also to fulfill the Hamiltonian prophecy, though in ways Hamilton could not have foreseen and might not have welcomed. Out of our material abundance we grew more intent on life satisfactions. Hence we demanded more of law, to create conditions favorable to life satisfactions or to repairing life damage. Our efforts led us into such impressive developments in law as the social security system. But at mid-20th century the future of this trend seemed in question. It was unclear that the electorate would show the will and self-discipline to provide the means required to move further in these new directions. Particularly in education and in the handling of crime and delinquency there appeared basic difficulties of policy development, both for want of adequate definition of programs and want of will to pay the bills.

Whatever the realm of men's purposes or institutions, certain general themes tended to give coherence to law's support functions in the growth of the United States. Both with respect to the individual and the social life, we tended to use law to maintain values of (1) continuity, (2) productivity, (3) context, and (4) community.

(1) *Continuity.* Man's growth in ideas and feeling, in competence to enlarge his satisfactions and to accomplish

inventive and protective adaptation to circumstance, rested on his capacity to develop a culture, that is, to store and use experience. Capacity to create and sustain culture determined the range and volume of communication, which determined what variety and quality of stimuli would exist to develop mind and emotion. Cultural inheritance provided the frame of stability without which man's mind could find no meaning or use in change, but only chaos. Culture provided sustainment for individuality as well as for the common life. A man grew as an individual by organizing ideas and emotions into relatively dependable habits of will which would press him beyond the limited objectives of his animal nature and sustain him against awareness of his lonely human condition. These conditions of man's growth made continuity of experience and its teachings basic to realizing meaning in his life, alone or in society. It may seem strange to emphasize continuity as a value in the life of a country relatively so young as the United States. But what men developed here, they developed by successive increments to a rich cultural inheritance. Moreover, our interest is in relations of legal to social order. In creating constitutional legal order amid accelerating scientific, technical, and organizational change, our experience was in some respects older than that of any other people, and at least as productive in its continuity as that of any other nation. That our experience was relatively short as measured by the clock, though relatively long as measured by certain criteria of legal accomplishment, only accents questions of the role of law in supporting cultural continuity.

Clock time ticked along with mechanical uniformity, its unvarying units and pace symbolizing physical and biological facts which man's awareness, feeling, or will could not alter. But man's creative competence in mind and emotion enabled him to slow or speed up, extend or compress what he experienced and what he did as an individual or collectively, changing the ratio of his experience or his effects to the pace of mechanical or physiological time. The leverage uses of law in United States history represented creative manipulation of time/experience and time/effects ratios to the end primarily of fostering fresh, original awareness and readiness of will, for decisions that would promote either stability or change. But fresh perception and will could grow only within the protection and by the stored nutriment of culture. Culture means continuity. There was need to manipulate time/experience and time/effects ratios, thus, by uses of law which would help sustain and enrich the continuity of the common life.

Continuity of individual life development was the product of formal and informal education shaped mainly outside law, by family, church, and job. So far as legal order cast its protection about family, religious, and market institutions, it indirectly sustained individual life structure. Certain values written into law probably relaxed the influence of family and church in channeling the individual life course, by supporting the extension of individual choice and responsibility. Law pointed in this direction by abolishing primogeniture, granting separate contract and property-owning capacity to married women, easing the legal terms of divorce, rejecting an established church, and legitimating the creation of independent religious associations. From the 1870's on, the functional discipline of factory and office jobs entered more and more into determining the shape and content of individual lives. The importance of these new disciplines to the quality and structure of the individual life was reflected in law after lags of one to two generations, first in health and safety legislation, then in workmen's compensation, later in unemployment insurance and old age and survivors' insurance and in legal sanctions of collective bargaining as the means to develop analogues of due process and equal protection doctrine in work relations. When man-made work discipline and dependence upon the market entered so intimately into the unfolding of individual life experience, there was insistence that law require that the job sector sustain life on at least minimally satisfactory terms. Of analogous import was law's support of the development of life and casualty insurance to provide means to overcome otherwise disastrous discontinuities in the course of individual family and business experience. The law's activity which most directly and powerfully affected the individual life course was the development of public education. Again, there were crosscurrents, hard to assess in net direction. McGuffey's Readers helped fashion and sustain striving middle-class morale; in a later day the technical and social emphases of the high school helped guide individuals into more status-conscious, consumption-oriented middle-class ambitions. In such ways for better or worse the public schools directly contributed to structuring individual life. On the other hand, and despite the acceptance of church schools within our tradition of free association, the compulsory school laws pre-empted for the state and away from family, church, and market the bulk of the creative hours of most young people during important formative years. In this aspect, law subtracted from the opportunities of influence of non-legal institutions traditionally significant in Western society in providing form and content for individual life.

Insofar as law directly or indirectly helped define roles and objectives and create and sustain attitudes which ordered individual lives, law made its most subtle, most potent contributions to the continuity of the society. Social continuity depended also, however, on great impersonal relations of time and circumstance. Our record was most uneven in the uses of law to affect general trends in social sequence. Two closely related types of sequence problem had peculiar urgency in the conditions of our growth. First was the problem of relative time preferences. Did the moving Present in any meaningful ways "owe" something either to Past or Future? Second was the problem of accommodating individual lives and social organization and functions to relatively abrupt discontinuities in the sequence of social experience.

If we ask whether the Present "owes" anything to Past or Future, do the metaphors symbolize relations that have meaning in legal history? We must distinguish whether we speak of sanctions or of values.

As a secular enterprise law can exert compulsion only over the will of the living, by the will of the living. Neither the dead nor the unborn can lobby for a bill or file a complaint in court. All secular power is by nature of the Present only, in the sense that it exists and is wielded only by the living. If by obligation we mean a claim enforceable by exertion of compulsion on the will or constraint of conduct, the Present "owes" nothing either to Past or Future.

But we still confront the question, by what criteria will the living use the practical power they have. In this aspect there may be meaning in the metaphors. Here we need distinguish among the dead, the living, the unborn, and the more and the less mature living. In a moral sense, the living "owe" nothing to the dead, for the dead are beyond benefit or hurt by the living. Because man's quality as man lies in his capacity for growth in awareness and in competence to direct his experience, the living diminish their own quality of experience if they lightly disregard the hard-won lessons of their culture. In this light the living owe it to their own human quality to strive for meaningful continuity with past experience, disciplining emotion and using knowledge so that for more gross or transient satisfactions they do not sacrifice their capacity to achieve more subtle and more lasting ones. Thus successive generations of the living in this country managed to hold on to a more self-respecting and respected life for the individual by at least minimal enforcement of the Bill of Rights to curb the excesses that common passion or fear might wreak in the name of security. Thus, to take a more positive example, successive generations built on knowledge both of biological science and of developing public administration to maintain increasingly effective measures of public sanitation.

In a moral sense the living "owe" something to the unborn, because the living can benefit or hurt the unborn. For like reason, the more mature living "owe" something to the less mature living. In both cases there is a relation of dependence inherent in facts. The matter returns to man's nature, the distinctive character of which lies in his capacity for growth in mind and feeling. Morally, the mature living owe to their own self-respect and quality of experience, and to the less mature living, and the defenseless unborn, not knowingly or negligently to make present choices which without good reason restrict or destroy the range of alternatives of choice for further growth. The Present "owes" the Future the chance to grow, because this is the only sense in which life has human meaning. This obligation is the more clearly defined toward the less mature living than toward the unborn, simply because men can make choices only on the limited knowledge and the emotional capacity they possess at a given time, and because it is inherent that man's capacity for growth itself makes his future uncertain by adding new variables. Thus the mature living cannot be deemed bound to choose present conduct according to estimates of purely speculative future conditions. "The Creator has made the earth for the living, not the dead."[45] Especially because science and technology show no limits to potential growth of knowledge, the Present is not bound to hoard all it has for a Future which is likely to find particular hoarded items no longer needed.[46] Still, the essential criterion stands. The Present is morally entitled to discount possible Future satisfactions in the light of uncertainty, and to live its own life. But, within the best knowledge and emotional self-discipline they possess, the living must not act so as unreasonably to destroy or limit capacity for future adaptation to changed circumstances or future choice of new lines of growth. To say otherwise would be to deny all that man can see of meaning in his experience.

[45] "Letter from Thomas Jefferson to Major John Cartwright, June 5, 1824," in THE COMPLETE JEFFERSON 296 (Padover ed. 1943).

[46] See Pinchot, *supra* note 26, at 27, criticizing the "indefensible" 1891 amendment to the New York Constitution forbidding the cutting of any trees, even for proper forestry practice, in the Adirondack reserve.

Nonetheless, under the temptations of our situation, such attitudes of restraint toward the future often failed to find expression in public policy. Tantalizing present opportunities, frustrations created by the gross imbalance of the factors of production (the abundance of natural wealth, the relative scarcity of labor and money), the spurs of unusually high levels of personal discontent under the drive of prevailing middle-class ambition—all biased our judgment toward undue preference of immediate over deferred satisfactions. Successive generations were entitled to little complacency on this score. The 19th century made highly debatable choices in spending natural wealth past practical points of reversible depletion. But the first half of the 20th century showed no better record in accepting drift toward costly and formless urban growth as the price of the immediate pleasures, conveniences, and status satisfactions derived from indulgent use of the automobile. Law rode with such currents more than it channeled them.

A different matter is involved when we ask whether Past and Future can be useful to the Present. Secular decision making occurs only in a Present, but this is a time span which can have greater or less extension and depth according to the perspective of the decision makers. By insisting on regular procedures and relating general and particular experience, that is, by promoting deliberation, law made past learning and future expectations more useful to decision by extending the scope of the Present to involve a more significant range of factors. As a sequence of passing moments the Present had little meaning for the quality of decision. The reach of men's thought and the discipline of their emotion depended on the spans of memory and foresight within which they ordered ideas and feelings relevant to determining behavior. By insisting that all secular power be held to account, and that decisions backed by law's force be taken only within regular procedures, this legal order promoted social continuity by enlarging the Present within which decision proceeded. It accomplished this in large measure because by slowing the pace of decision, it tended to bring a wider range of interests into play. Here law adjusted time/experience and time/effects ratios by expanding the time over which men exercised their competence, reducing the extent to which they acted with ignorant opportunism or impatience. Of course this states the matter only in terms of the law's positive contribution. Law was often a cumbersome mode of public decisions and its formal processes generated their own vested interests and made their own contributions to social drift. These factors sometimes meant that law produced delay rather than deliberation, so that law played no part in achieving a planned result, and decision went by default. Such was the relation of law to the events which produced practically irreversible depletion of the Lake States forest in the mid-19th century.

Law helped make the Past useful to the moving Present, a particularly important contribution in a country undergoing the turbulent growth of the United States. Law did this in part by fostering the accumulation of the useful Past. It did so most obviously by promoting public education, first largely through the proceeds of the public lands, later by taxing and spending. It did so by promoting the advance of knowledge, for example through the early establishment of the Bureau of the Census. By the stability and solemnity of its forms law sustained the morale of the active minorities which worked to preserve hard-won gains of past experience in popular government and in civil liberties; men's enthusiasm and devotion to procuring legislation or curbing abuses of official power might wax and wane on particular issues, but the processes of legislatures and courts abided. The vast development of the 20th century executive branch in national and state governments added a potent new sustaining element; the increased number and influence of professional administrators tended to bring to bear on present decision a weight of ordered experience or knowledge without counterpart in the 19th century United States.

Social continuity implied adaptation to resistless change of circumstance. Thus it was no less important that, despite its own contributions to inertia, law also was used to free the Present of the encumbering Past. I observed earlier that the leverage uses of law might be viewed functionally as a specialized type of the support uses of law; wherever law lent leverage to fresh awareness of relations and will to act upon fresh insight, it fostered a rationally and emotionally healthly irreverence toward the unexamined Past. The law's treatment of "vested rights" presented varied and subtle issues of time preferences. Both in its constitutional values and in its technical operations this society used private contract and property as organizing concepts too central to social power arrangements to permit of easy disturbance. In any given Present the allocation of functions in the society depended significantly on stability of contract and property arrangements. The range of fresh commitments (that is, the inclusion of the Future in present decisions) depended on reasonably assured expectations built largely on private contract and property. The stability of the currency and the public control of credit affected both these expectations and expectations based on public financial policy. The dominant temper of our 19th century politics was "conservative" in using law to underwrite such expectations, as the frustrated anger of agrarian political revolt testified. But this conservatism was not without material qualifications, which legal historians have not yet adequately defined. As a people we were too much committed to faith in the beneficent dynamics of increased productivity to permit past claims to thwart future promise. We did not evolve sharply defined principle on this matter. But in practice we tended to uphold vested rights only so long as they were felt to yield substantial present returns in social function. This was the basis on which the Taney court required that claims under old bridge or turnpike charters yield to the growth opportunities of the railroad.[47] In the 20th century it appeared that we might have moved into different, less manageable problems of "vested right." The 1930's depression and fast-grown dependence upon a rising standard of living taught a powerful public opinion to fear interruption of a rising curve of public and private spending. Reasonable expectations (that is, the inclusion of the Future in present decision) figured now in a different fashion than in the production-oriented 19th century. A central issue in the second half of the 20th century was whether the positive, resources-allocating and directing functions of law could be used with enough skill to generate such security in public opinion as would accept economic changes or risks that interrupted rising curves of income.

[47] See Taney, C. J., in Proprietors of the Charles River Bridge v. Proprietors of the Warren Bridge, 36 U.S. (11 Pet.) 420, 547-48, 552-53 (1837).

In largest part its culture was an unearned common inheritance of each generation. Law supported social continuity by enforcing free access to the inheritance and denying preemptive claims upon it which might give a few men unfair or unduly powerful holds upon their contemporaries. Law worked so through all the means by which it fostered social mobility in the United States—through public education, the sanction of a free press and free church, the prohibition of feudal tenures in land, the extension of the suffrage, the favor shown contract, and all other fashions in which law let individual talent use whatever of the common stock of knowledge and experience it could lay hand on. Law recognized the common right of free access to the cultural inheritance when it limited the years of a patent or copyright and also when it limited the extent to which businessmen might pre-empt the language by claiming protection for trade names. However ingenious the inventor, author, or advertiser, he built on too great an inherited stock of accumulated ideas and symbols to claim other than a marginal increment by his own creativity. In the 20th century, progressive income, gift, and inheritance taxes expressed analogous values. No man's accumulations represented entirely the result of his unique contributions to productive capacity. The law might properly thus return shares periodically to the common stock; the rates and manner of taxing might raise questions of expediency or secondary issues of fairness, but the primary justification of such taxes rested on man's nature as a social being.

Continuity with the future posed problems of special difficulty in the conditions of this country's growth. Every society must provide for the overhead costs of sustained organization and stored or cultivated resources; it must defer present satisfactions, to furnish the means of later ones. The weight of this overhead cost of continuity was indicated in the fact that almost nine tenths of the Wisconsin General Acts, 1853, concerned the support of existing institutions (mainly government and the market) and care of the sustaining physical and biological bases of life (for example, the navigability of streams and the preservation of fish and game). However, there was profound tension between the values we assigned present and future satisfactions. From this tension grew some of the greatest failures and most constructive effects in the support use of law.

Out of its middle-class origins, instructed in hope by the rich potential of the continent, this people believed in growth and gave change the benefit of the doubt, projecting their experience into the belief that the new would likely be better than the old. Even with the relatively limited means available in 1853, Wisconsin people provided by law for schools, for long-term improvement of the Fox and Wisconsin Rivers, and for wildlife conservation.

However, the same middle-class values which looked to the future included imperious demands for status mobility and for tangible results of striving. These attitudes made us impatient of slow, steady returns and desirous of immediately realized gains, whether in economic or social terms. This bias of attitude had reinforcement from the pressures of nearly 300 years' gross imbalance among the factors of production. We had abundant natural resources, but until the late 19th century we were relatively short of people and frustratingly short of fluid capital. This situation taught us, we thought, the practical wisdom of making extensive use of the land and relatively intensive use of men and money; since the land was cheap and men and money more costly, circumstances pressed us to seek maximum return from the more expensive factors. This situational pressure found strong expression, for example, in the persistent demands that the public domain be passed speedily into private hands, and in the popular agitation against private "speculators" in land who held it unimproved and out of current production while they waited for community growth to increase its value. But intensive use of men and money emphasized present (shorter-term) returns over future (longer-term) yields. Men are short-lived. Money has use in the market, whose function is primarily to strike the best bargain on terms immediately given. When law gave rein to the market, to individual contract, and to small-group ventures it gave impetus thus to short-term calculation in using natural resources. The bastard pragmatism that marked our working philosophy inclined us the more readily to follow the pressures our situation created toward short-term, limited-factor decisions. We did not begin to develop a broad or adequately implemented conservation policy until the first quarter of the 20th century. Then population growth, machine production, and the invention of more flexible procedures of mobilizing credit relaxed pressures for present preference, while growing scarcities taught us to put higher value on deferred returns from land, timber, mineral and waterpower. Of related effect was the greater concern in law for conserving human resources by expanding care for dependent persons and fixing minimum standards to protect men's long-term productivity and satisfactions from the immediacies of the market. Law supported preferences for future over present satisfactions most powerfully by cultivating its own independence; this theme, of fostering the separate force of political as against market or status calculus, belongs, however, to the next essay. Indirectly, law also helped lengthen the span of men's calculations by supporting non-legal institutions which worked to this effect. It did so by all the ways in which it supported the growth of a scale of business operation within which great firms took on institutional character and business management more the bent of professional administrators. It did so through grants of corporate status and favoring tax exemptions for charitable foundations devoted to basic research.

The second type of social continuity problem which had peculiar urgency in the conditions of our growth was that of adjusting to social changes of unusual pace and range. Pace and range of change had special effect here because they operated on elements of large size—a great, rich, unoccupied land mass, a fast-growing population, commitments of capital and manpower on the grand scale, scientific and technical innovations with unusual multiplier effects upon production and distribution of goods and services. A result was that in this country quantitative change tended to pass into qualitative difference. The United States underwent three periods of relatively abrupt, major transition—in the achievement of independence and the formation of the federal Union, in the Civil War and the generation of tumultuous industrial and financial growth that followed it, and in the depression of the 1930's and the impact of World War II. It attests the close support relations of law to the general structure of the society that the history of each of these generations of discontinuity is in large part a history of achievements or defaults in law. Large and abrupt discontinuity imperils the utility of the cultural inheritance which men need to sustain both creative change and stability. That in its time and place this country was specially subject to the strains of discontinuous growth underlines the importance of support functions of law, particularly as these related to holding the present ready to meet a disturbing future.

No wisdom or force mustered into legal controls could have held within neat channels the boisterous growth of the United States. However, a more modest support role for law—one with its plain analogues in the general evolution of life species—was to help allocate material and human resources so as to give the society capacity to adapt to the unexpected. It was dangerous for a society, as for a species, to attain a highly specialized adaptation to a particular environment, lest its specialization become too rigid to accommodate to substantial environmental change or to tolerate present variations which might contain the means of future adaptation. The distinctive potential of civilized society lay in creating and maintaining such a margin of resources that decisions need not be made under pressure of the most immediate necessities. Closely related was the danger of making present decisions which would have irrevocable consequences; this is a problem especially likely to present itself in the unfolding of complex social relations, where men do not, probably cannot, grasp all the variables and must hazard decisions without knowing all the available alternatives or the likely consequences. Such considerations give point to all that law did to promote a healthy pragmatism in public and private decision making. The public side of this belongs to the next chapter; here I note the matter for its bearing on non-legal institutions. In this respect the law's great positive contribution was its favor for large freedom in private association and private ventures —a policy calculated to encourage development of variation and experiment out of which the commonwealth might find means to meet new problems. However, there are puzzling problems of striking a balance in these matters. The large play which 19th century policy allowed to the market also permitted exploitation of some natural resources dangerously close to or past points of irreversible depletion. An example is the destruction of the Lake States pinery as a continuing productive asset. Especially in the 20th century, scientific and technical advances had great, often unforeseen impact in expanding categories of useful resources and yields of known resources. Rational calculation required that future satisfactions be discounted by the uncertainty attaching not only to their realization but to whether when the time came to realize them they would be needed or useful or as costly as present prophecy might suggest. So far as natural resources conservation was concerned, however, this comment speaks from hindsight; of the times in which much 19th century policy was made, the realistic verdict must be that too many decisions went by default rather than by rational discount of future uncertainties. The 20th century presented another distinctive problem. Productivity increasingly depended on complex technical and social organization, which typically meant increase in the time spans between committing resources and realizing upon them. Given the steady acceleration of scientific and technical knowledge, this meant that commitments were subject to increasing risks of obsolescence. In this aspect the Present could make stronger claims than before against the Future's demands for deferred realization of assets. Law came grudgingly to terms with this development, for example, in liberalizing depreciation allowances in business tax calculations. The issue was not without 19th century forecast (the *Charles River Bridge* case bore this aspect of legal weight given to obsolescence in social contrivances) but the problem became acute only after the '90's, as a prime example of major discontinuity with which law must come to terms.[48]

(2) *Economic Productivity.* Rising capacity to produce goods and services provided much of the dynamic of this country's growth. The reality of this trend, and popular confidence that it would continue and increase life satisfactions, supported the political and social values most distinctive to this society. Productive capacity was not the only cause at work for the nation's growth. An economy of large capital commitments, great impersonal markets, free private association, and high division of labor came into being here largely under the impetus of attitudes created out of political and social experience; there was prevailing belief in the rule of law to bulwark reasonable expectations and protect privacy; there was a confident sense of individuality, born as much from Western religious and

[48] *Ibid.* Legal procedures to deal with urban blight presented a major instance of problems of social obsolescence in the mid-twentieth century. The seriousness of the issues of discontinuity involved was reflected in the flexibility which constitutional doctrine allowed, both for areal treatment of the problems and in defining the extent to which the legislature must proceed by eminent domain and the extent to which it might invoke the police power. *Cf.* Berman v. Parker, 348 U.S. 26, 75 S. Ct. 98 (1954); David Jeffrey Co. v. City of Milwaukee, 267 Wis. 559, 66 N.W. 2d 362 (1954).

political development as from the teachings of trade. An enduring society must produce more than merely economic satisfactions; the following two subdivisions of this section note relations of law to other criteria of productivity in the individual and in the common life. Nonetheless, when men shaped a society on a vast, substantially unoccupied land mass, rich in natural potential, in times of surging scientific and technical advance, the rate of economic production could not but affect the whole form and content of their enterprise. For all its failures, North American society did show that men could build values of the spirit on a material base—more effective respect for individuality, more generosity and exchange among equals. Law's support of the rising curve of productivity thus had peculiar importance in United States history.

Natural abundance, development of new sources of physical and biological energy, and invention of more effective production, marketing, and financial organization initiated and sustained the rise in productive capacity. The law's support roles were secondary to these forces, but of critical importance to their realization. The record included failures, defaults, and dubious choices. But on the whole it showed remarkably creative use of legal processes.

Acceleration and uneven distribution of effects rather than simple flow and accumulation made rising productivity the shaping factor it was in our growth. Of first importance, thus, were uses of law to help us obtain multiplying returns from limited means. In societies less richly endowed by circumstance, the additions to productive capacity possible of achievement within a limited number of years were small relative to existing capital. This country had unusual means to achieve much larger increments to productive capacity. It had vast unoccupied acreage; the country's promise stimulated unprecedented immigration; its natural wealth and the rising tide of scientific and technical advance supported a great increase in the domestic population, which provided an expanding labor supply and expanding markets. Until late 19th century the contrast between abundance of land and relative scarcity of working force and fluid capital made us acutely aware of the challenge to obtain maximum returns for the use of labor and money in relation to land. From the beginning of our national life public policy emphasized a booster or multiplier criterion for the use of law to mobilize and allocate resources. We would use law so, where its use promised productive returns many times over. Out of grants or cheap sales of public lands we subsidized establishment of farms and the growth of bulk transport facilities to move farm produce to market. Public land policy in effect subsidized industry with cheap raw materials, notably timber and minerals; cheap food and low-cost lumber for town building helped the growth of urban population needed to provide labor and distribution facilities for industry. The scope of initiative we allowed private decision through contract and property law, the availability of the corporate form of doing business, and the provision of instruments of credit and long-term finance encouraged the emergence of scarce managerial talent and the muster and discipline of scattered capital. By chartering privately administered public utilities and leaving them long free of effective controls over rates or service, we delegated to them practical power to raise capital by levies on those who must use their facilities. By failing to enforce accounting for many of the social costs of business enterprise, in effect we subsidized the more rapid growth of trade and industry. In the 19th century, concentration on real property and excise taxes and the absence of progressive income, gift, or inheritance taxes promoted turnover and concentration of capital for commerce and industry. On the other hand, we used the taxing power to promote industry through protective tariffs. After mid-19th century, by an increasing measure of public education we subsidized development of the minimum skills required of the labor force in an economy where trade and factory discipline bulked larger and agriculture demanded more technical learning. By public health measures we underwrote the energy to sustain a more productive people. By grant of public utility franchises and by public subsidies for transport improvements, law helped create foci to attract foreign and domestic capital to new opportunities. The married women's property acts supported cultural trends which brought women more effectively into the labor force. Contract, property, and tort law favored initiative for action, creating a climate friendly to scientific and technical innovation; in the 20th century perhaps the most notable application of the multiplier criterion for use of law was the spending of public money and the allowance of tax exemptions to foster basic and applied research.

Closely related to the multiplier principle was public policy which promoted mobility or liquidity of economic resources. The commerce clause of the Federal Constitution protected free movement of capital and labor across state lines, and until the 1920's national policy on the whole favored immigration. Legislation provided procedures to discharge insolvent or bankrupt debtors and constitutional provisions abolished imprisonment for debt; these measures expressed humanitarian sentiment but also reflected the view that men should have means to shed the hampering past and to re-enter the market as fresh productive agents. The development of a complex legal apparatus to sustain credit and long-term finance fostered larger volumes of economic activity on a given capital base. In all respects in which law contributed to the growth of cities—as by the help given to bulk transport development, and hence the concentration of markets—it brought men into a life context that promoted specialization, division of labor, and realization of more varied talent.

To support larger increments to capital growth and to render human and money capital more mobile would have produced only limited results had it not been for two other aspects of public policy—the provision of a large theatre of operations and of substantial freedom to experiment with private organization. We created a successful federal system distinguished by firm power at the center to discipline parochial policies, and by provision for orderly expansion through admission of new states. Thanks to the will and imagination of Mr. Chief Justice Marshall, federalism provided an assured legal framework for the growth of markets of sectional or even national scope. Congress fostered the potential of the system by establishing a national postal system, aiding completion of a transcontinental railroad net, and contributing some ingredients of a national law of trade regulation. In a country of such vast distances, what federal and state law both did to promote and regulate means of bulk transport had basic importance for enlarging the possible scale of economic operations. This, in turn, spelled increase and diversification of farm markets. Cheap bulk transport was indispensable to the growth of towns and cities, hence to the growth of division of labor and commercial, financial, and industrial organization and development of the managerial talent and diversity of ideas necessary to such expansion. I observed earlier that, in general, law seconded initiatives for productive growth which originated elsewhere. If this judgment requires qualification, it is with reference to creation of a successful federalism and a bulk transport network, where the uses of law plainly lent tremendous impetus to economic processes.

The productive gains which this economy scored were achieved only through increasingly elaborate organization of human relations. Organization itself became a major productive asset, a distinctive product of modern man; in the 20th century United States, the factors of production became less important as prime determinants of economic decisions, and worked rather as limits upon the dynamic possibilities of new organization of effort and knowledge. Organization was especially essential to realizing the productive potential of large-scale operations; unless there were procedures to channel energy, it would expend itself into useless diffusion in a large field of relationships. We used law to support our need of organization. Patent and copyright law and the general law of property and tort offered protection to original ideas and to valuable human relationships. We turned to law the more because as organization became more intricate and far-reaching, it became more impersonal and dependent upon reliable, rationalized processes, and so required the support of legitimated forms. We used law to provide legitimate forms of association (notably the business corporation) and legitimate forms of transactions (notably in the market, where commitments must be made over time). In mid-20th century we made progress at hammering out legal supports for procedures of collective bargaining and job discipline and due process, as management-labor relations grew into closer-knit organization on both sides. No social institution more dramatically symbolized the new role of organization in productivity than did the city—in the 20th century, the metropolitan area. With considerable efficiency we devised workable legal forms for business association and market dealings. We did badly in devising legal arrangements to keep pace with urban growth. At mid-20th century this was the most serious area of failure of domestic public policy affecting social organization.

These relations of law to increase of economic productive capacity present a confusing mixture of deliberate promotion, ratification of initiatives taken outside law, and unplanned and largely unexpected aids and hindrances. The variety of problems posed for assessment make this an area deserving high priority in study of our legal history.

(3) *Context.* Alone and together, men achieve quality and content in life not only out of time (out of memory and foresight) but also in space (from the challenge and support of a constantly shifting network of relations among themselves and with the rest of nature). This is to look at determinants of individual and social life in successive cross-section, while attention to continuity and productive increase presents causes in depth. It was inherent in the character this society gave its legal order—the charge to scrutinize allocations of power, to enforce responsibility of power and regular procedures of its use, and to make useful distribution

of resources—that law embodied much concern for the efficiency and decency of the context in which individual and social life proceeded. But awareness and adjustment of context demanded close and continuous application of mind and discipline of will. Hence this was an area in which the bastard pragmatism in our culture—our impatient opportunism—produced much default and error in public policy. To order relations and mediate tensions arising within them was business to which legal agencies as sensitively representative as ours were peculiarly adapted. The care of context is thus a realm in which law rendered support functions mainly by its own direct contributions, and less by sustaining other social institutions. Accordingly, this section (which relates primarily to the law's support of nonlegal institutions) takes only brief note of context values, leaving further exploration to the following essay.

Values of context for the intimacies of individual life were defined and fostered primarily by institutions outside the law. These are the values which provide basic meaning for much of the law legitimating, preserving, and protecting relations of husband and wife, parent and child, communicant and church, and student and teacher. Law was too heavy-handed to enter deeply into these relationships; its concern typically was to validate and maintain basic forms within which individuals could work to make their own continuing adjustments. So far as law extended its range, it was not by more probing use of law itself but by support of insights and instruments that arose outside law. Two developments of this sort were particularly notable. Increase of ordered knowledge about psychology, psychiatry, and social work encouraged creation of new legal agencies to offer counsel and therapy in disturbed family relations. Recognition of the larger importance which job discipline had for the satisfaction and security of wage or salaried workers and their families was part basis for the law's support of collective bargaining, to develop standards of private due process of law in plant or office relations of authority and subordination.

Like any other society, this of the United States existed only by continuing adjustments of large relationships which fulfilled at least the minimal wants of the common life. These adjustments of social context became of increasingly critical and more difficult character in the growth of this society. For the United States found its elan in invention and energies released through wide dispersion of power, and its means in more and more intricate division of labor and interlock of function.

By legitimating and supporting broad freedom of private association for purposes of education, religion, welfare, and business, law made its main contribution to adjustment of social context by other than legal processes. To delegate to private hands the management of social relations of public importance was a policy already deep set by the early 19th century. Then the policy rested in large part on the inexperience of government and the difficulties of raising sizeable sums by taxation in an economy scarce of fluid capital. However, the practice of such delegation also expressed conviction of the political wisdom of dispersed power, grounded in our 17th century English inheritance. By mid-20th century, need, political faith and practice had made such delegation a tough-rooted element of our unwritten constitution. We had by no means resolved all the value problems posed by delegation. Bigness permitted organizations the margin of security which might encourage decisions that took the long view and weighed a broad range of factors—that is, which provided better both for social continuity and the integrity of social context. Large, integrated forest-products firms could practice a long-term sustained-yield policy on their timberlands which small operators could not afford or would not plan. Large trade unions in the garment trade enforced a decent level of working conditions which small, ill-financed employers would subvert. Yet, big organizations could and did push their special interests with more threatening effect than small ones. As the next chapter notes, the trends within the unfolding of the delegation principle led to enlarging law's balance of power role.

The market was a central institution of social adjustment in this culture. The degree of reliance we put on it magnified its defects. These defects occasioned most of the law's direct interventions in social context adjustment, considered in the next essay. But within its own frame of reference, the market was a most flexible and effective instrument for achieving workable contexts of dealing. The reality and contribution of this function was reflected in the dominance of contract in the law of the fast-growing 19th century. Out of market experience developed one specialized institution for adjustments of context, of an importance reflected in rich development of statute and case law. This was the device of insurance, which had almost as much significance for adjustment of current relations as it had for continuity. Through insurance certain costs of business risk might most effectively be accounted for, to be included in the price of goods and services. Sheltered by insurance, manufacturers and traders could venture commitments and enter relations of mutual dependence of a reach and scale which prudence would otherwise forbid. Another striking development—part of the market and part outside it—was the law's enforcement of relations of trust and dependence essential to widespread marketing and protection of private property. Out of its immediate functional needs, the market developed relations of agency which law enforced to permit trade at a distance and over time. The growth of trusts proceeded out of demands of more intricate property relationships and the need of obligations superior to the ordinary standards of the marketplace; here law played a more positive role in transforming an instrument of land tenure into an important means for managing fluid capital.

(4) *Community.* "[M]an is by nature an animal intended to live in a polis."[49] With the subjective satisfactions an individual derived from his unique response to experience, our law had nothing to do—beyond the vastly important matter of protecting the individual's right to be let alone in his thoughts and feelings. This was the profound significance for individuality of the general doctrine in this legal order that law concerned itself only with overt behavior. Herein lay law's root support of the pursuit of happiness; effective freedom called also for affirmative uses of law, but without this essential limitation organized power mocked liberty. However, man finds satisfaction even in his solitude out of memory and forethought bred from fruitful exchange with other men, living or dead. Social feelings and satisfaction are more the product than the cause of social

[49] THE POLITICS OF ARISTOTLE 5 (Barker trans. 1946).

relations. Typically, the individual enjoys the satisfactions of realized powers in himself only through considerable overt relation with his contemporaries. This was especially true—to a fault—in this energetic, mobile, middle-class society, with its emphasis upon achieved rather than ascribed status and its faith in the beneficent dynamics of material productivity and free and flexible association. Given the value we put on the individual life, it must be matter of concern for legal history what contributions legal order made to the success or failure of individuals in seeking satisfactions of mind and spirit through life in society.

Satisfaction from human relations rests on exchange of ideas and feeling and not on mere response to stimuli or mere technical performance; it rests on a sense of being useful for something or to someone outside oneself; it rests, too, on the self-respect and education that attend sharing in responsible decisions. In this last aspect, through its own processes law had important direct effect upon the worth men found in their common life. As with problems of the social context, attention to these direct effects of law belongs in the next chapter; here our concern is with law's relation to institutions other than legal, as these bore on the fulfillment or the frustration which individuals found in social living. Brief comment will suffice, for we are noting matters already discussed, observing merely how they relate to the morale of individuals as members of a community.

Law supported attitudes and institutions which made this North American society one of remarkable consensus through some 175 years of national growth. It was in this time a society not riven by internal wars of class or religion, nor were its common affairs hampered by pervasive, lasting, deep-seated distrust among major groups. Differences of interest, feeling, and program produced plenty of controversy. But moments of high crisis were fortunately few. On the whole our quarrels were within a commonly accepted frame of beliefs—in separation of church and state, the division of labor, the virtues of a fast-rising curve of productive power, the maintenance of substantial status mobility, the broad dispersion of power among private groups of diverse objects and interests. The tragic exceptions to this consensus were the problem of the Negro before and after slavery, and the closely related but not wholly dependent issue created by too gross an imbalance of sectional economies. The deep hurts which the whole country suffered from injustice to the Negro and the costs of Civil War and Reconstruction highlight by contrast the incalculable gains we had from our more general ability to hold within a common frame of values even strong and bitter contests.

This community consensus reflected the fact that men found life in this society on the whole remarkably satisfying—perhaps not happy, but carrying interest, challenge, hope, and sustenance for self-respect. In large measure this condition was the unearned gift of circumstance—of a vast, rich, unoccupied land, and fortunate timing which let our growth ride the surge of the industrial revolution and the general advance of science. Yet the record cannot all be written off to luck. Free religion upheld men's confidence in their own worth and equal claims to opportunity; free science and technology, and free associations of many purposes—for trade, education, care of the sick and incompetent, prosecution of works of public utility—multiplied the occasions for fruitful, rewarding joint effort; the market challenged the development of managerial abilities in farmers as well as in merchants, industrialists, and bankers; the city, largely the product of a growing technology of machines and production-distribution-financial procedures, invited unfolding of individual creativity, both through protecting privacy and expanding opportunities of communication. When law fostered and protected free religion, free private association, free access to market opportunities, and urban growth, it supported institutions which gave men wider chances for meaningful exchange of ideas and feeling, challenged them to find their functional roles in an increasingly complex division of labor, and taught them better to respect themselves as responsible makers and doers.

However, these dynamic attitudes and processes outside law developed trends which could frustrate as well as fulfill the individual's need of meaningful relation to his fellows. Individuality bred discontent as well as sense of worth. Status mobility cost men their bearings as well as set their course. Amid opportunities of fast-growing population and technique, market flexibility promoted such capital accumulation and concentration as might destroy the market as a theatre of diverse talent. Association multiplied occasions for fruitful joint effort, but also developed such size and intricacy of process and such centralization of energy sources as to deprive individuals of understanding or confidence that they performed meaningful functions or that they longer mattered. Increasing independence of the technical realm of life tended to rob work of its former capacity to create cultural satisfactions, while men had not yet learned to use leisure as an effective substitute. The growth of cities, and especially of metropolitan areas, increased men's freedom in privacy and exchange but also their aloneness as they dealt with each other on terms more and more specialized and impersonal and lost much of the emotional support that small, local groups had supplied.

Law entered into the creation of such tensions only remotely and by the unplanned, unforeseen consequences of its support of main lines of social development. Such resolution as could be hoped for many of these stresses could come only by cultivating morale through means subtler than law could use. Law's effective role to these ends consisted in providing legitimated forms within which other institutions could work out their salvation; legal sanction of private collective bargaining was an example. However, much of the tension which threatened or denied individual satisfactions from the common life expressed need to bring institutions or processes into more ordered relation to values outside their own frames of reference. The large ordering of relations of power, and of gain and cost, was business in which law had utility. This brings us to consider the direct and indirect force wielded by law—and to the next essay.

V

Force and Fruition

1

Upon the separation from England, Rhode Island did not adopt a constitution, but continued substantially the form of government set by the charter which Charles II had granted the former colony in 1663. This form of government contained no procedure for its amendment. It authorized the legislature to fix the qualification of voters, and under this authority successive legislatures, controlled by interests pleased with this situation, restricted the suffrage to freeholders. Opposition to this closed circle of power and frustration over legislative complacency and the want of a procedure of constitutional change finally burst forth in 1841 in the organization of popular associations favoring extension of the suffrage. Meeting no response from the constituted authorities, these associations of their own initiative caused the election of a popular convention according to voting procedures of their own contrivance. This convention framed a constitution extending the suffrage to all adult male residents, submitted its constitution to the broader electorate which it had defined, upon canvassing the returns declared the constitution adopted, and in 1842 superintended the election of a governor and legislature thereunder. Thomas Wilson Dorr, the idealistic lawyer who had headed the popular movement, was elected governor. The charter government pronounced the illegality of all these proceedings and put militia in the field against armed forces of the new government. The charter government's show of force prevailed. Meanwhile, in January, 1842, the charter government launched proceedings for a constitutional convention. This convention framed a constitution which the people ratified and to which the charter government relinquished power in May, 1843. In 1844 the state courts sustained the conviction of Dorr for the crime of treason by levying war against the state. The Rhode Island Supreme Court refused to examine the merits of Dorr's plea that his government had had legitimate title from the people. The court held that this presented a non-justiciable issue; the courts before which Dorr stood trial derived their authority from the 1843 constitution; thus they lacked authority to question the legitimacy of the charter government whose proceedings had brought the 1843 constitution into being.[1]

The matter came also before the United States Supreme Court, in *Luther* v. *Borden*.[2] To a suit for trespass to land, defendants answered that they entered the land as militiamen enforcing the action of the charter government to suppress insurrection. Plaintiff replied that the charter government had been duly supplanted by the Dorr government, because the latter had been ratified by popular vote; hence defendants' trespass lacked warrant in public authority. The Supreme Court held that the question posed was one not open to judicial inquiry and decision, but lay wholly in the domain of "the political department," as the state court

[1] "The Trial of Thomas Wilson Dorr for Treason, Rhode Island, 1844," 2 American State Trials 5 (Lawson ed. 1914). Dorr was pardoned after several years' imprisonment.

[2] 48 U.S. (7 How.) 1 (1849). See especially pp. 39, 42-44.

had ruled. This, said Mr. Chief Justice Taney, was clearly the proper decision as to the authority of the state courts. "[I]f a State court should enter upon the inquiry proposed in this case, and should come to the conclusion that the government under which it acted had been put aside and displaced by an opposing government, it would cease to be a court, and be incapable of pronouncing a judicial decision upon the question it undertook to try."[3] Nor was there authority in courts of the United States to adjudicate a revolution within a state. By the Federal Constitution, Article IV, section 4, "The United States shall guarantee to every State in this Union a Republican Form of Government, and shall protect each of them . . . on Application of the Legislature, or of the Executive (when the Legislature cannot be convened) against domestic Violence." Congress must necessarily decide what is the established government within a state, before it may admit as Senators and Representatives men claiming to be duly elected to Congress from the state; by admitting particular men as Senators or Representatives, the Congress adjudicates the legality and republican character of the state government under whose laws they claim election, as it had done here by seating men elected under the charter government. Moreover, by the act of February 28, 1795, Congress had delegated to the President to decide, upon application of a state government, that military aid should be supplied the state against domestic violence. In the Rhode Island situation the President had acknowledged the authority of the governor under the charter government by taking steps on his application to provide military support to that government; indeed it had been knowledge of this

[3] *Id.* at 40.

decision that ended armed opposition to the charter government. This determination by the President, under delegation from Congress, must be treated as binding upon the federal courts. The Supreme Court, Taney concluded, must decline to pass on "political rights and political questions" such as the plaintiff in *Luther* v. *Borden* urged upon it. By our accepted doctrine, in each state the sovereignty resides in the people. The people "may alter and change their form of government at their own pleasure. But whether they have changed it or not by abolishing an old government, and establishing a new one in its place, is a question to be settled by the political power. And when that power has decided, the courts are bound to take notice of its decision, and to follow it."[4]

Luther v. *Borden* raised issues of avowed political combat. Consider two later cases where large issues of power were at stake, but the nature of the conflicting claims was less clear.

On July 6, 1892, two private armies clashed and men died, as organized strikers at the Homestead, Pennsylvania, plant of the Carnegie Steel Company successfully prevented the landing of two barge-loads of 300 armed Pinkerton detectives. The strikers formed their battle array not only to support their wage claims, but to protect their union, the Amalgamated Association of Iron, Steel and Tin Workers; Henry Clay Frick, the company's general manager, had imported the Pinkertons not to fight a wage contest but to destroy the Amalgamated. For both sides, therefore, allocation of power was the ultimate stake.

One sequel to the violence of July 6 was the indictment

[4] *Id.* at 47.

of several strike leaders for treason by levying war against the state of Pennsylvania. Pennsylvania's Chief Justice Paxson charged the grand jury that there was treason "when a large number of men arm and organize themselves by divisions and companies, appoint officers and engage in a common purpose to defy the law, to resist its officers, and to deprive any portion of their fellow-citizens of the rights to which they are entitled under the Constitution and laws. . . ."[5] Later the treason charges were quietly dropped, after three strike leaders had been acquitted in prosecutions for murder growing out of the encounter.

English decisions before mid-18th century went far toward establishing that any riotous assembly to achieve a purpose of some public concern amounted to constructive treason. But the discussions in the Federal Convention and the carefully limited phrasing of the treason clause of the Federal Constitution, which became the model for state doctrine, showed that our policy opposed the expanded scope of the offense under English notions of constructive treason. Federal court decisions recognized and applied this restrictive approach, in effect ruling that only collective force exerted with specific intent to supplant the rule of law would suffice to make out treason by levying war. The abortive attempt to revive an extended concept of the crime in the Homestead cases met strong criticism. The *American Law Review* condemned the Homestead treason indictments as "a mass of stale, medieval verbiage."[6] The *Review* thought it absurd to "attempt to raise to the grade of treason the

[5] Commonwealth v. O'Donnell, 12 Pa. County Ct. 97, 105 (Court of Oyer and Terminer, Allegheny County, 1892).

[6] Note, 26 AM. L. REV. 912 (1892).

act of a lot of half-starved mechanics, or their governing committee . . . in taking unlawful measures to coerce their employer into compliance with their demands. The object is not to bring about any *political change* whatever, but to subject a party to an intended contract to a species of *duress,* such as will compel him to enter into a contract determined upon by the members of the unlawful combination."[7] This was undoubtedly an unlawful conspiracy, pursued by unlawful means. "But it is the wildest dream to dignify such a conspiracy with the name of treason."[8] Such, too, was the silent verdict of subsequent practice; the Homestead treason indictments stand alone in the record. The law had to deal thereafter with tumultuous assemblies, but it found all the doctrine it needed in the offenses of riot and unlawful assembly.

About three years after the Homestead indictments, the United States Supreme Court decided *In re Debs.*[9] The Court upheld convictions for contempt of court of leaders of the American Railway Union, for violating terms of a federal district court injunction issued *ex parte* at suit of the United States to enjoin any manner of interference with the business of railroads transporting the mails and goods and passengers in interstate commerce. Originating in a strike against the Pullman Company in the spring of 1894, by mid-summer the controversy had affected almost every railroad in the Middle West and threatened the national transport system, because of deadlock between the American Railway Union

[7] *Id.* at 914.

[8] *Ibid.* For further discussion of the Homestead trials, see Hurst, "Treason in the United States," 58 HARV. L. REV. 806, 823-25, 849-50 (1945).

[9] 158 U.S. 564, 15 S. Ct. 900 (1895).

whose members refused to handle any Pullman cars and the railroad General Managers Association which would not accept the boycott. As in the Homestead case, the background issue which peculiarly embittered the contest was not disagreement over a wage bargain but a struggle over the allocation of power. Under provocation the strikers broke into riot against the railroads' special deputies. Upon the plea of the General Managers Association that violence had become uncontrollable, and against the protest of Illinois' Governor Altgeld, President Cleveland sent federal troops to Chicago to restore order and protect the movement of mail and interstate commerce. Still the strike spread, the strikers' morale held firm, and violence increased. At this point the railroads persuaded the federal Attorney General to obtain an injunction. The jailing of the strike leaders under the injunction deprived the strike of direction and the men drifted back to work. The Pullman strike history encouraged widespread use of the injunction to break trade union organization, and launched the American Federation of Labor on a generation's battle for legislation to curb use of the injunction in labor disputes, which reached one climax in enactment of the Norris-LaGuardia Act in 1932.[10]

Brewer, J., for the Court, took pains to disclaim that the *Debs* injunction issued because there was a threat to sovereignty. On the record, the Court found, it did not appear that defendants were conducting a rebellion or inaugurating a revolution. On the other hand, the record showed that by organized means they were acting to obstruct the mails and interstate commerce. "If a State with its recognized powers

[10] 47 Stat. 70 (1932), as amended 29 U.S.C. ch. 6 (1958). See Lindsey, THE PULLMAN STRIKE (1942); Hurst, *supra* note 8, at 822 and n. 7.

of sovereignty is impotent to obstruct interstate commerce, can it be that any mere voluntary association of individuals within the limits of that State has a power which the State itself does not possess?"[11] Of course Congress might by statute make such obstruction a crime, and the Executive might use the army to remove the obstructions. "The entire strength of the nation may be used to enforce in any part of the land the full and free exercise of all national powers and the security of all rights entrusted by the Constitution to its care."[12] But the government was not limited to action after the event or of simply punitive nature. "Every government, entrusted, by the very terms of its being, with powers and duties to be exercised and discharged for the general welfare, has a right to apply to its own courts for any proper assistance in the exercise of the one and the discharge of the other . . . . The obligations which it is under to promote the interest of all, and to prevent the wrongdoing of one resulting in injury to the general welfare, is often of itself sufficient to give it a standing in court."[13] Thus, in contrast to the Homestead indictments, the *Debs* opinion took its stand on government's authority to provide for social order and function, apart from any revolutionary challenge, and to act preventively as well as by penalty or reparation.

Consider, now, two cases where again the allocation of power was in issue, indeed, the allocation of power over life, but the confrontation was between individuals and the state, rather than between groups and the state.

[11] 158 U.S. 564, 581, 15 S. Ct. 900, 905 (1895).
[12] *Id.* at 582, 15 S. Ct. at 905.
[13] *Id.* at 584, 15 S. Ct. at 906.

In 1841 the sailing ship *William Brown,* Liverpool to Philadelphia, sank after striking an iceberg. Into the long boat crowded 32 Scotch and Irish emigrant passengers, the mate and eight members of the crew, including seaman Holmes. The boat leaked, requiring constant bailing, and even under relatively favoring conditions of the sea, it was overloaded to the point that its gunwales rode only a few inches above the water. Heavy rain began, the sea rose and waves splashed into the boat. The mate ordered the crew to throw some of the passengers overboard to lighten the boat. Holmes helped another seaman throw 14 men into the sea. The next morning a ship sighted and rescued the survivors. Brought to trial in the federal circuit court in Philadelphia under indictment for manslaughter, Holmes was convicted, but received a light sentence in view of mitigating circumstances. Circuit Justice Baldwin charged the jury that the law, represented in court and jurors, must assert ultimate secular authority to determine whether proper cause existed to take life. Though the mate gave the order to jettison the passengers, his order did not protect the defendant. "[M]an, in taking away the life of a fellow being, assumes an awful responsibility to God, and to society; and . . . the administrators of public justice do themselves assume that responsibility if, when called on to pass judicially upon the act, they yield to the indulgence of misapplied humanity."[14]

In *Brown* v. *Mississippi*[15] the United States Supreme Court reversed a state court conviction of murder which rested

[14] Baldwin, Circuit Justice, in United States v. Holmes, 26 Fed. Cas. 360, 366 (No. 15, 383) (C.C.E.D. Pa. 1842). See Cahn, THE MORAL DECISION 61-70 (1955); Perkins, CRIMINAL LAW 849-50 (1957).

[15] 297 U.S. 278, 56 S. Ct. 461 (1936).

solely upon a confession "shown to have been extorted by officers of the State by brutality and violence."[16] The Court ruled that a conviction so obtained represented not mere error in trial "but . . . a wrong so fundamental that it made the whole proceeding a mere pretense of a trial"[17] and hence a violation of the due process of law required by the 14th Amendment of the Federal Constitution. That defendant was charged with the most serious offense against the sanctity of individual life did not warrant such violence by officers of the state as subverted the administration of justice. A state enjoys large freedom to regulate its court procedure according to its own conceptions of policy. "But," said Mr. Chief Justice Hughes, "the freedom of the State in establishing its policy is the freedom of constitutional government and is limited by the requirement of due process of law. Because a State may dispense with a jury trial, it does not follow that it may substitute trial by ordeal. The rack and torture chamber may not be substituted for the witness stand."[18]

Possession of the legitimate monopoly of violence within a territory was the most distinctive attribute of our law. In this society the law was not so much distinguished by its ends as by its means. To say that this was a constitutional legal order meant that law was not an end in itself, but existed to serve purposes which emerged out of private individual and group experience; on the whole, law shared its ends with other social institutions. This was true also in large measure of its means. The law shared rule making and the imposition of penalties with other social institutions.

[16] *Id.* at 279, 56 S. Ct. at 462.
[17] *Id.* at 286, 56 S. Ct. at 465.
[18] *Id.* at 285-86, 56 S. Ct. at 464-65.

Private clubs, trade associations, labor unions, religious congregations fixed terms of admission, made regulations for the behavior of members, and fined violators, or withdrew their privileges, or suspended or expelled them. Individuals governed much of their everyday relations by social customs which they enforced by recognized signs of social disapproval or by ostracism. But to take life, inflict physical pain, or confine the body were ways of enforcing rules which this legal order recognized as properly held only at the command of law. This was the respect in which the form of law was its most distinctive feature; force was not the sole, or even the normal, means of the state, but it was the means most specific to the state. Since this was a constitutional legal order, the law had title to use these modes of enforcement only for ends and by procedures legitimated by the most durable traditions of consent and approval of the people. As we entered the second half of the 20th century it appeared possible that men would learn more effective means of compelling the will than by violence. Bill of Rights guarantees of free speech and press, free religion, and peaceable assembly denied government the monopoly of indoctrination. Possibly law might find necessity to regulate private use of more subtle techniques of compelling the will to the ends of the manipulators; likewise it might become necessary to enlarge the categories of compulsion forbidden to government. This remained for the future, however. For our legal history to 1950, the law's claim to the legitimate monopoly of physical violence presented a subject whole in itself.

This does not mean that we exhaust the significance of the law's possession of force merely by reciting the instances when the law used force. The resort to violence or the potentiality of violence tended to satisfy man's most powerful feelings of hatred and aggression and to feed his deepest feelings of fear and guilt; violence might be used with deliberated measure for reasoned ends, but because it had its ultimate effect by physical rather than mental or moral compulsion upon the will its use or threat always exerted some pressure to displace reason and moral discipline and to install naked emotion in command of events. In using violence, law drew ultimately on energies of will rather than of reason—upon men's capacity to act, whatever the limits of their knowledge or moral control. Thus the use of violence was charged with peculiar dangers to man's realization of his distinctive qualities. Men's desires typically outran what they knew how to accomplish; their courage to achieve self-determined choice was constantly mocked by their fear that they could find no meaning; not far below the ordered surface of society there lurked always savage temptation to relieve discontent, frustration, and fear with the anodyne of obliterating action. The surgeon's knife cuts in order to heal, but the cutting is no less attended by risks of shock or infection. The historic meaning of the law's possession of force rests largely in the success or failure with which we developed secondary means to confine force and limit the social shock or infection which might accompany its use.

The significance of the law's monopoly of force lay also in its relation to the general distribution of power in the society. We must not let the dramatic character of men's conflicts lead us to exaggerate the relative place of conflict in their affairs. Man grew into increasing command of his environment because the development of his brain made him a creature capable of unusual competence in cooperating with his fellows. The interlock of function and intricacy of division of labor which marked the growth of this North American society attested that men could achieve a great preponderance of cooperation and creative competition over destructive conflict. The value our tradition put on enlarging the content and quality of the individual life expressed our sense of ability to make creation prevail over destruction. These perceptions we translated into the emphasis our legal order put on protection of individual privacy, private association, and the wide dispersion of decision making among individuals and groups. However, disagreement, friction, and some bad faith inevitably went with the operations of such a system of dispersed power. Individuals and groups required sanctions to enforce reasonable expectations of cooperation. Typically the legitimated sanctions were of a non-violent kind, as by suit for breach of contract; rarely, as in the individual's use of force to defend his life, they might involve private resort to violence. But if non-violent sanctions proved ineffective or were flouted, there was always the possibility that aggrieved individuals or groups would be goaded to attempt violence. This we would not legitimate. For good reasons we assigned to law the legitimate monopoly of violence. Moreover, another kind of problem required that law have the last word on the allocation and types of power in the society. The freedom our legal order gave to individual and group initiative invited more able, aggressive, and lucky individuals and associations to enlarge their economic, social, and political influence. Private power holders might thus exert non-violent but very effective compulsion to enforce their own interests in disregard of others. Given a society of wide dispersion of power, which encouraged infinitely varied initiative of will by private individuals and groups, the law could fulfill its charge and maintain its ultimate monopoly of force only by asserting authority to determine the kinds of power which private persons might wield. Moreover, the law must police private compulsion. To these ends law provided forms for peaceful resolution of disputes. To these ends law asserted ultimate authority to review the justification alleged for the individual's exercise of rights of self-defense and to define the legitimate areas and means of competition. To these ends, from the late 19th century on, law developed an increasing range and specialization of administrative regulation to put some limits of public interest upon the use of concentrated private power in public utilities, finance, and mass production industry. Thus the historic role of law's force is not confined to its direct exertion, but includes the superintending function which the law performed over the total distribution and use of power in the society.

Government mustered its greatest force for the conduct of war; it could do no less, where events put in issue the collective existence or self-determining capacity of the nation. The years of formal peace before and after World War II added a new dimension to the effects of the law's force functions upon the common life, as the federal government made unprecedented investments of manpower and money in maintaining readiness for war. The conduct of war, and more lately the preparation for war, caused major changes in the structure of government. Warlike conditions tended especially to increase the relative power of the executive and the difficulties of Congress in making effective use of its purse power to control the executive. They tended also to shift the balance of power between government and individuals and private association, in favor of government, as fear persuaded popular opinion to uncritical acceptance of demands made in the name of national security. The effects of war or threat of war upon law and its place in social order provide an important chapter in United States legal history. I note the relevance of the subject to pass it by, only because it is in itself too large a theme to fit within the present framework. This essay touches only functions and problems of law's force within the borders of domestic policy.

Within this compass the cases already stated present situations and values in terms of which we can examine relations which law's force bore to law's functions. (1) We believed that legal order was a necessary element of decent social order. Since we looked to law to help structure the common life, we required that law have effect and not merely symbolize an ideal. Thus in our conception law should successfully assert the legitimate monopoly of force within a territory; no less would do. So in Rhode Island the charter government and the Dorr claimants made mutually exclusive claims to title, and posed an issue that could not be resolved short of successful revolution or successful prosecution for treason. (2) The charge of treason pushed issues to the final point of political conflict. However, within social order which encourages diversity, men may come to many more limited issues of power. Corollary to its claim to monopolize ultimate force, law must hold the final judgment on the extent and manner of these more limited conflicts. But reason and prudence counsel not widening differences or promoting their development into irreconcilable positions. Whatever we think of the particular merits of the *Debs* case, the Court's limiting definition of what was there at stake represented the main trend, and the healthy trend, within which we kept order, in contrast to the invitation to extremes given by the Homestead treason indictments. (3) Treason was a crime of effective or attempted association, with foreign foes or domestic malcontents. More limited challenges to the law's monopoly of force might come from deviant individuals or from groups, as from the strikers of Homestead and Pullman on the one hand, and the alleged slayers, Holmes and Williams, on the other. Conceivably the law might distinguish the severity and manner in which it brought its force against individual and against group challenge. In fact the record was most uneven in this respect. (4) Its monopoly of violence made government itself the potential source of great harm, both to the integrity of individual life and to the individual's interest in fruitful relations with his fellows. Our tradition showed continuing awareness of this danger, but typically this awareness had effect only through the initiative of a few unusually energetic and courageous officials or private persons. This awareness found two expressions. One was in recognition that control of the government's force presented special issues of the separation of powers, reflected, for example, in Taney's opinion in *Luther* v. *Borden.* The other was in the development of Bill of Rights doctrine declaring limits upon the use of law's force in the interests of private individual and group freedom, as in the *Brown* case and in the Norris-LaGuardia Act. (5) Experience showed that direct force, though it might be necessary, was very costly in secondary results. Partly as the unearned gift of fortunate circumstances, partly as a matter of deliberate practice, our record showed a trend toward the preventive rather than the reparative uses of law. Typically this approach found expression in indirect, situation-structuring uses of law rather than the direct imposition of command or penalty. Though the *Debs* case was in other respects repudiated by later policy, the ruling there in support of the government's right to injunctive relief against public nuisance pointed to a main direction of legal development.

2

United States history shows enough occasions when law opposed its violence to the violence of large combinations outside the law to attest that legal force was a real and continuing aspect of law's functions in maintaining the political community. Of national importance were the defeat of Shays' Rebellion by the Massachusetts militia in 1786 which materially advanced the movement for a stronger central government, the vindication of the fledgling Federal Government by prompt suppression of the western Pennsylvanians' Whisky Rebellion in 1794, and the use of federal troops in the railroad strike riots of 1877 and in the Pullman strike of 1894. The greatest drama of law's force was played on the national stage over the claim of states to nullify federal acts they deemed unconstitutional and to secede from the Union as the ultimate expression of nullification. Avoided by political compromises in the Hartford Convention (1815) and in South Carolina's challenge to the federal tariff in 1833, the issue was submitted to arms in April, 1861, when the Charleston batteries fired on Fort

Sumter and President Lincoln called for 75,000 volunteers to put down combinations "too powerful to be suppressed by the ordinary course of judicial proceedings," and "to cause the laws to be duly executed."[19]

Few states are without record of use of major public force against the actual or threatened violence of private groups. The generally stable 19th century Wisconsin community, for example, saw a show of military force against opposition to the first Civil War draft in 1862 and the use of militia in the Milwaukee riots in the spring of 1886 growing out of the Eight Hour Day movement. The most sustained records of use of official force or officially sanctioned or tolerated private force against private group claims in the states occurred in the South—before the War in the armed "patrols" which operated under the constant fear of slave insurrections, after the War in official and private violence to deny Negro freedmen the vote and to keep the Negro in a subordinate social and economic status. After adoption of the 14th Amendment these impositions of official and officially tolerated violence upon the Negro—and analogous but more limited instances involving Spanish-speaking and Asiatic minority groups in the Southwest and in California—represented illegal use of official force against lawful claims of private persons. I note them here only because they formed so definite a pattern of policy that they require inclusion in any recital of the impact of law's force in the life of the society.

Save for the tragic discontinuity of the Civil War and its costly aftermath, this country achieved over 175 years of

[19] "Proclamation of April 15, 1861," in Richardson, 6 A COMPILATION OF THE MESSAGES AND PAPERS OF THE PRESIDENTS, 1789-1908, at 13 (1909).

national life with relatively little direct use of the law's force. The Civil War apart, if we look beyond the hot words of angry men to the record of action, instances of direct use of the law's violence against group violence appear as episodes and not as parts in a pattern.

Religious war was no part of United States history. From the 1820's, when Irish and German immigration first made the Roman Catholic church a substantial element among the country's religious associations, Protestant distrust of the institutional power of the Catholic church became a factor of weight in our politics. In the generation before the Civil War, Eastern cities witnessed some riotous attacks upon Catholic churches and convents. But these were local and passing incidents. In the 1850's the short-lived Know Nothing party and in the 1920's the Ku Klux Klan flourished for a time on appeal to anti-Catholic sentiment, well mixed with the fears that native white labor had for the job competition of immigrants and Negroes. These political movements carried more sinister threats of religious, national or racial disorder than had the convent burnings of the 1840's. But the longer term showed that there was a deep, emotional revulsion in our people against translating religious difference into violence. Thus, as we shall note later, law could contain Protestant-Catholic tension within measures such as the doctrine of separation of church and state which rested on the potential of law's force but did not require its direct use.

Class war was never a substantial reality in the life of the United States, though the polemics of agrarian politics and management-labor conflict sometimes sounded differently. The fears stirred in the early '80's by the German anarchist

Johann Most and the Chicago Haymarket bomb incident of May, 1886, and by the short career of the I.W.W. in the early 20th century, stood outside main currents of the country's life. Debtor farmers and striking workers were generally striving for middle-class status, conforming to the prevailing values of the society. Middle-class status meant that a man was respected for his individuality and was not subject to being pushed around by arbitrary outside force. Middle-class status meant that a man enjoyed fair opportunity to exercise his own creative initiative of mind and will—more particularly, in this market-oriented society, that he enjoyed some real bargaining power for his goods or services. Middle-class status meant that a man could fashion a private life in substantial degree, making only limited commitments to common institutions, so that he was vassal to no political creed, serf to no manor, zealot to no messiah. We were a people who believed in avoiding extremes in idea, emotion, and action. Those who set the dominant patterns of our settlement suffered the material and psychological hardships of tearing up Old World roots largely to flee extremes of poverty, of position and of political and religious dogma then familiar in England, Ireland, and the continent. The geographical and social situation of this unoccupied North America provided great room for physical movement and mobility in status. Inheritors of the Parliamentary Revolution, we put key political power in popularly elected assemblies whose natural way of business was compromise. The same political inheritance taught us faith that a healthy social environment for individuals was one in which power was widely dispersed; hence we naturally gave rein to the productive energies of the industrial revolution through large freedom for contract and property dealings in market, procedures which also daily indoctrinated men in habits of negotiation, bargain, and adjustment.

The whole pattern of our circumstances thus inclined disputing parties in the United States to a faith so deep-rooted that they rarely put it into words, that adjustments could be reached, that on the whole no group need fear that another sought its total destruction or subjugation, and hence that there was no need to adopt violence as a creed or program. Most occasions when law opposed its violence to that of private groups did not reflect the presence of irreconcilable principles or interests. Rather they reflected failures of legal order to make timely accommodation to demands of farmers or workers to be treated as sharers in the community of middle-class values. This is why, measured by the aftermath, these occasions typically proved to be episodes and not parts of a pattern of continued force.

Shays' Rebellion would not have come about, had the seaboard men who dominated the Massachusetts legislature not disregarded repeated peaceful petitions for help from the debt-ridden western counties, beset by long-depressed farm markets. The whiskey excise which provoked the outbreak of 1794 was not essential to the federal revenue, but was imposed rather as a symbol of federal authority in the back country; the violence against federal tax collectors could not go unchallenged, but it expressed the resentment which independent-minded men of small property felt toward what they interpreted as the arrogance of the wealthy East, rather than a challenge to the common legal order. Rioting railroad strikers in 1877 and 1894 were not pursuing social revolution, but venting their frustration at denial of fair chances to bargain in market for their services. Rather than a response to radical social division, the use of federal troops in 1877 and 1894 reflected the fact that neither law nor social practice had kept pace with the growth of heavy industry, to provide procedures within which management and labor might order relations which had quickly taken on a scale and impersonality quite new and posing novel issues of value.

Some of these occasions of resort to the law's direct force could have been avoided; Shays' Rebellion and the Dorr "government" were needless products of willful, shortsighted want of response by regular legal process to insistent social problems. The 1877 and 1894 railroad strikes present issues harder to assess. Given the rapidity with which new problems of industrial relations emerged, the unprepared state of popular or government opinion, the relative crudity and simplicity of existing executive processes, the want of established traditions of collective bargaining or of large-scale, well organized trade unions, we could hardly ask in 1877 or even 1894 that law meet these crises with an apparatus of Railway Labor Board, official fact finding and mediation or arbitration. For reasons hard to overcome, law will lag behind emergence of some issues which carry the threat of private violence. If the threat realized itself, the law must overcome private force with legal force. On the one hand, if we recognize that an explosion was produced by lagging adjustment of common principles to new conditions, we will avoid the error of interpreting resort to force to signify deeper divisions of principle or interest than in fact existed. On the other hand, to say that some situations of lagging legal and social adjustment were more excusable than others, because they were harder to remedy, did not mean that law must not oppose its violence to private violence. The use of law's force was costly, but the want of it would be costlier still to the values of the middle range to which this middle-class society was so firmly committed. No condition would more surely lead men to extremes of purpose and action than constant fear that any major private difference would evoke resort to force from the other party.

The secondary as well as the direct costs of violence are heavy. They are so great that reasonable men can ponder no more serious issue of legal order than whether circumstances warrant the use of force. I have suggested that the typical clash of force in this country's history was not over irreconcilable issues. This estimate requires that we study these instances of force more than we have, for the lessons they may yield about failures of efficient legal order; reconcilable conflicts should not be allowed to break into violence. Sometimes we profited rather quickly from hard lessons; Rhode Island's charter government simultaneously put down Dorr's Rebellion and called its own belated constitutional convention. Sometimes we have taken unwarranted, self-righteous satisfaction in the virtues of repairing order without sufficiently prodding our wit and energy to learn why order broke down. This was the expensive, often bloody history of developing a law of labor relations suitable to the scale and complexity of our economy. If 1877 or even 1894 were too early, yet it should not have taken us through the disorders of Lawrence and Paterson (1912), Gastonia (1929) and the South Chicago "Memorial Day Massacre" (1937) to find more constructive roles of law in this critical area of social order. If any one proposition emerged clearly from our experience of using and avoiding need of using law's force, it was this: In a society of individualist values and widely dispersed power, the failure of legal process to respond with "all deliberate speed" to deeply felt human needs or hurts could only invite costly social breakdown.[20] True conservatism lay in reasoned readiness for change.

Beyond this point, however, there always stood a final issue of the law's force. We should not allow reconcilable divisions to proceed into violence, and within the framework of this open society our experience showed that there were few, if any, truly irreconcilable divisions. But if blunder or wilfullness or fateful inability to do better brought men to a division that erupted into unsanctioned violence, the law must meet it with legitimate violence, else challenged legal order ceased to exist. Of course successful revolution might produce a desirable new legal order. But the risks were always great. "Prudence, indeed, will dictate that Governments long established should not be changed for light and transient causes. . . ."[21]

Discussion of the law's force in United States history must always return us to the massive enigma of the Civil War. The country lived through a generation of maneuver to avoid force through the flexible resources of legislative compromise. In logic there seems irreconcilable division between the positions of nullifier and constitutionalist, the exponent of indivisible Union and the advocate of the right to secede. Madison had put the case well for the need of binding federal authority:

> Every general act of the Union must necessarily bear unequally hard on some particular member or members of it, secondly the partiality of the members to their own interests and rights, a partiality which will be

[20] See Brown v. Board of Education of Topeka, 348 U.S. 294, 301, 75 S. Ct. 753, 757 (1955).

[21] THE DECLARATION OF INDEPENDENCE.

> fostered by the courtiers of popularity, will naturally exaggerate the inequality where it exists, and even suspect it where it has no existence, thirdly a distrust of the voluntary compliance of each other may prevent the compliance of any, although it should be the latent disposition of all. Here are causes and pretexts which will never fail to render federal measures abortive [if they have not compelling effect upon all].[22]

Could we have bought more time, the developing interdependence of the national domestic economy and more urgent need to present a common front in foreign affairs might have brought us to practical accommodations that would have surmounted the logical differences between Union and secession. In any case the values of national Union justified great risks. World experience before and after 1861 shows the human costs of excessive political division, and points up the incalculable values that resided in maintaining a single sovereignty over the great land mass which became the United States. Thus when the events of 1860-1861 brought secession to overt reality, there was full warrant not only in the formal requirements of legal order but also in the substantive human interests at stake, for the President to maintain Union by force. Madison had pointed to the basic subversion of order that the contrary decision would threaten: ". . . a distrust of the voluntary compliance of each other . . . [would thenceforth, otherwise] prevent the compliance of any, although it should be the latent disposition of all."

Judgments on the pre-Civil War generation are the more difficult to make, because inherently they are judgments of

[22] "Vices of the Political System of the United States" (1787), in 2 THE WRITINGS OF JAMES MADISON 361, 364 (Hunt ed. 1901).

more or less, on the degree of skill which various interests showed in exploiting opportunities of compromise within a general acceptance of the legitimacy of compromise. At least two points emerge with more clarity about Reconstruction and its aftermath, because issues were drawn in more absolute terms. First, the post-War period made plain how great were the costs to legal and social order when sustained use of force generated emotions and concepts of interest which put important questions long beyond compromise. Both to the South and to the whole country, the War's most lasting cost in legal order was artificially to channel all effective political maneuver in the South into one party. It showed the tough fibre of our representative legal order that the national political parties had been the last major associations to yield to sectional division. It showed the depth to which the costs of sustained violence reach, that we found it so hard to restore substantial diversity of political association. The one-party South spelled not only disfranchisement of the freedmen, but loss of proper voting effectiveness to white farmers, workers, and tradesmen who should have formed natural alliances with men of modest means in the North and West for a more effective balance of power amid the concentration of wealth and centralization of decision that emerged after 1870. The Populist upsurge in the South in the '90's showed the normal trend of interests. But its ultimate result was mainly to frighten Southerners of property or position into exalting the symbol of white supremacy to block an alliance of white and Negro tenant farmers. The artificial one-party system condemned the Southern Democratic Party to excessive personal factionalism and boss rule. And of course one-party rule served its prime declared purpose, to bar the Negro from the practical give and take of ordinary representative politics by which successive generations of the underprivileged in the North won their way to a share in power and standing. The region paid heavy costs for this condition in the fear which underlay its social life; the nation paid in loss of national morale and added exposure to the hazards of demagogic politics that attend all representative government. The second point which the experience of Reconstruction and its aftermath especially illuminates is the importance of a positive use of law to promote a healthy general social context, to overcome the costs of violence and the threat of its recurrence. If the United States ever needed to apply boldly the Hamiltonian multiplier principle, it was to help the South's total economy toward greater productivity and a better balance of agriculture and industry, after the War. The Radical Republican program for the freedmen showed some limited conception of the importance of creating conditions which would affirmatively help the Negro to realize his opportunities. But there was no effective leadership in Congress for such broad-scale help to the South as might have meant that the Negro's betterment would not appear simply in competition with white interests. The inherent difficulties of the situation were such as to tax the best leadership, and Lincoln's death deprived the country of its vision toward a constructive program. Not the least cost of sustained violence was that it disabled the North from a positive approach to the aftermath of war, leaving a public opinion weary, disgusted, and vengeful. Moreover, the North and West were soon so engrossed in the excitement of their own post-War expansion that by 1877 they were ready to seal the compromise by which Northern troops left the South, and national policy in substance resigned the region to its own devices. Only rarely has the use of force other than negative value, to prevent some result which would be more costly than the consequences of force. It was desirable to use force in 1861-1865 to prevent lasting disunion. But it was folly to expect to achieve positive results only from negative means. Fruitful Union required constructive investment after the law's force had preserved the opportunity for national growth. The prime default of our policy was that we did not see this, or were unable to muster the will and self-discipline to act on our wiser insights.

Through our history there was always the other realm of experience in which law used its force against violence and disorder without the law. This was the domain of the traditional criminal law, in which the state confronted the deviant individual or group whose challenge was not to the political order as such, but to social constraint upon private greed or passion.

To define or weight the functions that the force of the criminal law fulfilled in the growth of this society presents baffling problems for legal history. Challenges to general political order yield more readily to analysis. They were unique episodes, subject to appraisal in light of their special contexts, presenting events of large enough scale to be highly visible. But the excesses of private desire and emotion, the failures of private nerve or control which were the concern of the ordinary criminal law had significance for social order in their total weight and direction, not taken singly. A crime might be decisive for the individual life or the career of a private group. But if the challenge were not directly to political order, the particular offense usually had no meaning to the history of social order, save as it indicated the presence of a source of general infection. We may usefully study challenges to general political order for their particular impact. We need to generalize more widely to find meaning for social-legal history in the ordinary phenomena of crime.

Two prime difficulties confront this enterprise of generalization. First, it requires useful and dependable criminal statistics, but we have very little such data through the end of the 19th century and there is considerable dissatisfaction with the adequacy of classifications or the reliability of reporting procedures upon which the greater volume of 20th century material is based. Second, the conduct that becomes the concern of the ordinary criminal law by nature involves the interplay of self-centered or group-centered desires or feelings with values commonly held or emerging into common acceptance. Especially in a society which put the high estimate this did upon individuality and large scope for private venture, there are subtle problems in appraising these interactions of particular and general points of view. But study of the development of ideas and emotion in our culture has not yet attained the maturity that gives confidence for this undertaking.

The last point finds apt illustration in the difficulties we meet if we ask how much respect we showed for the rule of law at different stages of our development. Given a frame of representative, constitutional government, respect for law was a factor which directly affected the range and vigor with which we used the force of the criminal law.

We do not know much about the matter. It is at least clear that there were confusing crosscurrents of attitude. There were reasons in the structure of our middle-class philosophy and of our market-oriented, division-of-labor society why we had deep rational and emotional commitment to conducting life within rules and procedures set or sanctioned by law. We depended too much on mutual confidence and cooperation, on the assurance of reasonably reliable expectations of other people's behavior, to treat law lightly. We could not obtain the scope we wanted for expression of individual talent and achievement of individual status, unless we curbed the advantages which arrogance, malice, or cunning could win over the generality. There was a symbol of practical concern for the rule of law in the fact that three fourths of the support statutes in Wisconsin General Acts, 1853,—in a state still not far from frontier crudity—had to do with maintaining the structure of legal institutions.[23] On the other hand there were aspects of our character which at least created the appearance that we sometimes treated law lightly. The challenge of the opening continent and the recurrent frustrations of too little mobile capital with which quickly to exploit obvious opportunities made us chronically impatient. We wanted to get on with the job most immediately at hand. Our popular assemblies, our free religious congregations, the simplicity of our surroundings, and our need to use all the effort we could muster through government for the very tangible operations of building roads and schools and helping construct canals and railroads taught us a matter-of-fact attitude toward government; government belonged to us, and it was an instrument of utility, not an object of awe. The product of such habitual points of view was an instrumental attitude toward law—we would use it readily as a tool, and turn to another method where the job made another approach seem more useful—and a disposition of laymen to put little weight on formal processes of decision

[23] See Chapter IV, section 1, *supra.*

or action and to accept the legitimacy of contriving informal approaches to a desired end. Evangelical religion, such knobby Yankee independence as Thoreau preached, our constant practice in improvising out of scarce capital—all these factors combined to instill a confidence in individual judgment that did not easily yield to contrary official policy.

Such elements inclined us to shape or reshape official policy by the weight of informal popular practice. Thus the impatient drive for settlement in mid-19th century overleapt the federal survey and the slow procedures of public sales and issue of land patents, until Congress gave up even the form of calling the settlers squatters or trespassers and gave them legal status first as pre-emptors and then as homesteaders. So, too, in the Lake States during the lumber boom it was well nigh impossible to persuade local juries to convict men of timber trespass on the public domain. This was not because common opinion favored theft or anarchy, but because it believed that rapid economic growth was good for everyone, and hence that the sensible use of the forest was to cut it as fast as the midwest lumber market would buy the product. Analogously, in the 1920's a large-scale withdrawal of popular consent and cooperation brought an end to Prohibition. The flaunting of duly enacted public policy concerning the public domain or the public morals had serious consequences for general order; public complacency conspired with private greed and the unrestrained short-term pressures of the market to destroy the Lake States pinery; the breakdown of Prohibition cost the country much in corruption of local government and the rise of gangs whose power reached beyond ordinary crime to subvert the political process itself. Yet, so far as general attitudes are involved, these phenomena seem to show at work a costly and dangerous process of informal popular legislation, rather than disregard of legal order as such. Unscrupulous and dangerous individuals and groups cashed in on such popular attitudes to their own profit, in real contempt of legal order. This was part of the cost, but it did not show the character of popular values. One thing that such examples do suggest is the social importance of the education that law can give general opinion in the worth of adhering to formal processes of decision and the danger of blurring responsibility and concealing costs by substituting informal pressures and approaches to obtain substantive ends of large concern.

Though we lack reliable criminal statistics for most of our history, and confusing crosscurrents in popular attitudes make interpretation difficult, one trend emerges from the record in some clarity. There was a relative increase of emphasis in criminal law doctrine—and probably in criminal law administration—on invoking law's force to protect the integrity of social structure and social processes. Conversely, there was relatively less emphasis on ordinary crimes against person or property. Of course there was continuing need that law oppose its force against murder, rape, and robbery. However, the form and incidence of such classic offenses were sensitive to changes in social context. For example, violent crimes against person or property reached a peak in a northwestern Wisconsin county during the lumber era when men made up the bulk of the local population and many of them were transient workers; the relative number of such offenses fell off sharply as the county grew into a more balanced distribution of population and into quieter occupations. On the other hand, in the great cities prosecutions for serious felony increased faster than population. Moreover, in the 19th century Wisconsin lumbering county serious crimes of violence represented instances simply of individual aggression or breakdown, fostered, it is true, by crudities of the social situation, but rarely the product of calculated flaunting of legal order. But crimes of violence in 20th century metropolitan areas tended to represent more direct challenges to the rule of law; at second remove only, if not by immediate design, private violence in a metropolitan setting derived in threatening degree from organized effort—from gang organization of murder or robbery, or from gang-run gambling or narcotics traffic.

The shift of emphasis in criminal law from protection of individual interests of person or property to protection of collective interests in social structure and social processes appeared mainly, however, where the law did not have to meet the direct challenge of private violence. There was no institution outside the law on which we put more reliance for creating and administering social order, than the market. One sign of the preoccupation of criminal law doctrine with values of social structure and process was the degree to which protection of market processes came to predominate in the total category of values which we declared we would support with the force of the criminal law. Thus of 1113 distinct offenses defined in Wisconsin penal statutes in 1953, 501 (45 per cent) were crimes directly involving activity of the criminal or the victim in making a living by sale of goods or services. Of the other 612 heads of statutory crime, the bulk concerned the functioning of other social institutions: thus of these 612 heads, 256 involved the operation of government (23 per cent of the whole), 44 involved conservation of natural resources and 45 involved transport and communication. Of the whole 1113 heads of statutory crime, 241 (about 20 per cent) involved protection of interests of individual person or property. In comparison, of 240 separate heads of crime defined in the Wisconsin Revised Statutes, 1849, 44 (about 18 per cent) were offenses incident to market activity, 82 (about 34 per cent) involved the operation of government, 35 involved transport and communication (about 14 per cent—compared with about four per cent under the like category in the 1953 statutes), none concerned conservation, and 65 (about 27 per cent) involved protection of individual person or property.

The increased attention given in criminal law to security of social structure and social processes had other reflections besides the relative emphasis upon market crimes defined in state law. The number and range of federal offenses increased. In part this expressed the need for closer federal-state cooperation in policy in a more interdependent society, notably in federal offenses involving abuse of channels of interstate commerce, as for the transport of stolen goods. In large part the expanded catalog of federal crimes grew out of the growth in size and scope of market activity whose potential for harm reached beyond both the jurisdiction and the practical means of the states, as in the problems dealt with by the federal antitrust laws. A second reflection of the new emphasis on protection of social processes was the relative increase in crimes of negligence and of offenses so defined as to require no showing of any fault in the accused, compared with crimes of intent. Of the 1113 separate heads of offense defined in the Wisconsin Statutes, 1953, for example, only 407 (about 36 per cent) were so defined as to require proof of intent or reckless fault. Nearly two thirds of this catalog of statutory crimes required a showing only of ordinary negligence, or proof that the accused had performed forbidden overt acts or produced forbidden overt results. Most of the 706 statutory offenses of this type involved regulation of business, public health and safety, or the conservation of natural resources. The focus of such provisions was less upon penalizing antisocial attitudes than upon insuring the security or continuity of processes or environmental elements essential to the productivity of the society as a whole.[24]

This zeal to write into the criminal law protections for great impersonal social structures and social processes raises questions of interpretation. Where private violence flaunted legal order, there was obvious need to bring the force of the criminal law against the challenge. The point here was not that repression alone would deal with the lasting sources of trouble, but that a shield of order be provided behind which more constructive measures might be taken. Where private action threatened legitimate individual or social interests, but without violence, the criminal sanction was still necessary to deal with the stubbornly recalcitrant or those whose conduct would subvert the mutual confidence essential to operation of this market-focused, division-of-labor society. Hence we early expanded the criminal law pertaining to

[24] Except for the figures from the Wisconsin Revised Statutes of 1849—which are my own count, made for this essay—the specific references to Wisconsin penal legislation in this and the preceding paragraph are drawn from Laurent, THE BUSINESS OF A TRIAL COURT 35, tables 38 and 39 at pp. 116-17; Robinson, "Interests and Institutions Reflected in Wisconsin Penal Statutes," 1956 WIS. L. REV. 154; Remington, Robinson, and Zick, "Liability Without Fault Criminal Statutes—Their Relation to Major Developments in Contemporary Economic and Social Policy: The Situation in Wisconsin," *id.* at 625. More generally, see Conboy, "Federal Criminal Law," in 1 LAW, A CENTURY OF PROGRESS 1835-1935, at 295 (New York University School of Law ed., 1937); Hall, "The Substantive Law of Crimes—1887-1936," 50 HARV. L. REV. 616 (1937); Warner and Cabot, "Changes in the Administration of Criminal Justice During the Past Fifty Years," *id.* at 583.

commercial fraud and to breach of fiduciary relationships. However, when we extended the criminal law widely into problems of the social balance of power or the efficiency of social structure or process, there was ground to question whether we were extending the law's ultimate force into areas of regulation where it did not belong. The traditional emphasis of the criminal law was negative—repressive or at best deterrent—rather than designed affirmatively to restructure the context of action. There was reason to distrust our ready resort to the penal code to define and protect values. This was dramatic action, which conveyed the appearance of decisive resolution of problems. These features made it a type of legal action which too well fitted our native impatience and the strain of bastard pragmatism which preferred the more obvious, close-to-hand, shortly-accomplished action as compared with multi-factored, long-term planning and organization. Perhaps the expanded definitions of the criminal law which were so conspicuous a feature of 20th century legal development represented evasion of responsibility and hard thinking, and unwillingness to pay the large social overhead costs of constructive legal action.

Having raised this caution, we should also take care not to exaggerate the relative importance of the criminal law in the total range of the law's activity. Its occasional drama made the law of crimes a highly conspicuous area of legal action. But, compared for example with provisions for national defense, for public schools and roads, and compared with affirmative measures to promote public health and to develop market activity, criminal law making and administration always represented a relatively small part of the total overhead cost of legal order. Despite the enlarged scope of local, state, and federal penal legislation, criminal law administration at mid-20th century generated only a part of the overhead costs of law's regulatory activity; and the whole general overhead cost of law administration of the federal government was only about three per cent of its expenditures, that of the states about five per cent, and of local governments about nine per cent. Throughout our national life, the bulk of the law's functions concerned positive provision of aids and sustaining procedures for the productive activities of law-abiding men and women. The force aspects of law provided very important, if marginal, protections for these main currents of life, but they never constituted the principal business of government.

3

When law used its ordered violence, at best the effects were typically negative and so was the justification—that some worse consequence was avoided and opportunity preserved for more positive action. However, there were significant differences between force used and force reserved. The unused potential of the law's force could have affirmative as well as negative effect and justification. The threat of violence held in waiting might prevent trouble. Like violence realized, potential violence carried costs, but they need not have the severity of the price usually paid for overt force. Due in part to the vitality of constitutional limits and in part to good fortune, in this country men did not live repressed by constant fear of the law's threat. Moreover, the unused potential of law's force could and did have effect and warrant in helping create sources of productive action. In this aspect, through its legitimate monopoly of violence, law made major contributions to fashioning the structure and vital processes of the society.

The potential force of law had creative effect in two ways that particularly related to the value we put on wide dispersion of private and official capacity for decision. (1) Its reserved violence provided the ultimate sanction under which law legitimated a rich variety of private power. Within the values this society put on constitutional order, such an assured source for validating private power was necessary to realize full release of private energies. (2) The law's potential force provided the ultimate means to make the political process an effective, independent source of criticism and creation in social life. This independence of the political element was particularly necessary, and it particularly required institutional protection to bring about, because in the circumstances of this country's origins and growth the market and the limited range of values it promoted threatened to exert a supremacy inconsistent with the good life.

That all power to exert compulsion on men's wills must be legitimate was one of the organizing ideas which determined the social history of law in the United States. Compulsion of will touched the heart of individuality. Given the central value this culture assigned to the individual life, it followed that all such power of compulsion must be held under scrutiny. However, if the state were not totally to dominate the society, we must exercise this surveillance largely by delegation.

To be legitimate, power must serve the growth of individual life, and the source of power must in some way be held to account to criticism outside itself. This was no less true of the law than of other seats of power. We relied on a lively individualism and on large scope for private association as well as on institutional checks built into legal order, to furnish means to hold law accountable. On the other hand we relied on power mustered and directed through formal legal process to hold private power accountable; otherwise, popular distrust and resistance tended to limit realization of private energies which a substantial public opinion saw as irresponsible or threatening to achieve irresponsible command.

The next section considers the role of law's reserved force in providing the base from which the law reviewed the legitimacy of private power. The two following sections consider how the law's potential force was translated into a position of independent influence for the political process, and how we sought to protect individuals and maintain diversity of political opportunity as against abuse of law's force.

4

This country stayed fortunately free of factional, religious, or class war. It did so largely because we used the threat of law's potential force to set bounds to extreme claims of compulsion over individual lives.

The insistence that a Bill of Rights be added to the new Federal Constitution symbolized our refusal to accept absolute claims by the state. As *Brown* v. *Mississippi* reminds us, we would not admit the state's claim to pursue the individual by any effective means at its command, even when the state acted in the name of the sanctity of life.[25]

Our tradition of separation of church and state had its inconsistencies. But it worked to bar an establishment of

[25] See *supra* note 15.

religion and to forbid imposition by law of religious tests to condition the individual's exercise of his political, social, or economic capacities. In 1856-1857 a threat of federal armed force put down an anachronistic effort to maintain a theocratic state in Utah. This was the closest we came to using law's direct force to implement the separation of church and state. There were battles over the detailed definition of the principle, but we fought them out in public discussion and political maneuver and in legislatures and courts. In the 1920's a revived Ku Klux Klan moved an alarming way toward militant prosecution of anti-Catholic attitudes. There was some state legislation to curb the Klan, but the movement collapsed of internal rot before it posed sustained challenge to legal order. In over-all effect, legal sanction for separation of church and state legitimated free religious association and peaceable religious diversity in the United States, multiplying the sources for a wider range of policy initiative and policy criticism.[26]

The procedures and products of contract and property rights had honored prominence in late 18th and early 19th century constitutional guarantees and in common and statute law. Thereby we put the sanction of law's potential force behind the ventures of the entrepreneur, and the law's validation upon his social contributions. Within this assured legal framework the farmer, as producer for market, and the businessman, as manager of resources in trade and industry, won the highest prestige the society accorded any group—

[26] On the Mormons, see Hurst, "Treason in the United States," 58 HARV. L. REV. 806 at 849; on the Ku Klux Klan of the 1920's, see Hacker and Zahler, THE UNITED STATES IN THE 20TH CENTURY 241-42, 326, 327 (1952), and New York *ex rel.* Bryant v. Zimmerman, 278 U.S. 63, 49 S. Ct. 61 (1928).

higher, certainly, than common opinion assigned to public service or public office through most of the 19th century. What was "good for the farmer," what was "businesslike" or "efficient" had self-evident value. Conversely, in late 19th and early 20th century politics agrarian radicalism and Progressive middle-class revolt expressed the sharp-felt loss of status which farmers and small businessmen experienced from the rise of new concentrations of wealth in the Civil War and the generation following it. Its dignity offended, and fearing for its lost independence, the old middle class questioned the legitimacy of the new men of power who had displaced it. Dispersion of power through the market and through free private association (notably through business corporations and organized interest groups) invited emergence of new sources and styles of social influence, to the discomforture of the old. Thus the dispersion-of-power principle inherently invited the law to validate new power relations and make such adjustments of them to the old as might prevent overreaching and reduce tension by restoring security and position to those who felt threatened. From the 1870's to 1940 the growth of administrative regulation of railroads, banking, finance, and fair trade practice, the development of anti-trust doctrine, and the enactment of progressive taxes on personal and corporate income and on transfers by gift or inheritance, derived in large part from the search for acceptable terms within which law might confer legitimacy upon drastic rearrangements of private power relations.[27]

[27] As a symbol of this emphasis upon restoring, or finding a new basis for middle-class power and self-esteem, see Roosevelt, THE NEW NATIONALISM 3-5, 7-21, 23-33 (1910) (from Theodore Roosevelt's speech at the dedication of John Brown Battlefield, Osawatomie, Kansas, 1910).

The effort succeeded in a measure which warranted praise for the talent for accommodation that went into it. With only transient episodes of violence, the country grew through a revolutionary transformation of relations among different types of private power and between public and private centers of decision. The changes were not merely quantitative; the United States of 1940 was qualitatively a different society than that of 1870. To pass through such a transformation with national unity and a working morale manifest in increasing productivity of goods and services, was no mean accomplishment. To this end we relied on no technique more than upon the legitimizing functions of legal regulation. These functions rested on popular confidence that because law held in reserve the ultimate monopoly of force, it could be used to fix the terms of responsibility of private power.

We were not entitled to complacency over our success. Here, as in so many aspects of our record, complacency should be tempered by acknowledging that we enjoyed the unearned increments of good fortune. Science and technology provided the primary dynamics of the rising material productivity which time and again took the edge off otherwise sharp dissatisfactions. So the outrage of farmers and small business at the arrogance of the railroads provided no sustained political drive for effective regulation, let alone for the more drastic measure of public ownership, in the face of improved market conditions. "Trust busting" had passing tones of moral crusade. But in the long run popular opinion put too high a value on the comfortable standard of living which it associated with large-scale manufacturing and marketing to support real effort to dismantle great capital concentrations; over the years antitrust law operated rather to provide a minimum and often dubiously effective code of fair trade practice for big business than to provide a redistribution of market power into smaller units.

A rising material standard of living and habituation to life within the frame of institutions of increasing size and internal complexity turned the people in the 20th century more and more to concern with the consumption rather than the production interests of life. The strain of bastard pragmatism in our working philosophy already inclined us to be impatient or relatively indifferent toward the demands which large decisions made for sustained energies of mind and emotion. Reinforcing this influence, the consumption emphasis seemed to lessen popular concern for using law to shape acceptable terms of legitimacy of private power.

Mid-20th century seemed incapable of generating the moral energy for politics that had marked the Grangers or the Progressives. To the mid-20th century the zeal of its forerunners seemed somewhat naive. The Grangers and Progressives did show some naivete, especially in their misapplied confidence that resounding declarations of principle or dramatic changes in procedure, like the direct primary, would bring the social milennium. But they were not naive in sensing that the social and political health of this middle-class society depended upon self-respect and a sense of function and place among its members. Mid-20th century seemed itself naive, and somewhat crass, in trading this concern for creature comfort.

In fact the United States of the 1950's faced large, unresolved issues of the legitimacy of private power. In the economy, it confronted unsolved problems of the terms of legitimacy of the power wielded by self-perpetuating corporate management, and by leaders of trade unions whose membership, past the day of idealistic zeal, behaved more and more like stockholders who would not ask questions so long as dividends flowed. In the arenas of social and political debate and decision, the society confronted unsolved problems of the legitimacy of power wielded by increasingly structured, bureaucratized interest blocs. Their influence posed new problems not so much because it was more selfish than pressures exerted in the past but because it was more sustained, more potent, more conscious of its goals. These were fresh, troubling issues, and at mid-century we had not well come to grips with them. Nonetheless we had given the political process an independence among other social forces which bulwarked one great positive value—that no total, jealous ideology of creed or class or faction could readily master this fluid, diverse society.

5

So far as this society achieved the constitutional ideal—that there be no major center of power over men's wills which was not subject to substantial accountability to centers of power outside itself—the result depended as much on the relative independence of political processes from total constraint wielded by other social institutions or by any one political faction as it did on the relative independence of other social institutions from total constraint of law. Law's legitimate monopoly of violence thus served a constitutional function. It insured that law could insist effectively on reviewing the legitimacy of all other forms of social power; if power centered in some non-legal institution or some one faction met no effective check elsewhere, in the last resort it would meet check in the law. But this puts the matter in its extreme form. Law normally played this balance of power role through regulation, bargain, negotiation, adjustment, and compromise—that is, through political techniques. It was the constructive contribution of the reserved power of law—its potential but unused force—to provide the means by which political processes could operate, with resources not dependent upon the grace or favor of social, religious, or economic institutions. It was the constructive contribution of law's reserved force, also, to protect the honesty of political processes and to keep open the opportunities for diverse political expression, so that no one group could capture the whole power of the state.

In both of these respects the independent effect which political processes achieved in this society was, again, the product largely of good fortune—of an advantageous physical and social situation and a happy timing of events. Especially in legal history it does not do to neglect the large elements of unearned increment in the country's development; the presence of such factors constantly intrudes disquieting doubts whether prevailing social values, attitudes, and institutions were tough-fibred enough to stand up to severe pressure without benefit of such gifts of fortune. It is a consideration of particular point when we estimate the significance of the realized or potential force of the law.

Even in our colonial period we had the advantage of launching settlement long past the time when feudalism prevailed, with its blurring of economic, religious, and political sources of power. As a matter of timing, there was no need ever to fight out on the North American continent the question whether the state should hold supreme physical force over all other associations within its territory. The great expanse of land stretching west from the line of Atlantic settlement offered such scope for fresh venture as early to insure that neither feudal landlords nor an established church could sink firm roots against the growth of broadly representative, secular government—or, for that matter, against the manifold pulls and pressures created by the market and by free private association. The "Anti-Rent" riots and political agitation against patroon and manor lord in New York's upper Hudson Valley in the 1830's by their oddity and episodic character emphasize how far outside the main currents of our life was any serious issue between formal institutions of class or economic status on the one hand and broad-based, representative legal order on the other.[28] Likewise, our national growth came late enough so that our constitutions started with the concept that office was a public trust and not a form of private property. In practice we wavered, first under the impact of Jacksonian sentiment for wide sharing of public perquisites, later under the pressure of late 19th century plutocracy. But the central idea remained, that control of public policy was a distinct realm, not to be treated either as the property of any particular group nor as the peculiar source of honor or status for any particular group. This was an important item in

[28] Christman, TIN HORNS AND CALICO (1945), tells the story of the New York Anti-Rent movement, putting it in broad social context. That the New York agitation, despite its peculiar local setting, reflected broad and basic values of the society is indicated by references to it in the debates of the first Wisconsin constitutional convention concerning limitations on land monopoly and long-term agricultural leases. See THE CONVENTION OF 1846, at 328, 395, 449-50 (Quaife ed., 1919).

that value consensus which saved the United States from the heaviest costs of deep social division.

But the currents of growth ran too hard and fast to allow us to relax forever in the gifts of time and situation. We developed our own problems of maintaining the vitality of political processes. These grew out of the enormous success of the market, both in promoting new styles of economic power and in capturing popular imagination and individual talent away from the challenges of public policy.

The principal invention by which we resisted the tendency of the market to prevail over the political process was that of the national political party. The range of interests a party must accommodate to capture the Presidency and effective power in Congress tended to focus the national parties on men and office rather than on ideological divisions. This condition worked to enhance the independent power of the politician.

Our parties were mainly products of informal contrivance. In this lay sources of danger, for the informal organization of power too easily allows blurring or hiding responsibility. We saw this danger realized in the irresponsible power which the city political boss achieved in the late 19th century by exploiting the dislocations of urban life and regimenting the votes of relatively recent immigrants. We saw the danger realized in more direct relation to the challenge of the market through free use of money in electing wealthy men or their agents to high office, climaxed in the '90's when popular leaders could attack the Senate as a rich men's club. The reality of the market's competition with politics provided the basis of political reform movements at the turn of the century. The appeals which Robert M. LaFollette and Theodore Roosevelt made to the public conscience were largely appeals to the professional and entrepreneurial middle class of modest means, to put aside preoccupation with private affairs and dedicate energy and concern to public decision making. Favored political prescriptions of the Progressives—the direct primary, the short ballot, the initiative, referendum, and recall—were devices designed not only to give more leverage to the average voter, but also to curb the influence of informal (boss) government by increasing resort to more formal and hence openly responsible procedures of public decision. The devices proved relatively disappointing in effect. The direct primary, in particular, had ambiguous implications for popular government; by tending to increase the costs of campaigning it may well have done more to increase than to reduce the political power of private wealth. On the other hand, it probably strengthened the two-party system by reducing the need to organize third parties as instruments of reform and revolt, and thereby strengthened the independence of the professional politician—concerned with men and offices—against the divisiveness of focused ideologies or interests.

If some of the reformers' procedural devices worked with less dramatic effect than their proponents had hoped, this was perhaps because the reformers depended too much on specific contrivances to deal with conditions which only very general, situation-shaping measures could affect. The competition between market and forum for talent and loyalties, the unsettlement of values and functions attending the growth of metropolitan areas and the declining social and economic influence of rural life, the rapid concentration of control over invested capital and the loss of self-sufficiency of individuals caught up in intricately interdependent patterns of social organization—such factors challenged us to use law to maintain and re-create social order, but they also imposed upon political processes institutional tensions too great to be resolved by any particular voting devices. Yet the reformers grasped a sound principle when they focused upon the formal organization of power. This emphasis re-enlisted traditional values by which we had defined the distinctive character of law in this society—its review of all arrangements of power, its constitutionalism and insistence on procedural regularity, its role in resource allocation. Its formal structure gave law—and the organized political process which law supported—their most abiding influence. In established forms men found symbols to which they could give loyalty; within recognized forms of order could grow offices, procedures, and the professional morale that developed from sustained attention to defined functions; the existence of acknowledged forms for allocating and using power minimized occasions of irreconcilable conflict and thus enabled those holding formally sanctioned power to consolidate its influence by custom, precedent, and utility.

The political process fell to its low of social influence in the '70's and '80's, having retreated before the rising prestige of the market since the 1830's. However, partly by plan and partly by circumstance from the late 19th century we developed general forms within which public policy making again became a significant independent source of creative energies. The invention of the electorate as a distinct legal organ was the foundation on which Western culture erected the independence of constitutional political processes. On the whole we strengthened this foundation by extending the suffrage. True, the more who held the vote, the greater might be the number of the venal, ignorant, or weak who could be manipulated to serve the informal government of boss or moneyed interest. But it was also true, as Jefferson had pointed out, that a larger electorate enjoyed more independent power, if only because its size more heavily taxed the resources of those who would control it.[29] The right to vote and to hold office proved also to be one of the most potent means by which the underprivileged levered their way into higher status and a larger share of the material and psychological satisfactions the society could provide. The emotion and violence with which the South denied the vote to the Negro attested how real was the independent influence which the political process could achieve by extended suffrage. All this was familiar in our tradition. We added a new factor of great effect in the late 19th century when we adopted the secret ballot. This simple amendment of formal legal process enormously increased the practical power of the electorate over boss, magnate, or interest group. Indirectly it increased the role of the more continuously operating agencies—legislature, executive, and courts—by bringing control of parties and elections more fully under the control of the state. There were still election frauds. The indifference of voters continued to give leverage to boss and money. But the combination of an extended electorate and a secret ballot substantially reduced the possibilities of close manipulation. If this development also invited new styles of informal manipulation through mass media of communication, the fact did not negate gains made

[29] See "Notes on the State of Virginia (1781)," in THE COMPLETE JEFFERSON 567, 669 (Padover ed., 1943).

but simply reminded that we should expect no final solutions to the control of power.

From about 1900 two developments in the legislative and executive branches added much to the independent influence of political process as compared with other sources of decision making. Broad trends in the economy and in social organization helped create these legislative and executive developments.

Through the first three quarters of the 19th century, scarcity of mobile capital was a factor which made it difficult and even dangerous—as the Whisky Rebellion testified—to raise substantial public revenues from taxation. Toward the end of the century, the surge and cumulation of productivity made this less a limiting factor on the scope of legislative policy. As government made bolder use of the tax power, it expanded its range of services (as in providing education, roads, sanitation, and research affecting health and promotion of markets) and regulations (as of marketing practices, finance and credit, land use, and conditions of labor). Government's readier command of money gave to public policy some of the flexibility for growth and experiment that characterized the market. At the same time the growth of division of labor and specialization of functions made men more aware how much the gains and costs of social life depended upon the state of relations—complementary or competitive—among various interests. This awareness inclined them to turn more to law. Law's conceded functions included reviewing the over-all distribution of power in the society; hence the legal forum was the natural place of resort for argument of values which ranged beyond the frame of reference of any one social institution or social process.

Greater legislative activity naturally fostered growth of executive offices and independent administrative agencies. Moreover, this development on the executive side took on life of its own and made its own powerful contribution to the greater independence of the political process. From feeble beginnings in the '70's civil service reform grew to large importance in national and state government by mid-20th century. Civil service sheltered much uninspired routine. But it also symbolized the entrance of the competent career man in public service. In both its routine and its professional aspects the enlargement of civil service bore witness that the executive branch had become a greater institution of social control with its own momentum, its own growing power of specialized knowledge and its own vested interests. Thus, supported by law's reserved force, the tax collector provided a new range of independent action for the legislature, while an expanded field of regulatory and services legislation combined with more exacting demands of social function to increase the sustained influence of the executive and administrative arms. However one evaluated the substantive product of these trends, there could be no doubt that by mid-20th century they represented a much greater public consciousness of the state, and an extent of independent influence of the political process beyond any counterpart in 19th century United States history.

6

To maintain the independence of the political process and yet hold it to creative service to individual life required that we organize power to prevent total capture of the state by any one faction or interest or the abuse of its force by its own ministers. This concern was in our classic political tradition. We recognized that political control could be in itself a distinct object and instrument of ambition, greed, or fear, as much as religious, economic, racial, or national power. Hence, Madison observed, "The great desideratum in Government is such a modification of the sovereignty as will render it sufficiently neutral between the different interests and factions, to controul one part of the society from invading the rights of another, and at the same time sufficiently controuled itself, from setting up an interest adverse to that of the whole Society."[30] There was the more need to check the power held by law, because the law's functions required that it hold the ultimate means of violence, which because of their appeal to will over reason and to destructive over disciplined feeling offered peculiar prizes to men's dark desires and fears.[31] To these reasons deep in man's nature the growth of this society into more and more complex interdependence of parts added further cause for concern,

[30] Madison, *supra* note 22, at 368.

[31] Compare John C. Calhoun: "But Government, although intended to protect and preserve society, has itself a strong tendency to disorder and abuse of its powers, as all experience and almost every page of history testify. The cause is to be found in the same constitution of our nature which makes government indispensable. The powers which it is necessary for government to possess, in order to repress violence and preserve order, cannot execute themselves. They must be administered by men in whom, like others, the individual are stronger than the social feelings. And, hence, the powers vested in them to prevent injustice and oppression on the part of others will, if left unguarded, be by them converted into instruments to oppress the rest of the community. That by which this is prevented, by whatever name called, is what is meant by CONSTITUTION, in its most comprehensive sense, when applied to GOVERNMENT." "The True Nature of Constitutional Government," in 1 THE PEOPLE SHALL JUDGE 676, 679 (Univ. of Chic. ed. 1949) (from "A Disquisition on Government").

because now force exerted at the center or at a few key points in the interlocking structure might command the whole.

Four principles represent the safeguards we built into formal legal process, so that the law's legitimate monopoly of violence might not be subverted to destroy rather than protect constitutional order. These principles included civil control of the military, restraints on political disqualification, protection of limited political commitment and provision of procedures for calling to account all forms of civil authority.

(1) *Civil control of the military.* "The military shall be in strict subordination to the civil power," Wisconsin's constitution makers declared in 1848.[32] They spoke in a firm tradition. An army was the type of legally organized violence which might most decisively overawe the community. Our English and Revolutionary inheritance left their stamp on our constitutional tradition in clear-cut assertions that military power must always be subject to direction by civilians. Representative legislative bodies must supply the funds and civilian chief executives should be the commanders in chief of the national forces or the state militia. Only Congress might declare war. Congress might not allow the executive to build up permanent armed force beyond its recall; no appropriation for the army might be for a longer term than two years. It was significant that the basic assertions of civilian control ran in terms of legislative and executive action. When large issues were at stake, only the legislature's

[32] Wis. Const. art. I, § 20. It is significant that this and other declarations of fundamental individual rights in the constitution expressed principles of such common acceptance that they received no debate in the constitutional convention. See Brown, "The Making of the Wisconsin Constitution," 1952 WIS. L. REV. 23, 57.

power of the purse and its authority of investigation and only the status of the chief executive as steward of the commonwealth would suffice to control the power of arms. The courts were cautious in reviewing legislative or executive determinations of the need to invoke military force. The judges acted with most assurance to protect the jurisdiction of civil tribunals against imposition of trial of civilians by military courts where civil courts could operate.[33]

The formal pattern of values was clear enough. What was not clear was how deeply these values engaged popular understanding and concern. For most of our national life the shield of two oceans and the want of an aggressive foreign power on our continent allowed us to hold the standing army to the size of a reserve police force. The sweep and scale of domestic economic growth furnished ample vent for aggressive ambition. It was symbolic that through many years the elite branch of the army was the Corps of Engineers, concerned mainly with internal improvements. Thus we created no large military bureaucracy, and though a military record was a political asset, we did not create a class which saw the military establishment as its avenue to status and power. On the other hand, there were disquieting instances in which general opinion under stress of fear for the common security accepted stronghanded use of military force to supplant civil power. This was so of the executive suspension of habeas corpus in the Civil War; and though the Supreme Court finally condemned the resort to military tribunals in areas where the courts were functioning, its decision did not come until after the extreme tensions of

[33] See U.S. Const. art. I, §§ 8(1), 8(11)-(16), and 10(3); art. II, § 2; art. IV, § 4; amends. II, III, V, and VI. *Cf. Ex parte* Milligan, 71 U.S. (4 Wall.) 2 (1866).

war were past. There appeared no substantial popular concern when in 1944 the Supreme Court upheld the authority of Congress to provide for forcible removal of citizens from their homes for detention in camps under military control, to preserve the security of military zones defined by order of the President, the Secretary of War or a military commander designated by the Secretary.[34] Moreover, from the outbreak of World War II through the succeeding tensions of the cold war, the national government for the first time in our history was impelled to create a standing military establishment of a size great enough to become a major influence in the over-all economy. This establishment possessed centralized force whose destructive capabilities could give it such command in the society as had never before been within reach of the military. The size of the mid-20th century national defense effort, the increasingly specialized scientific and technical knowledge which conditioned major decisions on defense expenditure, and the security restrictions put on the flow of information about the development and execution of policy were factors which made it more and more difficult for Congress effectively to use its powers of purse and investigation, and even for the President as commander in chief, to assure full civil control of military policy. Among indications of new-felt concern over these issues were the creation of the National Security Council in 1947, reorganizations of the Defense Department in 1949 and 1953, numerous hearings of Congressional committees, President Truman's recall of General MacArthur and the hearings on

[34] See *Ex parte* Merryman, 17 Fed. Cas. 144 (No. 9, 487) (C.C.D. Md. 1861); *Ex parte* Milligan, *supra* note 33; Korematsu v. United States, 323 U.S. 214, 65 S. Ct. 193 (1944); Duncan v. Kahanamoku, 327 U.S. 304, 66 S. Ct. 606 (1946).

this action conducted jointly by the Senate Armed Services and Foreign Relations committees in 1951, and the zeal shown to maintain the state National Guards as a system of some dispersed military power to check force held at the center.[35] Plainly legal history was fast in the making in this area in the second half of the 20th century. There was danger that in the face of quite novel problems and a wholly different reality of challenge to civilian control than we had ever had to meet, we would rest too confident in an historic tradition which in fact had never been put to much test.

Civilian control of law's disciplined armed force presented another problem more pervasive and closer to ordinary affairs than direction of the military. The more common issue was civilian control of the police, who in proportion to their efficiency took on the character of semi-military organizations. The problem existed also with reference to correctional authorities—custodians of prisons and hospitals for the criminal insane.

For the most part immediate control of the police lay in town or village, county, or city legislative and executive officers. This story is but one of the many aspects of local legal history which wait writing. Many police operations require much initiative and discretion of individual officers. Thus the greatest contribution local civilian direction could make to responsible police work was to provide the conditions of qualification, training, pay, promotion, and tenure which would build that professional morale that leads an institution to exact high standards of itself and impose self-

[35] See Huntington, THE SOLDIER AND THE STATE 337, 375, 405, 422 (1957); Millis, Mansfield, and Stein, ARMS AND THE STATE 266, 282, 317-32 (1958).

discipline. Probably as we learn more of this aspect of local legal history we shall conclude that the achievements and shortcomings of civilian control of the police rested mainly in this factor, and that as late as mid-20th century this was a major area in which we defaulted on imagination and on willingness to pay the overhead costs of good legal order.

This aspect apart, civil control of the police was exercised mainly through the courts. State legislatures did more to create than to solve problems of controlling the discretion of enforcement officers. From the late 19th century, state legislation turned increasingly to criminal sanctions to implement policies that were better pursued by more affirmative means. The sheer multiplication of items of penal law increased the opportunities, indeed the necessity, for police and prosecutors to exercise discretion where to apply their force. As the volume of penal legislation increased, it was the more important regularly to review the statute book as a whole to eliminate obsolete provisions, and to maintain some fair consistency and balance among definitions of crimes and assignments of penalty. But in no respect did law revision lag more than in this. Likewise there were common, serious deficiencies in the quality of new matter added. Legislatures were prone to react out of quick alarm or righteous indignation to a particular phenomenon, without spelling out adequately the range of values involved, as for example in broad condemnations of gambling which did not square with community practice in distinguishing social from professional gambling. To some extent—as perhaps in the matter of gambling—draftsmen introduced calculated vagueness into penal statutes, to hedge against evasion. This was understandable, but such drafting did nothing to answer the problems of controlling police discretion. Statutes commonly failed to spell out whether the elements of a given offense included intent or some degree of negligence, or whether the offense was made out simply on proof that the accused's behavior had produced forbidden overt results. To require proof of a mental element was an effective substantive limit upon the scope of offenses; uncertainty in this element of definition thus greatly enlarged the freedom with which enforcement officers might fashion the practical content of the criminal law.

Such considerations highlight the role of the courts in limiting enforcement discretion and imposing at least minimum standards of enforcement performance. The courts wielded control of the police indirectly by holding unconstitutional as in violation of due process of law statutes whose unreasonably vague terms were deemed to give no fair warning of what they prohibited, or more often by giving a restrictive interpretation to the coverage of broadly framed penal legislation. The courts wielded more direct control of policing standards by enforcing Bill of Rights guarantees such as those against unreasonable search and seizure and self-incrimination, by excluding confessions or admissions shown to have been procured by physical or mental torture (as in *Brown* v. *Mississippi*),[36] and by insisting generally on observance of the procedural rights of the criminal accused on trial. Here, again, we lack the detailed studies which would allow us confidently to weigh the meaning and effect of civil control of the police. If we regard only appellate court opinions, we might plausibly conclude that courts imposed substantial limits on police and prosecution conduct.

[36] See *supra* note 15.

But this does not prove how broad was the carry-over in trial court practice, nor how far-reaching was the effect on police operations in the field. Conversely, we lack studies by which to evaluate criticisms, by police and prosecutors, that much appellate court doctrine rested on unrealistic assumptions of fact about problems of urban law enforcement and on unsound weighting of the relative interests of suspected persons and the community. This was an area of legal order that called as much as any for sustained, able legislative investigation; the want of such inquiry was one of the most telling indications how far the legislative branch fell short of realizing its creative possibilities as grand inquest of the state.

(2) *Limits on political disqualification.* The state must possess the legitimate monopoly of violence, but no one faction might monopolize the state. To hold the state's force accountable, men must be able to form and re-form political alignments and to accomplish peaceful transfers of power according to legitimated forms of decision and succession. Thus individuals must have legally recognized and protected access to political participation; those in power must not be able to exclude their opponents from the arena of peaceful political maneuver.

To this end we fixed in the Federal Constitution a limited definition of treason. Treason should consist only in levying war (that is, organizing violence against legitimate domestic legal order) or giving aid to foreign foes; those in power might not eliminate political opposition on charges of "constructive" treason. Likewise the Federal Constitution forbade Congress or the states to pass any bill of attainder or ex post facto law, lest a successful faction permanently seal its victory by despoiling the lives or fortunes of its opponents. Federal and state constitutions forbade that any religious test be made a qualification to public office or trust; no sect might formally engross the secular power. Constitutional guarantees of trial by jury interposed between the accused and the zeal of the executive an agency drawn fresh for each occasion from the body of the community, and so presented another curb on political use of the penal law by those entrenched in power.[37]

Conversely, we protected men in office from the worst excesses of political malignity by providing procedures of legislative trial on impeachment or joint address as the sole methods of removing a man from office short of the natural term of his tenure. The failures to convict upon the impeachment of Mr. Justice Chase (1805) and President Johnson (1868) set precedents of constitutional practice, that impeachment should not lie simply for differences of political policy of however high degree. We conferred on federal and state legislators an absolute constitutional privilege against criminal or civil liability for words spoken in legislative debate, as we conferred absolute privilege upon judges with regard to their disposition of cases.[38]

Because we trusted to the electorate to enforce ultimate responsibility upon government, and designed that the electorate do so chiefly through its delegates in the legislature with their powers of purse and inquiry, we declared as constitutional principle that legislative representation should

[37] See U.S. Const. art. I, §§ 9 (2)-(3), 10(1); art. III, §§ 2 (3), 3; art. VI; Wis. Const. art. 1, §§ 3, 5, 7, 10, 12, and 19.

[38] See U.S. Const. art. I, §§ 2 (5) and 3 (6)-(7); art. II, § 4; Wis. Const. art. VII, §§ 1 and 13; Hurst, THE GROWTH OF AMERICAN LAW: THE LAW MAKERS 69, 415-16 (1950).

be reasonably proportioned to population. Generally we relied on the political process to enforce this prescription, though state appellate courts supplemented the political sanction by asserting and cautiously using the power, on direct attack, to invalidate an apportionment which grossly offended fairness. The political process worked with much imperfection to correct inequalities in legislative representation. Indeed, there was no more common or serious invasion of the principle of fair access to the political process than by the gerrymander or by simple refusal or neglect of state legislatures to make prompt reapportionment following changes of population. True, the nature of the conflicting interests changed over time; in an earlier day the typical conflict was between older settlements and the under-represented back country; in the 20th century the tension was typically between rural and metropolitan areas. Whatever the content of conflict, legislative apportionment was continuously the area of greatest violation of the principle against political disqualification.[39]

(3) *Protection of limited political commitment.* We used law to help maintain the independence of the political process, and so to guard life against total compulsions upon it in the name of faith, class, or economic interest. It was the counterpart of this value that no man be compelled by law to surrender whole other aspects of his life as hostages for his political conduct. The political process must only rarely be allowed to exert total compulsion; the individual should not have to pay legal forfeit of freedom of his person,

[39] See State *ex rel.* Attorney General v. Cunningham, 81 Wis. 440, 51 N.W. 724 (1892); Hurst, *supra* note 38, at 41-43, 237-39.

his religion, or his fortune for the vote he cast, the candidate he supported, the petition he signed, the office he sought.

The most aggressive forces in politics typically seek expression through legislation or executive order, for in the legislature and executive reside the authority and means for law's most positive action. Hence it was natural that the constitution makers and the courts made the principal contributions to doctrine favoring limited political commitments. They built upon the solid base of our written and unwritten constitutional principle that a healthy society was one in which there was broad dispersion of all types of decision making capacity. It was a functional corollary of this idea that men should be protected in making only limited commitments of themselves to the political realm. However, the corollary was so basic in our attitudes toward the state that it was not often openly challenged and so was not often expressed. We must read it in the implications of other legal principles.

Perhaps the most pervasive expression of the policy protecting limited political commitment was in the insistence that law's proper concern was only with men's overt acts and not with their inner thought or feeling. This was the common base of the common law and the statute law of crimes and torts. It found constitutional expression in the protection of free speech and religion. Constitutional and judicial doctrine requiring reasonable equality in the levy and assessment of taxes was an important protection of men's limited commitment to public affairs. Control of discriminatory taxation had special importance for the principle of limited political commitment insofar as it protected a free press against fiscal counterattack by those in power. Political retaliation by local machines through unequal property tax assessments or unequal enforcement of licensing laws was probably the commonest invasion of the principle of limited commitment. The principle found expression also in the law's favor toward unlicensed private association. At least from the time of Chief Justice Shaw's opinion for the Massachusetts court in *Commonwealth* v. *Hunt,* it was sound doctrine that the state might proceed against a private association only on a showing that the association existed for an unlawful purpose or worked by unlawful means. Moreover, the law did not generally recognize guilt by mere association; to subject the individual member to penalty for unlawful conduct of an organization, the state must show that the individual directly participated in or lent his consent to the illegal activity.[40]

Like the policy of civil control of the military, the principle favoring limited political commitment existed for most of our history more as a tacitly assumed premise of the common life than as a doctrine well and repeatedly defined

[40] See the reflections of history and the varied evaluations of interests involved in the regulatory device of the test oath in American Communications Ass'n, C.I.O. v. Douds, 339 U.S. 382, 70 S. Ct. 674 (1950). Control of taxation to protect limited political commitment is explored in Grosjean v. American Press Co., 297 U.S. 233, 56 S. Ct. 444 (1936), and in Murdock v. Pennsylvania, 319 U.S. 105, 63 S. Ct. 870 and 891 (1943). On the distinction between providing legal remedies against particular discrimination in tax assessment and denying judicial intervention to halt the regular legislative process of providing for the ordinary overhead costs of legal order, see Bi-Metallic Investment Co. v. State Board of Equalization of Colorado, 239 U.S. 441, 36 S. Ct. 141 (1915). Support for the prima facie legality of private association is indicated by Commonwealth v. Hunt, 45 Mass. (4 Met.) 111, 38 Am. Dec. 346 (1842); De Jonge v. Oregon, 299 U.S. 353, 57 S. Ct. 255 (1937). The disfavor shown to guilt by association is expressed in Schneiderman v. United States, 320 U.S. 118, 63 S. Ct. 1333 (1943), and in Wieman v. Updegraff, 344 U.S. 183, 73 S. Ct. 215 (1952).

under fire. Thus we were ill-prepared when the principle emerged into sharp controversy under the stresses of the second quarter of the 20th century. The law of boycott reflected some of the new strain, as courts confronted cases where there was organized withdrawal of economic relations to enforce social or political claims.[41] Government posed its own challenge to the principle. Reviving the 16th and 17th century atmosphere of the test oath in the name of national security, the United States extended loyalty probes into the private lives not only of ordinary public employees but also of employees of government contractors and men compelled into public service by military draft.[42] The claims for national security were real and had their area of validity. On the other hand, there was costly experience of past intolerance behind the idea that the individual should be protected in making only limited commitments to the political realm of life. As we entered the second half of the 20th century, we were perforce making new legal history in this matter. As we did so, we were paying a price in dispute, suspicion, and inefficiency for want of assured definition of our principles.

(4) *The accountability of civil authority.* The least costly, and in the long run most effective, way to control law's force from abuse was not by matching high constitutional doctrine against crisis but by more everyday means to

[41] See "The Common-Law and Constitutional Status of Anti-Discrimi nation Boycotts," 66 YALE L. J. 397 (1957).

[42] See Edgerton, Circuit Judge, dissenting in Bailey v. Richardson, 182 F. 2d 46, 66, 72-74 (D.C. Cir. 1950), discussing the value conflicts involved in loyalty clearance of public employees. *Cf.* Greene v. McElroy, 360 U.S. 474, 79 S. Ct. 1400 (1959) (employee of government contractor).

keep government responsive to needs and tensions as they arose in the common life. Such was the teaching of Dorr's Rebellion, and by analogy of the Homestead riot and the *Debs* case. The conditions of good legal order were laid as much in the formal and informal processes by which we held to account the ordinary course of official action, as in more dramatic clashes of power and interest.

This is another respect in which legitimacy is a key concept. It was a substantial success for decency in our legal order, that we developed a wide array of legitimated procedures by which critics and protestants might require that official power show its warrant. Because legitimated procedures of inquiry and objection were available, men could make timely question of the justification for official action, and press their points, without on each occasion generating crisis or perforce yielding their small power before the weight of formal institutions.

To exercise this leverage upon established power was one function of the electorate, given flexibility by the invention of political parties and the legal guarantees of free press, free speech, assembly, and petition. This was a function, likewise, of the legislature's control of the public purse and its power to inquire into executive conduct. It was a function of the chief executive's veto and the veto which each house of a two-chamber legislature held over the other. It was a function for which statutes conferred investigative powers on independent administrative agencies.

Procedures to call official power to account sometimes worked through large-scale mobilization of opinion, feeling, and will. However, mostly we depended on individuals and relatively small groups to provide the initiative, intelligence, sustained energy and courage to make these procedures have effect. Men in numbers did not generate fresh insight, disciplined emotion, or the nerve for independent decision. But, given legitimate procedures of enlistment, they could be rallied to support creative leadership. It was a basic contribution of law's reserved force to protect the free political process, the parliamentary procedures, and the executive stewardship which allowed leaders, critics, and dissenters to make their voices heard above the crowd.

Because operation of procedures to check official power depended on individuals or small groups, this aspect of legal history highlights the position of the courts and the bar. If there has been exaggeration of judicial law making, there is not exaggeration in rating high the part the courts and the bar played in reviewing official action. Litigious procedures placed the power of the state in aid of individuals and small groups to draw issues into focus, elicit evidence in orderly fashion, bring opposing testimony to cross-examination, and pursue reasoned argument of values. Political, legislative and executive processes were serviceable primarily to leadership in making or criticizing the general terms of policy. The judicial process and lawyers' work auxiliary to the judicial process through counsel and advocacy were serviceable primarily to bring general policy under examination in particular context. This was a point of view essential to this constitutional legal order. Litigation and lawyers' work connected with it served to enforce the responsibilities of legal order to interests other than those of government. The availability of an independent bar, supported by private retainer, bulwarked the courage of individuals and groups to put officials upon their proof and justification, and provided more skill and knowledge than private persons typically could muster otherwise to meet the maneuvers of official power. There was testimony to the leverage which the judicial process could afford private individuals and groups against the state in doctrines by which courts limited the help they would give particular claimants. A litigant must show both a specific interest in fact and in law in the issue of public policy on which he sought a court's ruling. Even had he such an interest, he might not have a court decision upon a question—such as the legitimacy of a state government, in *Luther* v. *Borden*—which the courts believed suitable for decision only by political processes. Generally a statute would be presumed constitutional; to persuade the court to treat it as invalid, the litigant must sustain the burden of showing that reasonable legislators could not have found the facts or made the choices of value necessary to make the statute a reasonable means to serve a public interest. A suitor might be held estopped to contest the constitutionality of a statute under which he had sought and obtained a benefit. Where contemporary, long-continued, consistent practice of administrators had put working content into ambiguous statutory terms, the judges would give substantial weight to this practical construction against a contrary reading by a particular litigant.[43] So judicial doctrine sought to accommodate the checks which particular interest might

[43] The doctrines of judicial self-limitation which implicitly testify to the extent of power the judicial process might potentially afford individuals or groups in checking government processes are well noted in various facets in Luther v. Borden, *supra* note 2; Buck v. Kuykendall, 267 U.S. 307, 316, 45 S. Ct. 324, 326 (1925); Norwegian Nitrogen Products Co. v. United States, 288 U.S. 294, 315, 53 S. Ct. 350, 358 (1933); and in the concurring opinion of Brandeis, J., in Ashwander v. Tennessee Valley Authority, 297 U.S. 288, 341, 56 S. Ct. 466, 480 (1936).

put on official power, to the social interest that government be capable of positive decision and generalization of policy; the considerable judicial effort that went into maintaining the accommodation bore witness that the opportunities which litigation afforded the challenger of state action could have material effect in the over-all balance of power.

7

The possession of the legitimate monopoly of violence was the means of influence most specific to law, but it was only one of an array of legal techniques which grew in number and diversity over the years. Moreover, law had social influence through this means typically because it held potential force rather than because it used force. The complement of these propositions was the trend to increase preventive compared with reparative uses of legal power. The point may be put with somewhat different emphasis. In increasing measure we employed law to affect social situations by indirection rather than by direct action, or by helping organize relations which would induce desired conduct or make it the easier to pursue, instead of relying on admonition and penalty.

The outstanding symbol of the stress on preventive law was the wider use of licensing and administrative rule making under statutory delegation. The expansion of the service roles of government showed the law's influence by indirection, or by structuring men's situations to induce or facilitate desired behavior. Government's practical monopoly of key informational services, like the census or the weather bureau, and public subsidies for development of bulk transport and mail carriage were the oldest, most continuous examples of ways in which by indirection we used law to affect the development of the economy. Originating somewhat later, the large-scale public provision of highways and public schools represented very influential techniques for affecting the course both of economic and social activity without much direct command. Behind all such styles of preventive and indirect legal influence lay the expansion in use of taxation and public spending as prime instruments of law's social effects. Money was neutral and flexible, and with growing funds at its disposal, government could act in the 20th century with a range, flexibility, and pervasive influence unknown in the 18th or 19th century United States. Back of the tax collector stood the law's force, but fiscal techniques worked in an expanding economy with a relative smoothness which moved the underlying force factor farther and farther into the background.

When law explicitly defined standards of conduct or sought to fix the limits of power relations—as in regulation of public utilities or market practices or the concentration of private economic power—the fact that law's peculiar sanction was its command of force was nearer the front of attention. But even in its regulatory features, law tended to apply direct compulsion less and operate the more by organizing situations to induce desired action or at least to reduce the sharp pinch of grievance. This effort to regulate situations by structuring them was involved, for example, in the growth in prominence of the consent decree in antitrust law, the trade practices conference procedure of the Federal Trade Commission, the use of advisory committees drawn from the regulated field by federal and state administrative agencies especially in the area of labor regulation, the negotiated character of much of the regulation of rates and quality of service of public utilities and the insurance industry. Perhaps the most widely felt type of legal regulation in the economy at large was wielded by indirection when government acted to affect the availability of money and credit and investment capital. Law operated so through Congress' control of the currency and bank reserve requirements, through the decisions of the Treasury on public borrowing and of the Federal Reserve System on costs of lendable funds, or through the joint control of the Federal Reserve Board and the Securities and Exchange Commission over margin trading on the stock exchange. Again, we are brought back to the enormous increase in flexibility of government action and the extension of its potential influence that attended the larger use of fiscal means of control.

That the direct use of law's force should be relatively rare and even the threat of its reserved force be held typically in the background were conditions desirable for efficiency and functional in the kind of society we developed. The use of force was costly, especially in its secondary and often unforeseen consequences; the effectiveness of law's potential force depended on husbanding it, for except when it was mobilized against extreme crisis it typically rested on resources very limited compared to the general resources of the society. The functional integrity of a high division-of-labor society in which individual and collective life depended on continuity in an intricate flow of relations would not consist with much direct use of force or with pervasive fear of the realization of potential force.

Nonetheless there were disquieting aspects to the fact that law operated more and more blandly, by indirection and inducement and complex organization of situations, with the underlying basis in force more and more covered up and forgotten in ordinary opinion. If the best safeguard against abuse of law's force was to keep law responsive to main currents of the common life, this responsiveness nevertheless required that the common life include some responsiveness to the facts of public policy making and administration. However, the indirection and technical specialization of 20th century legal order posed mounting difficulties for obtaining public understanding, and—more basic—for enlisting the necessary minimum of motive at least among a substantial body of opinion leaders to maintain knowledge of the practical nature and directions of legal order. Two factors of government operations especially increased these difficulties. One was the greater prominence of the budget and of fiscal measures generally among the methods of legal influence. Lay opinion could dramatize and understand in dramatic terms public issues that took form in direct regulation of conduct; the classic pattern of representative control upon abuses of public or private power was the conflict of "good" men versus "bad" men, of Jackson against the Bank, the Grangers against the railroads, the Progressives against the trusts. It was harder to understand, and almost impossible to dramatize, techniques of legal influence that expressed themselves through the incidence of taxation or the relative allocations of dollars to highways as compared with schools or public welfare institutions. Closely related was the fact that the development of more indirect and technical types of legal operation made inside knowledge and experience an increasing source of official power as against the increasing ignorance of the outsiders. The common inclusion of public information officers in the tables of organization of mid-20th century public agencies reflected disquiet over the questions of legitimacy that this development created. But there was evidence that this device could work as much to help hoard knowledge and withhold facts as to improve the representative quality of an agency's performance.

We could not afford to forget the basis of force on which legal order rested. Under constitutional limitations, the law's legitimate monopoly of force guaranteed peaceful continuity of succession in the management of the society, contributed to release productive energies by reducing constraints of fear and distrust, provided ultimate safeguards of the conditions of social context needed to maintain a highly organized common life, and promoted a vital community of interests by helping secure men against the control of any total ideology or interest. But because law held the ultimate means of violence, possession of the state was itself a natural prize of ambition, greed, and passion. We could not rest complacent in the faith that our constitutional tradition provided all the security we needed against abuse of official power. The range and depth of social change at mid-20th century posed new questions of the relevant content of constitutional limitations upon the force of law which required answer in terms relevant both to contemporary reality and to the teachings of our experience.

Sources

The footnotes in this volume identify only material quoted in the text or illustrative material of such special character that the reader might have difficulty in tracing it. The purpose of the essays is to suggest themes which offer fruitful results in the development of United States legal history research. Because most of the material invoked to this end deals with events or trends familiar to readers possessing a general knowledge of the country's history and legal order, more elaborate citation would serve little use.

On the other hand, I am conscious of debts owed many people for instruction in this effort (1) to find relevance for legal history in the work of men of other disciplines than law and (2) to present legal history in aspects which may render it more useful to non-lawyers. I shall make only general acknowledgment of my obligations to brothers in law; the kinds of learning and sources these essays draw on will be obvious enough to them. Because my debts to some more general theoretical works and to sources from social science may be less easy to identify, I present the following list of books which provided direct support in this enterprise, both by way of general framework and particular data. I am keenly aware that the list probably omits items which in fairness should be included, but which have entered so generally into my work that I have lost sight of their specific influence.

Adams, Charles Francis, Jr., and Henry Adams, CHAPTERS OF ERIE (Ithaca: Great Seal Books, 1956).

Adams, Henry, THE DEGRADATION OF THE DEMOCRATIC DOGMA (New York: Macmillan, 1920).

Adler, Mortimer J., THE IDEA OF FREEDOM (New York: Doubleday, 1958).

Aristotle, THE POLITICS OF ARISTOTLE (Barker trans.; Oxford: Clarendon Press, 1946).

Aron, Raymond, GERMAN SOCIOLOGY (Bottomore trans.; Glencoe: The Free Press, 1957).

Barker, Charles A., HENRY GEORGE (New York: Oxford, 1955).

Barnard, Chester I., THE FUNCTIONS OF THE EXECUTIVE (Cambridge: Harvard University Press, 1946).

Benson, Lee, MERCHANTS, FARMERS AND RAILROADS (Cambridge: Harvard University Press, 1955).

Berle, Adolph A., Jr., NATURAL SELECTION OF POLITICAL FORCES (Lawrence: University of Kansas Press, 1950).

————————, POWER WITHOUT PROPERTY (New York: Harcourt, 1959).

———, THE 20TH CENTURY CAPITALIST REVOLUTION (New York: Harcourt, 1954).

Berlin, Isaiah, HISTORICAL INEVITABILITY (London: Oxford University Press, 1954).

Blum, John Morton, THE REPUBLICAN ROOSEVELT (Cambridge: Harvard University Press, 1954).

Boorstin, Daniel J., THE AMERICANS: THE COLONIAL EXPERIENCE (New York: Random House, Inc., 1958).

———, THE GENIUS OF AMERICAN POLITICS (Chicago: University of Chicago Press, 1953).

Boulding, Kenneth E., THE ORGANIZATIONAL REVOLUTION (New York: Harper, 1953).

Brinton, Clarence C., THE ANATOMY OF REVOLUTION (New York: Norton, 1938).

Cahn, Edmond N., THE SENSE OF INJUSTICE (New York: New York University Press, 1949).

Chamberlain, John, FAREWELL TO REFORM (2nd ed.; New York: Day, 1933).

Childs, Marquis W., and Douglass Cater, ETHICS IN A BUSINESS SOCIETY (New York: Harper, 1954).

von Ciriacy-Wantrup, S., RESOURCE CONSERVATION: ECONOMICS AND POLICIES (Berkeley: University of California Press, 1952).

Clark, John Maurice, ECONOMIC INSTITUTIONS AND HUMAN WELFARE (New York: Knopf, 1957).

Cochran, Thomas C., and William Miller, THE AGE OF ENTERPRISE (New York: Macmillan, 1942).

Commager, Henry Steele, THE AMERICAN MIND (New Haven: Yale University Press, 1950).

Commons, John R., LEGAL FOUNDATIONS OF CAPITALISM (Madison: University of Wisconsin Press, 1957).

Coon, Carleton S., THE STORY OF MAN (New York: Knopf, 1954).

Curti, Merle, THE GROWTH OF AMERICAN THOUGHT (New York: Harper, 1943).

Dewey, John, JOHN DEWEY (Edman ed.; Indianapolis: Bobbs, 1955).

———, THE PUBLIC AND ITS PROBLEMS (New York: Holt, 1927).

Dobzhansky, Theodosius, THE BIOLOGICAL BASIS OF HUMAN FREEDOM (New York: Columbia University Press, 1956).

Dorfman, Joseph, THE ECONOMIC MIND IN AMERICAN CIVILIZATION (3 vols.; New York: The Viking Press, Inc., 1946, 1949).

Drucker, Peter, THE NEW SOCIETY (London: Wm. Heinemann, Ltd., 1951).

Dulles, Foster Rhea, LABOR IN AMERICA (New York: Crowell, 1949.)

Durkheim, Emile, THE RULES OF SOCIOLOGICAL METHOD (Solovay and Mueller trans., Catlin ed.; Glencoe: The Free Press, 1950).

Easton, David, THE POLITICAL SYSTEM (New York: Knopf, 1953).

Edwards, Corwin, MAINTAINING COMPETITION (New York: McGraw, 1949).

Eiseley, Loren, DARWIN'S CENTURY (Garden City: Doubleday, 1958).

__________, THE IMMENSE JOURNEY (New York: Random House, Inc., 1957).

Fabricant, Solomon, THE TREND OF GOVERNMENT ACTIVITY IN THE UNITED STATES SINCE 1900 (New York: National Bureau of Economic Research, 1952).

Ferrerro, Guglielmo, THE PRINCIPLES OF POWER (Jaeckel trans.; New York: Putnam, 1942).

Galbraith, John Kenneth, AMERICAN CAPITALISM (Boston: Houghton, 1952).

Geyl, Pieter, DEBATES WITH HISTORIANS (New York: Meridian Books, 1958).

Ginger, Raymond, ALTGELD'S AMERICA (New York: Funk, 1958).

Gouldner, Alvin W., PATTERNS OF INDUSTRIAL BUREAUCRACY (Glencoe: The Free Press, 1954).

Guérard, Albert L., FOSSILS AND PRESENCES (Stanford: Stanford University Press, 1957).

Gulick, Luther Halsey, AMERICAN FOREST POLICY (New York: Duell, Sloan & Pearce, 1951).

Hacker, Louis, THE TRIUMPH OF AMERICAN CAPITALISM (New York: Simon & Schuster, Inc., 1940).

Hall, Jerome, LIVING LAW OF DEMOCRATIC SOCIETY (Indianapolis: Bobbs, 1949).

Hamilton, Walton, THE POLITICS OF AN INDUSTRY (New York: Knopf, 1957).

Handlin, Oscar, and Mary Flug Handlin, COMMONWEALTH: MASSACHUSETTS, 1774-1861 (New York: New York University Press, 1947).

Handlin, Oscar, THE UPROOTED (New York: Grossett, 1951).

Hartz, Louis, ECONOMIC POLICY AND DEMOCRATIC THOUGHT: PENNSYLVANIA, 1776-1860 (Cambridge: Harvard University Press, 1948).

Herskovits, Melville J., THE ECONOMIC LIFE OF PRIMITIVE PEOPLES (New York: Knopf, 1940).

Hoebel, Edward Adamson, THE LAW OF PRIMITIVE MAN (Cambridge: Harvard University Press, 1954).

Hofstadter, Richard, THE AGE OF REFORM (New York: Knopf, 1955).

———, THE AMERICAN POLITICAL TRADITION AND THE MEN WHO MADE IT (New York: Knopf, 1948).

Holcombe, Arthur N., THE MIDDLE CLASSES IN AMERICAN POLITICS (Cambridge: Harvard University Press, 1940).

Hunter, Robert, REVOLUTION (New York: Harper, 1940).

Johnson, E. A. J., and Herman E. Krooss, THE ORIGINS AND DEVELOPMENT OF THE AMERICAN ECONOMY (New York: Prentice-Hall, Inc., 1953).

Jordy, William H., HENRY ADAMS: SCIENTIFIC HISTORIAN (New Haven: Yale University Press, 1952).

de Jouvenel, Bertrand, THE ETHICS OF REDISTRIBUTION (Cambridge: Cambridge University Press, 1951).

Kapp, Karl William, THE SOCIAL COSTS OF PRIVATE ENTERPRISE (Cambridge: Harvard University Press, 1950).

Key, Valdimer O., Jr., POLITICS, PARTIES AND PRESSURE GROUPS (New York: Crowell, 1942).

———, SOUTHERN POLITICS IN STATE AND NATION (New York: Knopf, 1949).

Knight, Frank H., THE ETHICS OF COMPETITION (New York: Harper, 1935).

Krooss, Herman E., AMERICAN ECONOMIC DEVELOPMENT (Englewood Cliffs: Prentice-Hall, Inc., 1955).

Lasswell, Harold D., NATIONAL SECURITY AND INDIVIDUAL FREEDOM (New York: McGraw, 1950).

———, THE POLITICAL WRITINGS OF HAROLD D. LASSWELL (Glencoe: The Free Press, 1951).

Lasswell, Harold D., Charles E. Merriam, and T. V. Smith, A STUDY OF POWER (Collection) (Glencoe: The Free Press, 1950).

Leighton, Alexander H., THE GOVERNING OF MEN (Princeton: Princeton University Press, 1945).

Linton, Ralph, THE STUDY OF MAN (New York: Appleton-Century-Crofts, Inc., 1936).

Lubell, Samuel, THE FUTURE OF AMERICAN POLITICS (New York: Harper, 1952).

Lynd, Robert, KNOWLEDGE FOR WHAT? (Princeton: Princeton University Press, 1939).

Lynd, Robert, and Helen Lynd, MIDDLETOWN (New York: Harcourt, 1929).

—————, MIDDLETOWN IN TRANSITION (New York: Harcourt, 1937).

MacIver, R. M., THE MODERN STATE (Oxford: The Clarendon Press, 1926).

—————, SOCIAL CAUSATION (Boston: Ginn, 1942).

—————, SOCIETY (New York: Rinehart & Co., 1949).

Maurer, Herrymon, GREAT ENTERPRISE (New York: Macmillan, 1955).

McCloskey, Robert Green, AMERICAN CONSERVATISM IN THE AGE OF ENTERPRISE (Cambridge: Harvard University Press, 1951).

Merriam, Charles E., SYSTEMATIC POLITICS (Chicago: University of Chicago Press, 1945).

Merton, Robert K., SOCIAL THEORY AND SOCIAL STRUCTURE (Glencoe: The Free Press, rev. ed., 1957).

Mills, Charles Wright, THE NEW MEN OF POWER (New York: Harcourt, 1948).

—————, WHITE COLLAR (New York: Oxford, 1951).

Myers, Francis M., THE WARFARE OF DEMOCRATIC IDEALS (Yellow Springs: Antioch Press, 1956).

Myrdal, Gunnar, AN INTERNATIONAL ECONOMY (New York: Harper, 1956).

—————, THE POLITICAL ELEMENT IN THE DEVELOPMENT OF ECONOMIC THEORY (Streeter trans.; London: Routledge & Paul, 1953).

Nef, John U., CULTURAL FOUNDATIONS OF INDUSTRIAL CIVILIZATION (Cambridge: Cambridge University Press, 1958).

Otto, Max Carl, THE HUMAN ENTERPRISE (New York: F. S. Crofts & Co., 1940).

—————, SCIENCE AND THE MORAL LIFE (New York: New American Library, 1949).

Parsons, Talcott, THE STRUCTURE OF SOCIAL ACTION (Glencoe: The Free Press, 2d ed., 1949).

Perlman, Selig, A THEORY OF THE LABOR MOVEMENT (New York: A. M. Kelley, 1928).

Perry, Ralph Barton, THE THOUGHT AND CHARACTER OF WILLIAM JAMES (New York: George Braziller, brief version 1954).

Pinchot, Gifford, BREAKING NEW GROUND (New York: Harcourt, 1947).

Polanyi, Karl, THE GREAT TRANSFORMATION (New York: Farrar & Rinehart, Inc., 1944).

Popper, Karl R., THE POVERTY OF HISTORICISM (Boston: Beacon Press, 1957).

Pound, Roscoe, THE FORMATIVE ERA OF AMERICAN LAW (Boston: Little, 1938).

——————, INTERPRETATIONS OF LEGAL HISTORY (New York: Macmillan, 1923).

——————, THE SPIRIT OF THE COMMON LAW (Boston: Marshall Jones Co., 1921).

Rieff, Phillip, FREUD: THE MIND OF THE MORALIST (New York: The Viking Press, Inc., 1959).

Riesman, David, Reuel Denney, and Nathan Glazer, THE LONELY CROWD (New Haven: Yale University Press, 1950).

Rostow, Walt W., THE PROCESS OF ECONOMIC GROWTH (New York: Norton, 1952).

Russell, Bertrand, POWER (New York: Norton, 1938).

Sabine, George H., A HISTORY OF POLITICAL THEORY (New York: Holt, rev. ed., 1950).

Schlesinger, Arthur M., THE RISE OF THE CITY, 1878-1898 (New York: Macmillan, 1933).

Schumpeter, Joseph A., CAPITALISM, SOCIALISM, AND DEMOCRACY (New York: Harper, 2d ed., 1947).

——————, IMPERIALISM AND SOCIAL CLASSES (Sweezy ed., Norden trans.; New York: A. M. Kelley, 1951).

Seligman, Edwin R. A., THE ECONOMIC INTERPRETATION OF HISTORY (New York: Columbia University Press, 1902).

Smith, Henry Nash, VIRGIN LAND (Cambridge: Harvard University Press, 1950).

Social Science Research Council, Committee on Historiography, "The Social Sciences in Historical Study," SOCIAL SCIENCE RESEARCH COUNCIL BULLETIN No. 64 (New York, 1954).

Stone, Julius, THE PROVINCE AND FUNCTION OF LAW (Cambridge: Harvard University Press, 1950).

Strout, Cushing, THE PRAGMATIC REVOLT IN AMERICAN HISTORY (New Haven: Yale University Press, 1958).

de Tocqueville, Alexis, DEMOCRACY IN AMERICA (2 vol. Bradley ed.; New York: Knopf, 1951).

Truman, David B., THE GOVERNMENTAL PROCESS (New York: Knopf, 1951).

Walker, Charles R., STEELTOWN (New York: Harper, 1950).

Warner, William Lloyd, and others, DEMOCRACY IN JONESVILLE (New York: Harper, 1949).

Weber, Max, FROM MAX WEBER: ESSAYS IN SOCIOLOGY (Gerth and Mills ed.; New York: Oxford, 1946).

———, GENERAL ECONOMIC HISTORY (Knight trans.; Greenberg, Publisher, Inc., 1927).

———, MAX WEBER ON LAW IN ECONOMY AND SOCIETY (Shils and Rheinstein trans., Rheinstein ed.; Cambridge: Harvard University Press, 1954).

———, THE THEORY OF SOCIAL AND ECONOMIC ORGANIZATION (Henderson and Parsons trans., Parsons ed.; New York: Oxford, 1947).

Whipple, Leon, THE STORY OF CIVIL LIBERTY IN THE UNITED STATES (New York: Vanguard, 1927).

Whitehead, Alfred North, ADVENTURES OF IDEAS (New York: Macmillan, 1933).

———, THE FUNCTION OF REASON (Princeton: Princeton University Press, 1929).

Whorf, Benjamin Lee, LANGUAGE, THOUGHT AND REALITY (Carroll ed.; Cambridge: The Technology Press of the Massachusetts Institute of Technology, 1956).

Whyte, William Foote, PATTERN FOR INDUSTRIAL PEACE (New York: Harper, 1951).

Whyte, William H., THE ORGANIZATION MAN (New York: Simon and Schuster, Inc., 1956).

Wiener, Norbert, THE HUMAN USE OF HUMAN BEINGS (Boston: Houghton, 1950).

Williams, Robin M., AMERICAN SOCIETY (New York: Knopf, 1951).

Woodward, Comer Vann, REUNION AND REACTION (Boston: Little, 1951).

Wyllie, Irwin G., THE SELF-MADE IN AMERICA (New Brunswick: Rutgers University Press, 1954).

Index